JUMP Math 7.1

Book 7 Part 1 of 2

Contents

jump math™

MULTIPLYING POTENTIAL.

JUMP Math
One Yonge Street, Suite 1014
Toronto, Ontario M5E 1E5
Canada
www.jumpmath.org

Writer: Dr. Sindi Sabourin
Editors: Megan Burns, Liane Tsui, Natalie Francis, Janice Dyer, Wendy Scavuzzo, Joe Zingrone
Layout and Illustrations: Linh Lam, Gabriella Kerr, Marijke Friesen, Pam Lostracco
Cover Design: Blakeley Words+Pictures
Cover Photograph: © Gary Blakeley, Blakeley Words+Pictures

ISBN 978-1-927457-47-4

Third printing June 2021

Printed and bound in Canada

Welcome to JUMP Math

Entering the world of JUMP Math means believing that every child has the capacity to be fully numerate and to love math. Founder and mathematician John Mighton has used this premise to develop his innovative teaching method. The resulting resources isolate and describe concepts so clearly and incrementally that everyone can understand them.

JUMP Math is comprised of teacher's guides (which are the heart of our program), interactive whiteboard lessons, student assessment & practice books, evaluation materials, outreach programs, and teacher training. The Common Core Editions of our resources have been carefully designed to cover the Common Core State Standards. All of this is presented on the JUMP Math website: **www.jumpmath.org**.

Teacher's guides are available on the website for free use. Read the introduction to the teacher's guides before you begin using these resources. This will ensure that you understand both the philosophy and the methodology of JUMP Math. The assessment & practice books are designed for use by students, with adult guidance. Each student will have unique needs and it is important to provide the student with the appropriate support and encouragement as he or she works through the material.

Allow students to discover the concepts by themselves as much as possible. Mathematical discoveries can be made in small, incremental steps. The discovery of a new step is like untangling the parts of a puzzle. It is exciting and rewarding.

Students will need to answer the questions marked with a ▯ in a notebook. Grid paper notebooks should always be on hand for answering extra questions or when additional room for calculation is needed.

Contents

Unit 4: The Number System: Rational Numbers

Unit 5: Ratios and Proportional Relationships: Ratio and Percentage Problems

Unit 6: Geometry: Constructing Triangles and Scale Drawings

Unit 7: The Number System: Multiplying and Dividing Integers

Unit 8: Statistics and Probability: Probability Models

PART 2

Unit 1: The Number System: Multiplying and Dividing Rational Numbers

Unit 2: Ratios and Proportional Relationships: Multistep Ratios and Proportions

Unit 3: Expressions and Equations: Equations, Ratios, and Inequalities

Unit 4: Geometry: Angles and Areas

Unit 5: The Number System: Repeating Decimals and Terminating Decimals

Unit 6: Geometry: Volume, Surface Area, and Cross Sections

Unit 7: Statistics and Probability: Statistics

RP7-1 Patterns

1. Find the number that was added or subtracted each time. Then extend the pattern.

a) 4 , 7 , 10 , <u>13</u> , <u>16</u>

b) 9 , 7 , 5 , _____ , _____

c) 2 , 4 , 6 , _____ , _____

d) 11 , 7 , 3 , _____ , _____

e) 43 , 51 , 59 , _____ , _____

f) 82 , 74 , 66 , _____ , _____

> If you know the **rule** for a sequence, you can create the sequence.
>
> Examples: The rule is: Start at 2 and add 3 each time. The sequence is: 2, 5, 8, 11, …
>
> The rule is: 2, 7, 1, then repeat. The sequence is: 2, 7, 1, 2, 7, 1, …

2. State the rule for the sequence.

a) 22, 27, 32, 37   The rule is: _____

b) 49, 46, 43, 40   The rule is: _____

c) 8, 4, 8, 4, 8, 4   The rule is: _____

d) 85, 81, 77, 73   The rule is: _____

3. Create the sequence from the rule.

a) Start at 7 and add 5 each time. _____, _____, _____, _____

b) Start at 45 and subtract 4 each time. _____, _____, _____, _____

c) 0, 6, then repeat. _____, _____, _____, _____

4. Does the sequence **increase** (go up), **decrease** (go down), or **repeat**?

a) 2, 4, 8, 16, 32, 64 _____

b) 3, 7, 1, 3, 7, 1 _____

c) 29, 27, 25, 23, 21 _____

d) 2, 6, 10, 14, 18 _____

e) 11, 9, 6, 11, 9, 6 _____

f) 61, 56, 51, 46, 41 _____

5. A marina rents sailboats at a rate of $8 for the first hour and $5 for every hour after that. How much does it cost to rent a sailboat from the marina for 4 hours?

6. Rani has a roll of 85 stamps. She uses 9 each day for 4 days. How many are left?

7. Match each sequence with the correct description (**A**, **B**, or **C**).

a)   **A.** increases by 5 each time
     B. increases by different amounts
     C. repeats

     8, 12, 18, 22, 24, 28 _____

     7, 12, 12 , 7, 12, 12 _____

     7, 12, 17, 22, 27, 32 _____

b)   **A.** increases and decreases
     B. decreases by different amounts
     C. decreases by the same amount

     18, 16, 14, 12, 10 _____

     31, 29, 25, 13, 9 _____

     6, 9, 14, 10, 5 _____

8. Make 3 sequences that match the descriptions. Write the sequences out of order.
Ask a partner to match each sequence with the correct description.

  A. increases by 4 each time   _____ _____

  B. increases by different amounts   _____ _____

  C. increases and decreases   _____ _____

9. a) Find the numbers that were added. Then extend the pattern.

    1 , 1 , 2 , 3 , 5 , 8 , 13 , 21 , 34 , _____, _____, _____

  b) The sequence in part a) is called the **Fibonacci sequence**. How can you get
    each term in the sequence from the previous two terms?

    _____

  c) Complete the table by writing "E" for even and "O" for odd.

Number	1	1	2	3	5	8	13	21	34
Even or Odd?									

    Write the rule for the even-odd pattern in the Fibonacci sequence.

    _____

10. Find the gaps between the gaps and extend the patterns.

    (+3)
  (+2) (+5)
  1 , 3 , 8 , 17 , 31 , 51 , _____, _____, _____

Bonus ▶ Find the gaps and extend the pattern.

    10 , 11 , 9 , 12 , 8 , 13 , _____, _____, _____

RP7-2 T-tables

Tom creates an **increasing pattern** with squares.

Figure	Number of Squares
1	4
2	7
3	10

Figure 1   Figure 2   Figure 3

The number of squares in the figures are 4, 7, 10, ...

Tom writes a rule for the number of squares: Start at 4 and add 3 each time.

1. Tom makes other increasing patterns with squares. How many squares does he add to make each new figure?

   Write your answers in the circles. Then write a rule for the pattern.

   a)

Figure	Number of Squares
1	2
2	7
3	12
4	17

   Rule:

   _____

   _____

   b)

Figure	Number of Squares
1	6
2	14
3	22
4	30

   Rule:

   _____

   _____

   c)

Figure	Number of Squares
1	12
2	25
3	38
4	51

   Rule:

   _____

   _____

2. Use a T-table to find out how many toothpicks will be required to make the fifth figure in each pattern.

   a)

   b)

3. Wang has $79 and spends $3 per week. Kam has $84 and spends $4 per week. How many weeks will it take for them to have the same amount of money left?

Bonus ▶

a) Draw a T-table to predict the number of shaded parts in Figure 5 of this pattern.

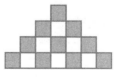

Figure 1   Figure 2   Figure 3   Figure 4

b) Will the number of shaded parts in Figure 15 be even or odd?

4. Extend the columns. What is the rule for how you get the numbers in the second column from the first column?

a)

Add 10	Add 10
2	5
12	
22	
32	

_____

b)

Add 4	Add 4
7	3

_____

c)

Subtract 2	Subtract 2
38	45

_____

5. Maria continues two sequences for the same number of steps:

Start at 4 and add 13.   Start at 9 and add 13.

When the first sequence reaches 251, what number will the second sequence reach? _____

6. Marco had $35 and Ava had $40. Then, they both started earning $17 an hour for mowing their friends' lawns. When Ava has $210, how much money will Marco have?

7. Extend the columns. What is the rule for how you get the numbers in the second column from the first column?

a)

Multiply by 2	Multiply by 2
2	6

_____

b)

Divide by 3	Divide by 3
9	18

_____

c)

Multiply by 10	Multiply by 10
6	3

_____

8. Josh continues two sequences for the same number of steps:

Start at 9 and multiply by 8   Start at 90 and multiply by 8.

When the first sequence reaches 36,864, what number will the second sequence reach? _____

9. Yu had $96 when Raj had $160. They both spend half their money every week.

When Yu has $12 left, how much money will Raj have left? _____

RP7-3 Lowest Common Multiples

The whole numbers are the numbers 0, 1, 2, 3, and so on.

The **multiples** of a whole number are the numbers you get by multiplying the number by another whole number.

Examples: $2 \times 3 = 6$, so 6 is a multiple of both 2 and 3.
$0 \times 5 = 0$, so 0 is a multiple of both 0 and 5.

1. a) Skip count to write the multiples of 3 up to 3×10.

   ___0___, ___3___, _____, _____, _____, _____, _____, _____, _____, _____, _____

   b) Use your answers in part a) to circle the multiples of 3.

   12   17   22   24   25   27

2. Mark the multiples of each number on the number lines.

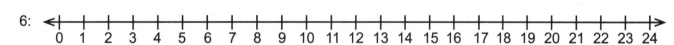

A number is a **common multiple** of two numbers if it is a multiple of both of them.

3. Find the first 2 common multiples (after 0) of …

   a) 2 and 5: _____, _____

   b) 3 and 6: _____, _____

   c) 2 and 4: _____, _____

   d) 3 and 4: _____, _____

   e) 4 and 6: _____, _____

   f) 2 and 6: _____, _____

4. a) How can you find the second common multiple of two numbers from the first?

   b) The first common multiple of 18 and 42 is 126. What is the second common multiple?

5. a) Write the first 4 common multiples of 2 and 3, after 0. _____, _____, _____, _____

   b) Extend the pattern from part a). Predict the fifth common multiple of 2 and 3. _____

The number 0 is a multiple of every number. The **lowest common multiple (LCM)** of two numbers is the smallest whole number (not 0) that is a multiple of both of them.

The common multiples of two numbers are the multiples of the LCM.

6. Find the lowest common multiple of each pair of numbers.

a) 4 and 10

4: *4, 8, 12, 16, 20*

10: *10, 20*

LCM = _____

b) 3 and 6

3:

6:

LCM = _____

c) 8 and 10

8:

10:

LCM = _____

d) 6 and 8

6:

8:

LCM = _____

To find the lowest common multiple of two numbers, write the first few multiples of the larger number until you see one that is also a multiple of the smaller number.

Example: Find the LCM of 3 and 5.
    The first few multiples of 5 are 5, 10, and 15. Stop here because 15 is a multiple of 3.

7. Find the LCM.

a) 6 and 10

10, 20, 30

LCM = ___30___

b) 9 and 12

LCM = _____

c) 7 and 10

LCM = _____

d) 6 and 30

LCM = _____

e) 6 and 15

LCM = _____

f) 8 and 9

LCM = _____

g) 5 and 8

LCM = _____

h) 6 and 9

LCM = _____

RP7-4 Models of Fractions

A fraction names a part of a whole.

The pie is cut into 4 equal parts.
3 parts out of 4 are shaded.

So $\frac{3}{4}$ of the pie is shaded.

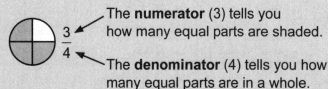

The **numerator** (3) tells you how many equal parts are shaded.

The **denominator** (4) tells you how many equal parts are in a whole.

1. Name the fraction shaded.

a) _____

b) _____

c) _____

d) _____

2. Draw lines to divide each figure into equal parts. Then write what fraction of each figure is shaded.

a) _____

b) _____

c) _____

d) 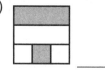 _____

3. Use a centimeter ruler to divide the box into equal parts. What fraction is shaded?

a)

_____ is shaded.

b)

_____ is shaded.

4. Using a centimeter ruler, complete the figure to make a whole.

a)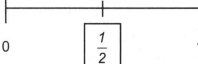

b)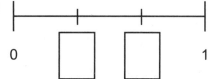

5. Name the fractions marked on the number line.

a)

b)

c)

Fractions can name parts of a set.

Example: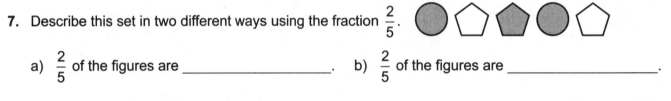

$\frac{1}{5}$ of the figures are squares, $\frac{1}{5}$ are circles, and $\frac{3}{5}$ are pentagons.

6. Fill in the blank.

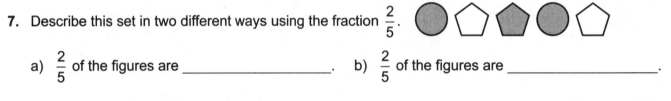

a) _____ of the figures are circles.

b) _____ of the figures are white.

c) _____ of the figures are white circles.

d) _____ of the figures are shaded pentagons.

e) $\frac{4}{7}$ of the figures are _____.

f) $\frac{5}{7}$ of the figures are _____.

Bonus ▶ $\frac{0}{7}$ of the figures are _____.

7. Describe this set in two different ways using the fraction $\frac{2}{5}$.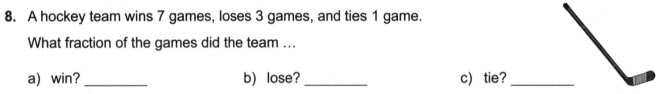

a) $\frac{2}{5}$ of the figures are _____.

b) $\frac{2}{5}$ of the figures are _____.

8. A hockey team wins 7 games, loses 3 games, and ties 1 game.

What fraction of the games did the team …

a) win? _____

b) lose? _____

c) tie? _____

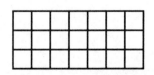

9. A box contains 1 blue marble, 5 red marbles, and 3 yellow marbles.

What fraction of the marbles are *not* blue? _____

10. There are 27 students in a class. Each student chose to do a science project on animals or on plants.

The chart shows the number who chose each topic.

a) Fill in the missing numbers in the chart.

b) What fraction of the students chose to study animals?

c) What fraction of the girls chose to study plants?

	Animals	Plants
Boys	8	5
Girls		
Students	14	

11. What fraction of the squares are on the outside of the figure? _____

RP7-5 Comparing Fractions Using Equivalent Fractions

Two or more fractions are equivalent if they can be shown by the same part of the same whole.

Example: $\frac{2}{3}$ and $\frac{4}{6}$ are equivalent fractions.

$\frac{2}{3} =$ $\frac{4}{6} =$

1. What equivalent fractions do these pictures show?

$\frac{1}{2}$ =   =   =

2. Shade the same part to find a fraction equivalent to the first fraction.

a)

$\frac{3}{4}$ =

b)

$\frac{1}{3}$ =

c)

$\frac{3}{5}$ =

3. Fill in the blanks.

A   B

a) A has _____ times as many parts as B.

   A has _____ times as many shaded parts as B.

A   B

b) A has _____ times as many parts as B.

   A has _____ times as many shaded parts as B.

4. Compare the numerators and denominators by multiplication.

a) $\frac{1}{4}$ and $\frac{2}{8}$

   2 is _____ times as much as 1.

   8 is _____ times as much as 4.

b) $\frac{4}{5}$ and $\frac{12}{15}$

   12 is _____ times as much as 4.

   15 is _____ times as much as 5.

You can multiply the numerator and denominator by the same number to get an equivalent fraction.

Example: A $\dfrac{3}{4} \xrightarrow[\times 2]{\times 2} \dfrac{6}{8}$ B

B has twice as many **parts** as A.
B has twice as many **shaded parts** as A.

5. Draw lines to cut the pies into more pieces. Then fill in the numerators of the equivalent fractions.

a)

    4 pieces   6 pieces   8 pieces

    $\dfrac{1}{2} = \dfrac{}{4} = \dfrac{}{6} = \dfrac{}{8}$

b)

    6 pieces   9 pieces   12 pieces

    $\dfrac{1}{3} = \dfrac{}{6} = \dfrac{}{9} = \dfrac{}{12}$

6. Cut each pie into more pieces. Then fill in the missing numbers.

a) $\dfrac{2}{3} \xrightarrow[\times 2]{\times 2} \dfrac{}{6}$

b) $\dfrac{3}{4} \xrightarrow[\times 2]{\times 2} \dfrac{}{8}$

c) 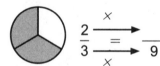 $\dfrac{2}{3} \xrightarrow[\times]{\times} \dfrac{}{9}$

    This number tells you how many pieces to cut each slice into.

7. Use multiplication to find the equivalent fraction.

a) $\dfrac{1 \times 2}{3 \times 2} = \dfrac{}{6}$

b) $\dfrac{1 \times}{2 \times} = \dfrac{}{10}$

c) $\dfrac{4}{5} = \dfrac{}{10}$

d) $\dfrac{3}{4} = \dfrac{}{8}$

e) $\dfrac{1}{3} = \dfrac{}{12}$

f) $\dfrac{4}{5} = \dfrac{}{25}$

g) $\dfrac{7}{8} = \dfrac{}{16}$

h) $\dfrac{9}{10} = \dfrac{}{100}$

i) $\dfrac{2}{9} = \dfrac{}{72}$

8. Write five fractions equivalent to $\dfrac{3}{10}$.

    $\dfrac{3}{10} = \boxed{} = \boxed{} = \boxed{} = \boxed{} = \boxed{}$

9. Shade the fractions provided. Then order the fractions from least to greatest.

$\frac{3}{5}$ $\frac{1}{5}$ $\frac{4}{5}$ $\frac{2}{5}$ ⬡

☐ < ☐ < ☐ < ☐

10. Two fractions have the same denominators (bottoms) but different numerators (tops). How can you tell which fraction is greater?

_____

11. Circle the greater fraction in each pair.

a) $\frac{1}{8}$ or $\frac{3}{8}$ b) $\frac{4}{9}$ or $\frac{2}{9}$ c) $\frac{5}{11}$ or $\frac{8}{11}$ d) $\frac{9}{31}$ or $\frac{6}{31}$

12. a) Write an equivalent fraction with denominator 12.

i) $\frac{2}{3} = \frac{}{12}$ ii) $\frac{5}{6} = \frac{}{12}$ iii) $\frac{3}{4} = \frac{}{12}$ iv) $\frac{1}{2} = \frac{}{12}$

b) Write the original fractions from part a) in order from least to greatest.

☐ < ☐ < ☐ < ☐

Pedro wants to compare $\frac{3}{4}$ and $\frac{5}{6}$. He turns them into fractions with the same denominator.

$\frac{3 \times 6}{4 \times 6} = \frac{18}{24}$ and $\frac{5 \times 4}{6 \times 4} = \frac{20}{24}$, so $\frac{3}{4} < \frac{5}{6}$.

---

13. Turn the fractions into fractions with the same denominator. Then compare the fractions. Show your answer using < or >.

a) $\frac{5}{7} = \frac{}{28}$ and $\frac{3}{4} = \frac{}{28}$ b) $\frac{5}{7} = \frac{}{}$ and $\frac{7}{10} = \frac{}{}$ c) $\frac{1}{2} = \frac{}{}$ and $\frac{3}{4} = \frac{}{}$

so $\frac{5}{7}$ ☐ $\frac{3}{4}$.   so $\frac{5}{7}$ ☐ $\frac{7}{10}$.   so $\frac{1}{2}$ ☐ $\frac{3}{4}$.

14. Compare $\frac{5}{6}$ and $\frac{7}{8}$ by using the smallest common denominator that you can.

The LCM of 6 and 8 is _____, so use _____ as the common denominator.

$\frac{5}{6} = \frac{}{}$ and $\frac{7}{8} = \frac{}{}$, so $\frac{5}{6}$ ☐ $\frac{7}{8}$.

15. In the grey box above, what smaller denominator could Pedro use to compare $\frac{3}{4}$ and $\frac{5}{6}$? _____

RP7-6 Fractions and Ratios

A fraction compares a part to a whole. A **ratio** can compare a part to a part, or a part to a whole.

Example: ○ ○ ☐ ☐ ○

> The **part-to-part ratio** of circles to squares is 3 to 2 or 3 : 2.
>
> The **part-to-whole ratio** of circles to shapes is 3 to 5 or 3 : 5.

1. ☆ ☾ ○ ☐ ○ ○ ○ ☐ ☆ △ ○ ☆ ○ ☾ ☐

    a) The ratio of moons to circles is ____ : ____.   b) The ratio of triangles to moons is ____ : ____.

    c) The ratio of stars to squares is ____ : ____.   d) The ratio of triangles to shapes is ____ : ____.

2. Build a model or draw a picture that could be described by the ratio 3 : 4.

3. a) Write the ratio of vowels (a, e, i, o, u) to consonants (other letters) in the word.

    i)   star   _____ : _____   ii) moon   _____ : _____

    iii) circle   _____ : _____   iv) square   _____ : _____

    v)   triangle   _____ : _____

    b) Are the ratios you found in part a) part-to-part ratios or part-to-whole ratios?

    _____

4. Circle the part-to-whole ratios. Underline the part-to-part ratios.

    a) vowels in "band" : letters in "band"   b) vowels in "blog" : consonants in "blog"

    c) buses : trucks   d) school buses to buses

    e) school days to days of the week   f) days in January to days in September

5. Write the ratio of the lengths.

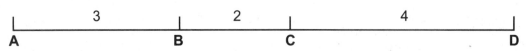

    a) AB to CD = ____ : ____   b) BC to CD = ____ : ____

    c) AB to AC = ____ : ____   d) CD to AD = ____ : ____

6. Which ratios from Question 5 are part-to-whole ratios? _____

A part-to-whole ratio can be thought of as a fraction.

Example: ◯◯△△△
The ratio of circles to shapes is 2 to 5 or 2 : 5, so $\frac{2}{5}$ of the shapes are circles.

7. Write a ratio and a fraction.

a) ◯◯◯△△△△

circles to shapes = _____ : _____

_____ of the shapes are circles.

b) ◯◯△△△△△

circles to shapes = _____ : _____

_____ of the shapes are circles.

A part-to-part ratio can sometimes be changed to a fraction.

Example: There are 3 circles for every 5 triangles in a set of circles and triangles.

◯◯◯△△△△

There are 3 circles for every 8 shapes, so $\frac{3}{8}$ of the shapes are circles.

8. Write the number of boys (b), girls (g), and students (s) in each class.

a) There are 8 boys and 5 girls in a class.   b: __8__   g: __5__   s: __13__

b) There are 9 girls in a class of 20 students.   b: _____   g: _____   s: _____

c) There are 3 boys in a class of 10 students.   b: _____   g: _____   s: _____

9. Write the fraction of students in the class who are boys and the fraction who are girls.

a) There are 5 boys and 8 girls in the class.   b: ☐   g: ☐

b) The ratio of boys to girls in the class is 5 to 9.   b: ☐   g: ☐

c) The ratio of girls to boys in the class is 6 : 7.   b: ☐   g: ☐

10. In Mr. X's class, $\frac{2}{5}$ of the students are girls. In Ms. Y's class, $\frac{5}{8}$ of the students are girls.

a) What is the ratio of girls to boys in each class?   Mr. X's class   Ms. Y's class

= _____ : _____   = _____ : _____

b) Whose class has more girls than boys? How can you tell from the fraction?
How can you tell from the ratio?

RP7-7 Equivalent Ratios

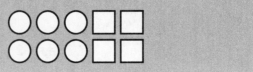

In the picture, there are 3 circles for every 2 squares.
There are also 6 circles for every 4 squares.

The ratios 3 : 2 and 6 : 4 are **equivalent**.

1. Find two equivalent ratios for each picture.

a)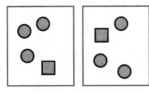

circles to squares = 3 : _____ = 6: _____

b)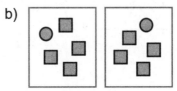

circles to squares = 1 : _____ = 2 : _____

c)

circles to squares = 2 : _____ = 6: _____

d)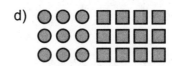

circles to squares = 3 : _____ = 9 : _____

2. Complete the pictures so the ratio of triangles to squares is the same in each column. Then create a sequence of equivalent ratios.

Triangles	△△	△△　△△	
Squares	☐☐☐		☐☐☐ ☐☐☐ ☐☐☐
Ratio	2 : 3		

Triangles	△△△	△△△ △△△	
Squares		☐　☐	☐　☐　☐
Ratio		6 : 2	

3. Skip count to write a sequence of three equivalent ratios.

a) 3 : 2 = _6_ : _4_ = ____ : ____

b) 3 : 5 = ____ : ____ = ____ : ____

c) 5 : 8 = ____ : ____ = ____ : ____

d) 3 : 10 = ____ : ____ = ____ : ____

e) 5 : 4 = ____ : ____ = ____ : ____

f) 4 : 9 = ____ : ____ = ____ : ____

4. Skip count to write a sequence of five equivalent ratios.

4 : 3 = ____ : ____ = ____ : ____ = ____ : ____ = ____ : ____

There are 5 girls for every 2 boys in a class. There are 20 girls.

To find out how many boys are in the class, write out a sequence of equivalent ratios. Stop when there are 20 girls.

There are 8 boys in the class.

Girls		Boys
5	:	2
10	:	4
15	:	6
20	:	8

5. Write a sequence of equivalent ratios to solve each problem.

a) There are 5 boys for every 4 girls in a class with 20 boys. How many girls are in the class?

Boys   **Girls**

b) There are 4 red beads for every 3 blue beads in a bracelet. The bracelet has 12 red beads. How many blue beads are in the bracelet?

Red   **Blue**

c) A recipe for soup calls for 3 cups of cream for every 5 cups of tomatoes. How many cups of cream are needed for 15 cups of tomatoes?

Cream   **Tomatoes**

d) A team has 2 wins for every loss. They won 10 games. How many games did they lose?

Wins   **Losses**

e) A mixture for green paint has 5 cups of blue paint for every 6 cups of yellow paint. How much blue paint would you need if you have 30 cups of yellow paint?

There are 3 boys for every 2 girls in a class of 20 students.

To find out how many boys are in the class, write out a sequence of equivalent ratios. Stop when the terms add to 20.

12 boys + 8 girls = 20 students, so there are 12 boys in the class.

Boys		Girls	Total
3	:	2	5
6	:	4	10
9	:	6	15
12	:	8	20

6. Write a sequence of equivalent ratios to solve each problem.

a) There are 5 boys for every 4 girls in a class of 27 students. How many girls are in the class?

Boys   **Girls**   **Total**

b) There are 2 red marbles for every 7 blue marbles in a box. If the box has 45 marbles, how many marbles are blue?

Red   **Blue**   **Total**

c) A recipe for punch calls for 3 cups of orange juice for every 4 cups of mango juice. How many cups of orange juice are needed to make 21 cups of punch?

Orange   **Mango**   **Total**

d) A team has 5 wins for every 2 losses. They played 35 games. How many games did they lose?

Wins   **Losses**   **Total**

e) A mixture for green paint has 2 cups of blue paint for every 3 cups of yellow paint. How much blue paint would you need to make 20 cups of green paint?

Ratios and Proportional Relationships 7-7

RP7-8 Ratio Tables

To create an equivalent ratio, multiply each term in the ratio by the same number.

Example: Draw 2 circles and 1 square four times.

There are now 2 × 4 circles and 1 × 4 squares. So the ratio of circles to squares is:

$$\times 4$$
$$2 : 1 = 8 : 4$$
$$\times 4$$

1. What number are both terms being multiplied by to make the second ratio?

× ___

a) 1 : 3 = 4 : 12

× ___

b) 2 : 5 = 6 : 15

× ___

c) 3 : 4 = 18 : 24

× ___

d) 3 : 5 = 12 : 20

× ___

e) 2 : 3 = 6 : 9

× ___

f) 1 : 4 = 13 : 52

2. Multiply both terms by the same number to make an equivalent ratio.

a) × 4 (2 : 3) × ___
___ : ___

b) × 5 (2 : 5) × ___
___ : ___

c) × 5 (3 : 4) × ___
___ : ___

d) × ___ (4 : 5) × 3
___ : ___

e) × ___ (2 : 7) × 4
___ : ___

f) × ___ (3 : 8) × 2
___ : ___

3. Fill in the blanks.

× ___

a) 4 : 3 = 12 : ___

× ___

× ___

b) 8 : 7 = ___ : 21

× ___

× 5

c) 3 : 4 = ___ : ___

× ___

4. Multiply the first term by the same number the second term was multiplied by.

a) 3 : 4 = _____ : 16

b) 6 : 7 = _____ : 35

c) 2 : 5 = _____ : 20

d) 4 : 5 = _____ : 20

e) 1 : 5 = _____ : 25

f) 2 : 3 = _____ : 18

A **ratio table** has equivalent ratios in every row. To make a ratio table, make a list of equivalent ratios.

Example: $3 : 5 = 6 : 10 = 9 : 15 = 12 : 20$

Then put each ratio into a separate row.

First Term	Second Term
3	5
6	10
9	15
12	20

5. a) Repeatedly draw 2 circles and 3 squares until you have 20 shapes.

b) Make a list of equivalent ratios using your picture.

$2 : \underline{\quad 3 \quad} = 4 : \underline{\qquad} = 6 : \underline{\qquad} = 8 : \underline{\qquad}$

c) Finish the ratio table.

Circles	Squares
2	3
4	
6	
8	

6. Use multiplication to complete a ratio table for each ratio.

a) 4 : 1

4	1
8	2
12	3
16	4

First row
First row × 2
First row × 3
First row × 4

b) 2 : 3

2	3

c) 5 : 2

5	2

7. Find the missing number in each ratio table.

a)

4	10
8	

b)

3	20
9	

c)

7	4
21	

d)

2	6
	24

8. Circle the tables that are ratio tables.

2	5
4	10

3	8
12	2

2	5
4	7

6	8
12	16

3	5
6	15

4	9
12	27

2	9
6	18

7	5
14	10

Ratios and Proportional Relationships 7-8

Two quantities are **proportional** if the T-table comparing their values is a ratio table.

9. Is the price of a drink proportional to its size?

a)

Apple Juice	
Cost ($)	Drink Size (oz)
1	4
2	8
3	16

_____

b)

Orange Juice	
Cost ($)	Drink Size (oz)
1	3
2	6
3	12

_____

c)

Fruit Punch	
Cost ($)	Drink Size (oz)
2	8
4	16
6	24

_____

d)

Milk	
Cost ($)	Drink Size (mL)
2	100
4	300
6	500

_____

10. Are the children's allowances proportional to their ages?

a)

Family A	
Allowance ($)	Age (years)
8	5
16	10
24	15

_____

b)

Family B	
Allowance (¢)	Age (years)
25	4
100	8
200	12

_____

c)

Family C	
Allowance ($)	Age (years)
8	3
16	6
24	12

_____

d)

Family D	
Allowance (¢)	Age (years)
5	2
15	6
30	12

_____

11. Did you need to look at the units ($ or ¢) to answer Questions 9 and 10? Explain.

_____

_____

RP7-9   Unit Ratios

In a **unit ratio**, one quantity is equal to 1. Unit ratios are easy to work with because
1 is easy to multiply and divide by.

Example: Each apple costs 30¢, so the unit ratio of cents to apples is 30 : 1.

1. Multiply to find the missing information.

   a) 1 book costs $5   b) 3 miles in 1 hour   c) 1 melon costs $3

   4 books cost __$20__   _____ miles in 5 hours   6 melons cost _____

2. Divide to find the missing information.

   a) 3 notebooks cost $24   b) 2 jackets cost $20.   c) 5 pears cost $20

   1 notebook costs _____   1 jacket costs _____   1 pear costs _____

3. Complete the ratio tables.

   a)
3	12
1	
5	
   ÷3
   ×5

   b)
3	15
1	
8	
   ÷
   ×

   c)
4	12
1	
5	

4. Which is a better deal?

   a) 3 T-shirts for $24   or   5 T-shirts for $45

      1 T-shirt for _____   1 T-shirt for _____

   b) 5 pens for 35¢   or   4 pens for 32¢

      1 pen for _____   1 pen for _____

   c) 7 CDs for $56   or   6 CDs for $42

      1 CD for _____   1 CD for _____

   d) 8 DVDs for $72   or   6 DVDs for $48

      1 DVD for _____   1 DVD for _____

Bonus ▶ Which is the best deal? Hint: Which price is better than 1 T-shirt for $10?

   8 T-shirts for $92   28 T-shirts for $273   35 T-shirts for $357

5. The unit ratio for 3,506 : 14,024 is 1 : 4. What is the unit ratio for 14,024 : 3,506? _____

In a ratio table, all the rows are equivalent ratios. So each row is equivalent to the same unit ratio.

6. Find the unit ratio in each row. Then circle the tables that are ratio tables.

a)
8	40	*1 : 5*
10	50	*1 : 5*
11	55	*1 : 5*

b)
5	15	_____
6	18	_____
9	27	_____

c)
2	8	_____
6	24	_____
9	54	_____

d)
6	42	_____
10	70	_____
11	66	_____

e)
3	24	_____
7	63	_____
9	72	_____

f)
4	24	_____
9	54	_____
10	60	_____

7. Find the unit ratio. How can you get the second column from the first column?

a)
2	6
4	12
5	15

b)
4	16
3	12
8	32

c)
7	35
8	40
100	500

a) _1_ : _3_

multiply by 3

b) _____ : _____

_____

c) _____ : _____

_____

The **constant of proportionality** of a ratio is the number the unit ratio tells you to multiply by.

Example: The unit ratio for the ratio 5 : 20 is 1 : 4. The constant of proportionality is 4.

8. Find the constant of proportionality. Then find the missing number in the ratio table.

a)
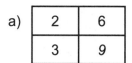
2	6
3	9

_3_

b)
5	15
	18

_____

c)
4	20
6	

_____

d)
2	
3	12

_____

e)
	16
20	80

_____

f)
4	
9	45

_____

RP7-10　Tape Diagrams and Ratio Problems

> A **tape diagram** uses blocks of the same size to show a situation.
>
> Example: There are 3 times as many girls as boys.
>
> girls: [ ][ ][ ]
>
> boys: [ ]

1. Use a tape diagram to represent the numbers of girls and boys.

    a) There are 4 times as many boys as girls.

    girls: [ ]

    boys: [ ][ ][ ][ ]

    b) There are twice as many girls as boys.

    girls:

    boys:

    c) There are 5 times as many boys as girls.

    girls:

    boys:

    d) There are 6 times as many girls as boys.

    girls:

    boys:

2. All the blocks are the same size. What is the size of one block?

    a)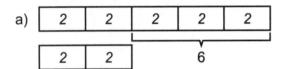

    b)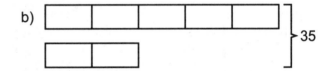

    c)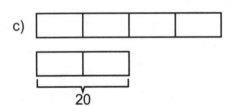

    d)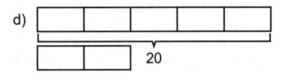

3. Show the amount on the picture that represents 12 beads. What is the size of each block?

    a) There are 12 red beads.

    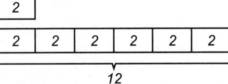

    b) There are 12 beads in total.

    green: [ ]

    red: [ ][ ][ ]

    c) There are 12 more red beads than green.

    green: [ ][ ][ ]

    red: [ ][ ][ ][ ][ ]

    d) There are 12 green beads.

    green: [ ][ ][ ]

    red: [ ][ ]

4. The bars below represent the number of red (r) and green (g) beads in a box. Fill in the blanks.

a) g: ▢▢▢

   r: ▢▢▢▢▢

   10 more red than green

   1 block = _____ beads,

   so _____ beads in total

b) g: ▢▢▢▢

   r: ▢▢▢

   35 beads altogether

   1 block = _____, so _____ green beads

   so _____ green beads

5. This tape diagram shows the number of girls and boys in a class. Each box represents the same number of students.

girls: ▢▢▢

boys: ▢▢

Complete the table.

If each box represents …	… then there are ___ girls	… and ___ boys
1 student	3	2
2 students	6	
3 students		
4 students		
5 students		

Is this a ratio table? _____

6. Use the model to find the number of red and green beads in each problem.

a) green beads : red beads = 2 : 3

   10 more red beads than green beads

   g: ▢▢

   r: ▢▢▢

   green: _____

   red: _____

b) green beads : red beads = 7 : 3

   30 beads altogether

   g: ▢▢▢▢▢▢▢

   r: ▢▢▢

   green: _____

   red: _____

7. Find the number of cups of blue (b) and yellow (y) paint needed to make green paint.

a) blue paint : yellow paint = 4 : 5

   45 cups altogether

   b: ⬚⬚⬚⬚

   y: ⬚⬚⬚⬚⬚

   blue: _____

   yellow: _____

b) blue paint : yellow paint = 5 : 3

   8 more cups of blue paint than yellow

   b: ⬚⬚⬚⬚⬚

   y: ⬚⬚⬚

   blue: _____

   yellow: _____

c) blue paint : yellow paint = 3 : 7

   12 more cups of yellow paint than blue

   b: ⬚⬚⬚

   y: ⬚⬚⬚⬚⬚⬚⬚

   blue: _____

   yellow: _____

d) blue paint : yellow paint = 7 : 5

   36 cups altogether

   b: ⬚⬚⬚⬚⬚⬚⬚

   y: ⬚⬚⬚⬚⬚

   blue: _____

   yellow: _____

e) blue paint : yellow paint = 4 : 7

   33 more cups of yellow than blue

   b:

   y:

   blue: _____

   yellow: _____

f) blue paint : yellow paint = 5 : 2

   42 cups of paint altogether

   b:

   y:

   blue: _____

   yellow: _____

8. Draw a model to answer the question.

a) There are 35 students in a class. The ratio of girls to boys is 3 : 2. How many girls and how many boys are in the class?

b) There are 44 marbles in a jar. The marbles are blue and red. The ratio of blue marbles to red marbles is 5 : 6. How many red marbles and how many blue marbles are in the jar?

c) Clara collects American and Canadian stamps. She has 6 more American stamps than Canadian stamps. The ratio of Canadian to American stamps is 3 : 5. How many of each kind of stamp does she have?

9. Peter is 6 times as old as Ella.

a) What is the ratio of Peter's age to Ella's age?

b) Peter is 15 years older than Ella. How old are Peter and Ella?

RP7-11 Solving Proportions

1. There are 3 cats for every 2 dogs. Write the quantity you know in the correct column. Write a question mark for the quantity you don't know.

		Cats : Dogs
a)	There are 12 dogs. How many cats are there?	3 : 2
		= ___ : ___
b)	There are 12 cats. How many dogs are there?	3 : 2
		= ___ : ___
c)	There are 18 dogs. How many cats are there?	3 : 2
		= ___ : ___
d)	There are 48 cats. How many dogs are there?	3 : 2
		= ___ : ___

A **proportion** is an equation that shows two equivalent ratios. Example: 1 : 4 = 2 : 8

When a proportion is missing a number, finding the missing number is called **solving the proportion**.

Example: To solve the proportion 10 : 3 = 50 : ?, notice that $10 \times 5 = 50$, so the missing number is $3 \times 5 = 15$.

2. Solve the proportions from Question 1 to fill in the blanks.

   a) There are _____ cats.   b) There are _____ dogs.

   c) There are _____ cats.   d) There are _____ dogs.

3. Five bus tickets cost $9. Write and solve a proportion to answer these questions.

   a) How many bus tickets can you buy with $45?   b) How much will 45 bus tickets cost?

   dollars : bus tickets   dollars : bus tickets

   = ___ : ___   = ___ : ___

   = ___ : ___   = ___ : ___

4. Jake can run 3 laps in 5 minutes. At the same rate …

   a) how many laps can he run in 30 minutes?   b) how long would 30 laps take?

   laps : minutes   laps : minutes

   = ___ : ___   = ___ : ___

   = ___ : ___   = ___ : ___

5. Solve the proportions. Did you multiply the rows or the columns?

   a) Nina can run 4 laps in 10 minutes. At the same rate, how long will it take her to run 20 laps?

Laps	Minutes
4	10
20	?

   It will take _____ minutes to run 20 laps.

   I multiplied the _____.

   b) A muffin recipe calls for 3 cups of flour for 12 large muffins. Tony has 5 cups of flour. How many muffins can he make?

Cups of Flour	Muffins
3	12
5	?

   He can make _____ muffins.

   I multiplied the _____.

   c) Two centimeters on a map represents five actual kilometers. If a lake is 6 cm long on the map, what is its actual size?

Map Size (cm)	Actual Size (km)

   The lake is _____ km long.

   I multiplied the _____.

6. Two centimeters on a map represents eight actual kilometers. If a lake is 5 cm long on the map, what is its actual size?

7. A baseball field 360 ft long has first base and home plate 90 ft apart. Kim wants to make a baseball field with the same proportions in a park 120 ft long. How far from home plate should she put first base?

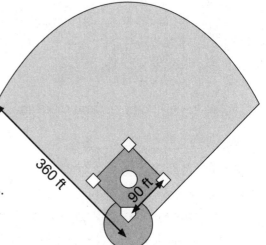

8. On a test with 30 math questions, Carl got 25 correct answers. At that rate, how many questions would he get right on a test with 90 questions?

9. An animal shelter has 4 dogs for every 5 cats. The shelter estimates that it spends $25 per month on each cat, and $40 per month on each dog. The shelter has a total of 45 cats and dogs. How much does it spend each month on all of the animals?

10. Zara wants to make 40 cups of orange paint. She uses 3 cups of red paint for every 5 cups of yellow paint. She already has 12 cups of red paint, but no yellow paint.

   a) How much red paint does she need to buy?

   b) How much yellow paint does she need to buy?

   c) Paint costs $8 for each cup. How much does Zara need to spend on paint?

         Ratios and Proportional Relationships 7-11

NS7-1 Integers

An **integer** is any one of these numbers: ..., −4, −3, −2, −1, 0, 1, 2, 3, 4, ...

1. Label the following integers on the number line with their letters.

   T. 6   **O.** −3   **S.** −7   **P.** −5   **R.** 3

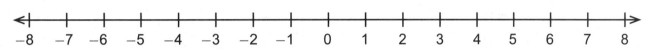

One integer is greater than another if it is:

   • higher up on a vertical number line or
   • farther right on a horizontal number line

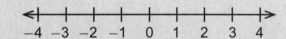

Write < for "is less than" and > for "is greater than."

2. a) Circle the integers on the number line: 2   −3   −7   −2   8

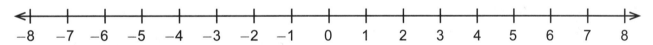

   b) Write the integers you circled in order from least to greatest.

   _____ < _____ < _____ < _____ < _____

3. Use the number line to answer the questions.

   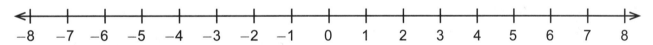

   a) Write < or > in the box.

   i) 2 ☐ 7   ii) −6 ☐ 5   iii) 8 ☐ −2   iv) −4 ☐ −6

   b) Put the integers into the boxes in order from greatest to least.

   4, −2, 7, −8, −1   ☐ > ☐ > ☐ > ☐ > ☐

   c) Write three integers that are less than −5. _____, _____, _____

   d) How many integers are between −4 and 2? _____

   e) Which integers are closer together, −3 and 3 or −4 and 4? _____

Integers that are **greater than 0** are called **positive integers**.
Integers that are **less than 0** are called **negative integers**.

4. How many negative integers are greater than (to the right of) −4? _____

5. Which other number is the same distance from 0 as the number marked?

a) 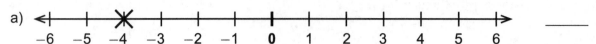 _____

b) _____

c) _____

d) _____

Opposite integers are the same distance from 0, but in opposite directions.

6. Write the opposite integer. Hint: Look at your answers to Question 5.

a) −4 _____   b) 3 _____   c) −2 _____   d) 6 _____

Positive numbers are sometimes written with a + in front.
Example: 3 can be written as 3 or +3, but −3 is written only as −3.

The opposite of an integer has the same whole number part, but the opposite sign (+ or −).
Example: The opposite of −100 is +100 or 100.

7. Write the opposite integer.

a) −83 _____   b) 76 _____   c) −800 _____   d) +510 _____

8. Use the number line to compare the positive numbers and their opposite negative numbers. Write < or > in each box.

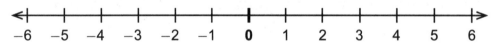

a) 2 ☐ 6 and −2 ☐ −6

b) 4 ☐ 1 and −4 ☐ −1

c) 5 ☐ 3 and −5 ☐ −3

d) 4 ☐ 6 and −4 ☐ −6

e) 3 ☐ 4 and −3 ☐ −4

f) 4 ☐ 0 and −4 ☐ −0

9. Make a prediction by writing < or > in the box.

835 < 846, so −835 ☐ −846.

10. Read the numbers from left to right. Circle the first pair of different digits you find.
Then write the greater number in the box.

a)   8 2, 4 ⑥ 3
    8 2, 4 ⑤ 8

[   ]

b)   ③ 8 4, 6 0 7
         3, 8 4 6

[   ]

c)   8 5, 6 4 1
    9 5, 3 8 0

[   ]

11. Write the correct inequality sign ($<$ or $>$) in the box.

a) 8,653 ☐ 8,486

b) 15,332 ☐ 16,012

c) 9,000 ☐ 7,999

d) 2,382 ☐ 589

e) 3,289 ☐ 10,104

f) 9,614 ☐ 90,614

> If you can compare positive numbers, you can compare their opposite negative numbers.
>
> Example: 30 is **less than** 40, so -30 is **greater than** -40.

12. Compare the positive integers, then compare the negative integers.

a) 5,438 ☐ 5,416

So $-5{,}438$ ☐ $-5{,}416$.

b) 35,463 ☐ 32,574

So $-35{,}463$ ☐ $-32{,}574$.

c) 90,608 ☐ 9,608

So $-90{,}608$ ☐ $-9{,}608$.

d) 72,035 ☐ 2,035

So $-72{,}035$ ☐ $-2{,}035$.

e) 863 ☐ 51,382

So -863 ☐ $-51{,}382$.

f) 85,417 ☐ 85,423

So $-85{,}417$ ☐ $-85{,}423$.

13. Do you need to compare the numbers 58 and 47 to compare -58 to $+47$? Explain. _____

_____

_____

14. Compare the fractions. Hint: Look at the signs first. Only look at the number parts
if you have to.

a) $-\dfrac{2}{5}$ ☐ $-\dfrac{4}{5}$

b) $-\dfrac{3}{4}$ ☐ $+\dfrac{1}{4}$

c) $-\dfrac{2}{3}$ ☐ $-\dfrac{1}{3}$

d) $-\dfrac{1}{2}$ ☐ $-\dfrac{3}{5}$

e) $+\dfrac{2}{3}$ ☐ $-\dfrac{3}{4}$

f) $-\dfrac{2}{3}$ ☐ $-\dfrac{3}{5}$

$= -\dfrac{\;\;\;}{10}$ $= -\dfrac{\;\;\;}{10}$

$= +\dfrac{\;\;\;}{12}$ $= -\dfrac{\;\;\;}{12}$

$= -\dfrac{\;\;\;}{15}$ $= -\dfrac{\;\;\;}{15}$

NS7-2 Integers in the Real World

Integers can be used to describe opposite directions from a chosen point. This point becomes the 0.

Examples:

- Temperature: degrees warmer than 0°F (+), or degrees colder than 0°F (−)
- Elevation: feet above sea level (+), or feet below sea level (−)
- Time zones: hours ahead of London, England (+), or hours behind London, England (−)

1. Write the integer to represent the situation. Include the units.

a) three degrees colder than 0°F ___−3°F___

b) four degrees warmer than 0°F _____

c) two feet above sea level ___+2 feet_____

d) eight feet below sea level _____

e) five hours ahead of London, England _____

f) four hours behind London, England _____

g) thirty-four meters below sea level _____

h) eight hundred seven degrees warmer than 0°F _____

+45°F is warmer than +32°F, so the integer +42 is greater than +32.

2. The thermometer shows average temperatures of the eight planets in our solar system.

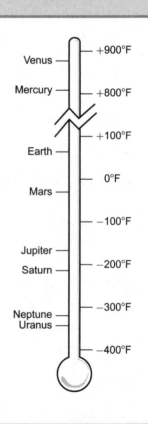

a) Which planet is warmest? _____

Its temperature is about _____ °F.

b) Which planet is coldest? _____

Its temperature is about _____ °F.

c) How many planets are warmer than Earth? _____

d) How many planets are colder than Earth? _____

e) About what is Earth's average temperature? _____

f) Which planet is about 300°F colder than Earth?

_____

g) About how much warmer is Mercury than Earth? _____ °F

Integers can be used to describe opposite values that cancel each other out.

Examples:

- Money: gaining money (+) and losing the same amount of money (−)
- Football: gaining yards (+) and losing the same number of yards (−)
- +/− rating: points in favor (+) and the same number of points against (−)

3. Write the integer that represents the situation. Include the units.

   a) a gain of $5 _____   b) a loss of $9 _____

   c) 4 points against _____   d) 3 points for _____

   e) a gain of 2 yards in football _____   f) a loss of 3 yards in football _____

4. Show the gains and losses by marking the letters on the number line.

   A. a gain of $4   **B.** a loss of $3   **C.** a gain of $5   **D.** a loss of $6

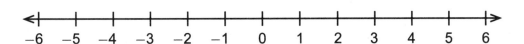

A bank statement shows a **credit** (+) when you add money to your account, and a **debit** (−) when you take money out of your account.

5. Write the integer that represents the action. Include the units.

   a) a debit of $3   b) a credit of $5   c) a debit of $4   d) a credit of $7

   ___−$3___   _____   _____   _____

6. Four people have bank account balances.

   Jake +$3   **Sally** +$6   **Ethan** −$4   **Mandy** −$5

   a) Show each person's balance on the number line.

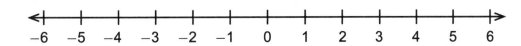

   b) Write the four names in order from least balance to greatest balance.

   _____ < _____ < _____ < _____

   c) Whose bank account balance would you most like to have? _____

   d) Whose bank account balance would you least like to have? _____

NS7-3 Adding Gains and Losses

1. Was it a good day (+) or a bad day (−)?

   a) $+5-3$ __+__   b) $+3-5$ _____   c) $-4+3$ _____   d) $+6-9$ _____

   e) $-3+2$ _____   f) $-6+7$ _____   g) $+7-2$ _____   h) $+7-10$ _____

2. How much was gained or lost overall?

   a) $+6-5$ b) $-5+3$ c) $+5-5$ d) $-6+6$

   _____   _____   _____   _____

   e) $+4+2$ f) $-1-3$ g) $+6-2$ h) $+3-3$

   _____   _____   _____   _____

To add many gains and losses:

Step 1: Circle the gains.

Step 2: Add the gains and losses separately.

Example: $(+3)-4-5(+6)(+2)-5(+1)$
$= +12 - 14 = -2$

---

3. Circle the gains. How much was gained or lost overall?

   a) $(+3)-2-8(+4)$
      $= +7 - 10$
      $= -3$

   b) $+6+5-3-7+6-4$

   c) $-5-6+9-8+10$

   d) $-9+7-2+1+1$

   e) $-1-1-1-1$

   f) $+1-2+3-4+5-6+7-8$

   Bonus ▶ Find an easier way to add $+1-2+3-4+5-6+7-8$.

4. Cancel out as much as you can before adding.

a) $\cancel{-3} + 5 \cancel{+3} - 8$
   $= +5 - 8 = -3$

b) $+5 - 4 \cancel{-3} + 2 \cancel{+3}$
   $= \boxed{+5} - 4 \boxed{+2}$
   $= +7 - 4 = +3$

c) $+9 - 5 - 6 + 5 + 3 - 9$

d) $+1 + 2 + 3 - 2 - 3 - 4$

e) $-7 + 4 + 5 - 4 + 7 + 6 - 1$

f) $+3 + 2 - 8 + 7 - 3 - 5 + 8$

g) $-8 + 5 + 3 - 7 - 5 + 7 + 5$

h) $-6 + 4 + 8 - 5 - 4 - 8 - 1$

Pairs that add to 10 are easy to see. When a positive pair adds to $+10$ and a negative pair adds to -10, you can cancel them out.

Example: $+4 + 6 - 3 - 5 - 7 = -5$ because $+4 + 6$ and $-3 - 7$ cancel each other out.

---

5. Cancel out pairs that add to $+10$ with pairs that add to -10. Then add the integers.

a) $+5 - 4 + 5 - 3 - 7$

b) $+8 + 3 + 2 - 1 - 9$

c) $+6 + 2 - 5 + 4 - 7 - 2 - 3 - 5 + 10$

d) $-1 + 2 - 3 + 5 + 8 + 5 - 4 - 7 - 6$

Bonus ▶ Cancel out pairs that add to $+100$ with pairs that add to -100. Then add the integers.

a) $-50 + 40 - 30 - 20 + 60 - 80$

b) $+62 - 41 - 59 + 38 - 69$

NS7-4 Opposite Actions and Opposite Integers

Opposite actions **cancel each other out**. The result is as though nothing happened.

Examples:

• A gain of $4 followed by a loss of $4 results in no gain or loss.

• A 4-yard gain in football followed by a 4-yard loss results in no gain or loss.

1. Write the integers that represent the amounts that cancel each other out.

   a) a gain of $3 and a loss of $3

   __+3__ and __−3__

   b) a loss of $5 and a gain of $5

   _____ and _____

   c) a gain of 4 yards and a loss of 4 yards

   _____ and _____

   d) a loss of 3 yards and a gain of 3 yards

   _____ and _____

Protons and electrons have electric charges that cancel each other out.

A proton has a charge of $+1$. ⊕   An electron has a charge of -1. ⊖

2. Describe the total electric charge as an integer.

   a) ⊕⊕   b) ⊖⊖⊖   c) ⊕⊕⊕⊕⊕⊕⊕

   _____   _____   _____

3. Draw a picture to show the given electric charge using protons () or electrons ().

   a) −4   b) +3   c) −2   d) −1

   ⊖⊖⊖⊖

4. Circle the electric charges that cancel each other out. Then find the resulting total electric charge.

   a) $+2 - 4 =$ __−2__

   ⊕⊕⊖⊖⊖⊖

   b) $+4 - 3 =$ _____

   ⊕⊕⊕⊕⊖⊖⊖

   c) $+3 - 4 =$ _____

   ⊕⊕⊕⊖⊖⊖⊖

   d) $+6 - 3 =$ _____

   ⊕⊕⊕⊕⊕⊕⊖⊖⊖

   e) $+5 - 1 =$ _____

   ⊕⊕⊕⊕⊕⊖

   f) $+3 - 5 =$ _____

   ⊕⊕⊕⊖⊖⊖⊖⊖

   g) $+3 - 3 =$ _____

   ⊕⊕⊕⊖⊖⊖

   h) $+2 - 2 =$ _____

   ⊕⊕⊖⊖

> REMINDER: A bank statement shows a credit (+) when you add money to your account, and a debit (−) when you take money out of your account.

5. Draw a picture to find the resulting balance. Hint: Circle the amounts that cancel each other out.

   a) a debit of $3 and a credit of $5   b) a credit of $1 and a debit of $3

 _+$2_

                                                                              _____

   c) a credit of $4 and a debit of $1   d) a debit of $3 and a credit of $2

                   _____   _____

   e) a credit of $4 and a debit of $4   f) a debit of $3 and a credit of $3

                   _____   _____

> When you add opposite integers, the result is 0:
>
> A **gain of $4** followed by a **loss of $4** results in **no** gain or loss.
>
>   (**+4**)   +   (**−4**)   =   **0**

6. Finish the equation.

   a) $(+3) + (−3) =$ _____   b) $(−5) + (+5) =$ _____

   c) $(−7) +$ _____ $= 0$ d) $(+2) +$ _____ $= 0$

7. Write an addition equation to show the situation.

   a) When Alex adds $3 to his bank account and then takes out $3 from his account, his account is the same as when he started.

      _$(+3) + (−3) = 0$_____

   b) When Bev walks 5 steps east (+) and then 5 steps west (−), she ends up where she started.

      _____

   c) When Cam's football team loses 4 yards and then gains 4 yards, it ends up where it started.

      _____

8. Describe a situation in which opposite quantities combine to make 0. _____

_____

_____

NS7-5 Adding Integers on a Number Line

Gaining $5, or adding +5, is the same as adding 5.

To add a **positive** number, move **right**.
Example: To find +3, move 3 units right.

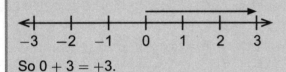

So $0 + 3 = +3$.

Losing $5, or adding −5, is the same as subtracting 5.

To add a **negative** number, move **left**.
Example: To find $(+3) + (−5)$, move 3 units right, then move 5 units left.

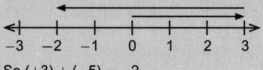

So $(+3) + (−5) = −2$.

1. Use the number line to add the positive and negative numbers.

a)
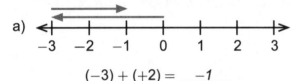

$(−3) + (+2) = \underline{\quad −1 \quad}$

b)
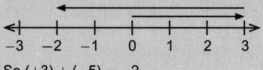

$(+2) + (−5) = \underline{\qquad}$

c)

$(−2) + (+1) = \underline{\qquad}$

d)
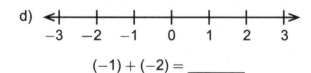

$(−1) + (−2) = \underline{\qquad}$

e)
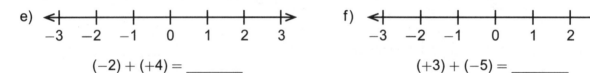

$(−2) + (+4) = \underline{\qquad}$

f)
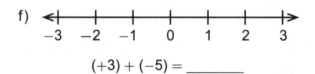

$(+3) + (−5) = \underline{\qquad}$

g)
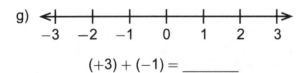

$(+3) + (−1) = \underline{\qquad}$

h)
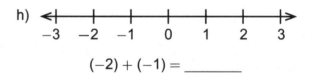

$(−2) + (−1) = \underline{\qquad}$

i)
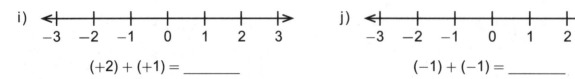

$(+2) + (+1) = \underline{\qquad}$

j)
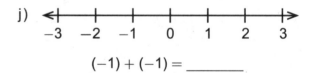

$(−1) + (−1) = \underline{\qquad}$

k)
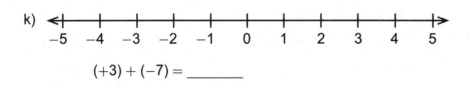

$(+3) + (−7) = \underline{\qquad}$

Expressions with brackets can be rewritten without brackets.

Example: Since adding -3 is the same as subtracting 3, you can write $(+5) + (-3) = +5 - 3$.

You can change the notation by using the rule: $+(+) = +$ $+(-) = -$

2. Write the addition without brackets.

a) $(-3) + (+6)$ b) $(+2) + (+3)$ c) $(-2) + (-5)$ d) $(+2) + (-4)$

   $\underline{\quad -3 + 6 \quad}$ $\underline{\qquad\qquad}$ $\underline{\qquad\qquad}$ $\underline{\qquad\qquad}$

e) $(+2) + (+6)$ f) $(-4) + (+1)$ g) $(+5) + (-1)$ h) $(-3) + (-3)$

   $\underline{\qquad\qquad}$ $\underline{\qquad\qquad}$ $\underline{\qquad\qquad}$ $\underline{\qquad\qquad}$

i) $(+3) + (-7)$ j) $(-8) - (+9)$ k) $(-4) - (-7)$ l) $(-7) - (+8)$

   $\underline{\qquad\qquad}$ $\underline{\qquad\qquad}$ $\underline{\qquad\qquad}$ $\underline{\qquad\qquad}$

3. Use the number line to add the integers.

a) number line: -3 -2 -1 0 1 2 3

   $(+3) + (-2) = \underline{\quad +3 - 2 \quad} = \underline{\quad}$

b) number line: -3 -2 -1 0 1 2 3

   $(-3) + (+4) = \underline{\qquad\qquad} = \underline{\quad}$

c) number line: -3 -2 -1 0 1 2 3

   $(-2) + (+5) = \underline{\qquad\qquad} = \underline{\quad}$

d) number line: -6 -5 -4 -3 -2 -1 0

   $(-3) + (-2) = \underline{\qquad\qquad} = \underline{\quad}$

4. Without using a number line, add the integers by first dropping the brackets.

a) $(-5) + (-5)$ b) $(+3) + (-6)$ c) $(-9) + (+4)$ d) $(+4) + (+7)$

   $= \underline{\quad -5 - 5 \quad}$ $= \underline{\qquad\qquad}$ $= \underline{\qquad\qquad}$ $= \underline{\qquad\qquad}$

   $= \underline{\quad}$ $= \underline{\quad}$ $= \underline{\quad}$ $= \underline{\quad}$

e) $(-5) + (+7)$ f) $(-3) + (-4)$ g) $(+5) + (+4)$ h) $(+4) + (-6)$

   $= \underline{\qquad\qquad}$ $= \underline{\qquad\qquad}$ $= \underline{\qquad\qquad}$ $= \underline{\qquad\qquad}$

   $= \underline{\quad}$ $= \underline{\quad}$ $= \underline{\quad}$ $= \underline{\quad}$

Bonus ▶

i) $(+2) + (-3) + (-1) + (+4) + (-5) = \underline{\qquad\qquad\qquad\qquad} = \underline{\qquad\quad}$

j) $(+2,000) + (-5,000) + (-3,000) = \underline{\qquad\qquad\qquad\qquad} = \underline{\qquad}$

NS7-6 Using Pictures to Subtract Integers

To subtract $+5$ from $+3$, you can write $+3 - (+5)$ or $(+3) - (+5)$.

1. Write a subtraction equation for the picture.

a) ⊖ ⊖ ⊖ ⊖ ⊖

$\underline{(-5) - (-2) = -3}$

b) ⊖ ⊖ ⊖

_____

c) ⊕ ⊕ ⊕ ⊕

_____

d) ⊕ ⊕ ⊕ ⊕

_____

e) ⊕ ⊕ ⊕ ⊕ ⊕

_____

f) ⊖ ⊖ ⊖ ⊖ ⊖ ⊖

_____

2. Draw a picture for the subtraction. Then finish the equation.

a) $+5 - (+3) = \underline{\;+2\;}$

⊕ ⊕ ⊕ ⊕ ⊕

b) $+4 - (+1) = \underline{\qquad}$

c) $(+3) - (+2) = \underline{\qquad}$

d) $-5 - (-3) = \underline{\qquad}$

e) $(-4) - (-1) = \underline{\qquad}$

f) $-3 - (-2) = \underline{\qquad}$

Bonus ▶ $-15 - (-8) = \underline{\qquad}$

3. What integer is represented? Hint: Circle the positives and negatives that cancel each other.

a) ⊕ ⊕
   ⊖ ⊖ ⊖ ⊖ ⊖

$\underline{\;-3\;}$

b) ⊕ ⊕ ⊕
   ⊖ ⊖

$\underline{\qquad}$

c) ⊕ ⊕ ⊕
   ⊖ ⊖ ⊖ ⊖ ⊖

$\underline{\qquad}$

d) ⊕ ⊕ ⊕ ⊕ ⊕
   ⊖

$\underline{\qquad}$

e) ⊕ ⊕ ⊕ ⊕ ⊕
   ⊖ ⊖ ⊖ ⊖

$\underline{\qquad}$

f) ⊕ ⊕
   ⊖ ⊖ ⊖ ⊖ ⊖ ⊖ ⊖

$\underline{\qquad}$

To subtract +3 − (−2), draw a picture for +3. Keep adding 0 (one positive and one negative) until you can take away −2.

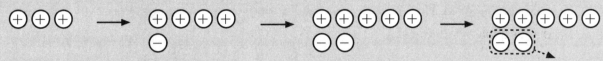

I can't take away −2.

I still can't take away −2.

Now I can take away −2.

So +3 − (−2) = +5.

4. Subtract.

a) +2 − (−3)

⊕⊕ → ⊕⊕⊕⊕⊕ → ⊕⊕⊕⊕⊕ → ⊕⊕⊕⊕⊕
            ⊖⊖⊖   ⊖⊖⊖

+2

Now I can take away −3.

+2 − (−3)

+2 − (−3) = _____

b) −3 − (+1)

⊖⊖⊖ → ⊖⊖⊖⊖ → ⊖⊖⊖⊖ → ⊖⊖⊖⊖
            ⊕   ⊕

−3

Now I can take away +1.

−3 − (+1)

−3 − (+1) = _____

c) +2 − (+5)

⊕⊕ → ⊕⊕⊕⊕⊕ → ⊕⊕⊕⊕⊕ → ⊖⊖⊖
            ⊖⊖⊖   ⊖⊖⊖

+2

Now I can take away +5.

+2 − (+5)

+2 − (+5) = _____

5. Finish drawing the pictures, then subtract.

−2 − (−3)

⊖⊖ → ⊖⊖⊖ →   →
            ⊕

−2

Now I can take away −3.

−2 − (−3)

−2 − (−3) = _____

6. Draw a picture of the first number so you can subtract the second number.

a) +5 − (−3)   b) −2 − (+3)   c) +2 − (+3)   d) −1 − (−4)

NS7-7 Subtracting Integers on a Number Line

You can subtract 5 − 3 on a number line by asking, "How do you get from 3 to 5?"

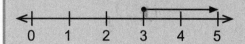

Move **2** units **right**, so 5 − 3 = **+2**

You can subtract 3 − 5 on a number line by asking, "How do you get from 5 to 3?"

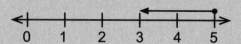

Move **2** units **left**, so 3 − 5 = **−2**

1. Use the number line to subtract the positive and negative numbers.

a)
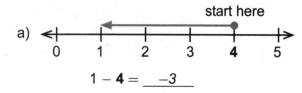
1 − **4** = ___−3___

b)
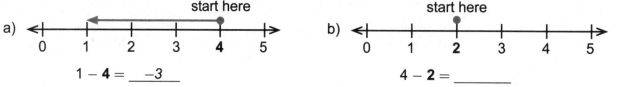
4 − **2** = _____

c)
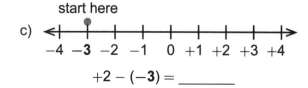
+2 − (−**3**) = _____

d)
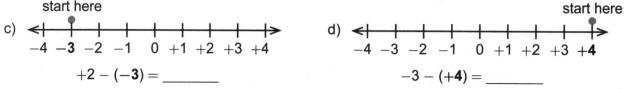
−3 − (+**4**) = _____

e)
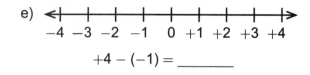
+4 − (−1) = _____

f)
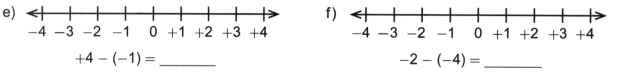
−2 − (−4) = _____

g)
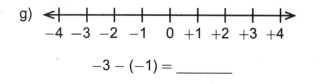
−3 − (−1) = _____

h)
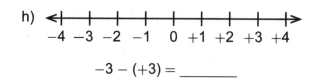
−3 − (+3) = _____

i)
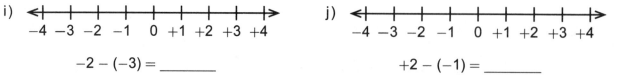
−2 − (−3) = _____

j)
−2 − (−3) = _____

+2 − (−1) = _____

k)
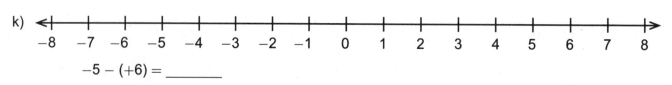
−5 − (+6) = _____

The Number System 7-7

REMINDER: A distance is always positive.

2. Do both subtractions. Then circle the subtraction that tells you how far apart the integers are.

a) $7 - 4 = \underline{\ \ 3\ \ }$

$4 - 7 = \underline{\ \ -3\ \ }$

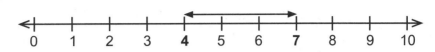

b) $3 - 2 = \underline{\quad}$

$2 - 3 = \underline{\quad}$

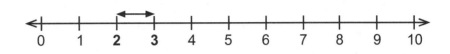

REMINDER: When subtracting integers, people sometimes write both numbers in brackets.

Example: $+5 - (-3) = (+5) - (-3)$

c) $(-1) - (+3) = \underline{\quad}$

$(+3) - (-1) = \underline{\quad}$

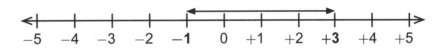

d) $(-2) - (-5) = \underline{\quad}$

$(-5) - (-2) = \underline{\quad}$

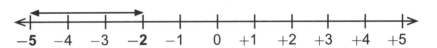

e) $(+2) - (-4) = \underline{\quad}$

$(-4) - (+2) = \underline{\quad}$

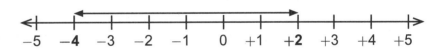

3. Which subtraction will give the distance between -2 and $+6$?

$(+6) - (-2)$ \qquad or \qquad $(-2) - (+6)$

How do you know? _____

_____

The **absolute value** of a number is its distance from 0. The notation $|-3|$ is short for "the absolute value of -3."

Examples: $|-3| = 3$ and $|+8| = 8$

4. Write the absolute value.

a) $|-3| = \underline{\quad}$ \qquad b) $|+5| = \underline{\quad}$ \qquad c) $|-15| = \underline{\quad}$ \qquad d) $|0| = \underline{\quad}$

e) $\left|-\dfrac{1}{2}\right| = \underline{\quad}$ \qquad f) $\left|-\dfrac{5}{6}\right| = \underline{\quad}$ \qquad g) $\left|+\dfrac{3}{8}\right| = \underline{\quad}$ \qquad h) $\left|+\dfrac{5}{2}\right| = \underline{\quad}$

The distance between two integers is the absolute value of their difference.

Example: 4 and 7 are $|4 - 7| = |-3| = 3$ units apart.

5. Subtract. Then take the absolute value to find the distance apart.

   a) $|(-3) - (+2)| = |\underline{\ -5\ }| = \underline{\ 5\ }$,

   so -3 and $+2$ are $\underline{\ 5\ }$ units apart.

   b) $|(-5) - (-1)| = |\underline{\hspace{1cm}}| = \underline{\hspace{1cm}}$,

   so -5 and -1 are $\underline{\hspace{1cm}}$ units apart.

   c) $|(+18) - (-4)| = |\underline{\hspace{1cm}}| = \underline{\hspace{1cm}}$,

   so $+18$ and -4 are $\underline{\hspace{1cm}}$ units apart.

   d) $|25 - 100| = |\underline{\hspace{1cm}}| = \underline{\hspace{1cm}}$,

   so 25 and 100 are $\underline{\hspace{1cm}}$ units apart.

   e) $|(-6) - (-15)| = |\underline{\hspace{1cm}}| = \underline{\hspace{1cm}}$,

   so -6 and -15 are $\underline{\hspace{1cm}}$ units apart.

   f) $|(-9) - (-9)| = |\underline{\hspace{1cm}}| = \underline{\hspace{1cm}}$,

   so -9 and -9 are $\underline{\hspace{1cm}}$ units apart.

6. Show your answer to these questions on a vertical number line.

   a) How much warmer is $+3°F$ than $-2°F$?

   b) Which temperature is warmer, $-5°F$ or $-8°F$? How much warmer?

   c) A bird is flying 500 m above sea level and a fish is swimming 200 m below sea level, directly below the bird. How far apart are the bird and the fish?

   d) Jennifer lives 5 blocks south of the library, and Rob lives 8 blocks north of the library on the same street. How far apart do they live?

NS7-8 Patterns in Subtraction

1. Subtract from 0 on the number line.

a)
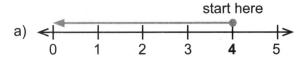

$0 - \mathbf{4} = \underline{\quad -4 \quad} \leftarrow$ move 4 spaces left

b)
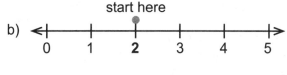

$0 - \mathbf{2} = \underline{\qquad}$

c)
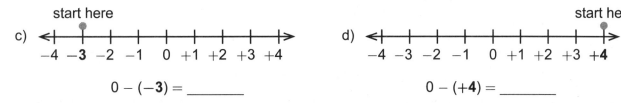

$0 - (\mathbf{-3}) = \underline{\qquad}$

d)

$0 - (\mathbf{+4}) = \underline{\qquad}$

e)
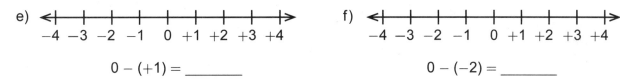

$0 - (\mathbf{+1}) = \underline{\qquad}$

f)

$0 - (\mathbf{-2}) = \underline{\qquad}$

2. Subtract from 0 without using the number line.

a) $0 - (-8) = \underline{\qquad}$

b) $0 - (+5) = \underline{\qquad}$

c) $0 - (+7) = \underline{\qquad}$

d) $0 - (-6) = \underline{\qquad}$

e) $0 - (-90) = \underline{\qquad}$

Bonus ▶ $0 - (+14{,}300{,}000) = \underline{\qquad\qquad}$

Subtracting -1 is the same as adding $+1$.

 $\longrightarrow$ $\longrightarrow$ $\longrightarrow$

Start with $+3$.   Add zero.   Take away -1.   So $+3 - (-1) = +4$.

---

3. Subtract -1.

a) $-2 - (-1)$

$= \underline{\quad -2 + 1 \quad}$

$= \underline{\quad -1 \quad}$

b) $+4 - (-1)$

$= \underline{\qquad}$

$= \underline{\quad}$

c) $-3 - (-1)$

$= \underline{\qquad}$

$= \underline{\quad}$

d) $+8 - (-1)$

$= \underline{\qquad}$

$= \underline{\quad}$

4. Subtracting -1 is the same as adding $+1$ because adding 0 (a ⊕ and a ⊖),
then taking away the ⊖ is the same as just adding the ⊕.

Explain why subtracting $+1$ is the same as adding -1.

You can subtract an integer by adding its opposite: $-(+) = -$ $-(-) = +$

5. Subtract.

a) $(+4) - (-3)$

= ___+4 + 3___

= ___+7___

b) $(-3) - (+2)$

= _____

= _____

c) $(+7) - (+2)$

= _____

= _____

d) $(+4) - (-8)$

= _____

= _____

e) $(-1) - (+5)$

= _____

= _____

f) $(-4) - (-1)$

= _____

= _____

REMINDER: $+(+) = +$ $+(-) = -$ $-(+) = -$ $-(-) = +$

---

6. Add or subtract.

a) $(+7) - (-8)$

= ___+7 + 8___

= ___+15___

b) $(-8) + (-5)$

= _____

= _____

c) $(-3) - (-5)$

= _____

= _____

d) $(+9) - (-6)$

= _____

= _____

e) $(-10) + (+3)$

= _____

= _____

f) $(-5) - (+8)$

= _____

= _____

7. Use the number line to continue the pattern.

a)
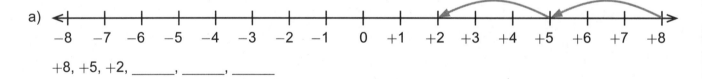

+8, +5, +2, _____, _____, _____

b)
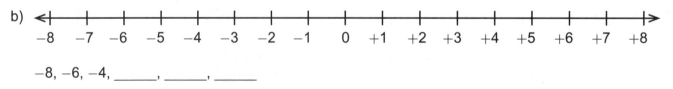

−8, −6, −4, _____, _____, _____

8. The temperature in the evening was 3°F. It dropped 4°F overnight. What was the temperature in the morning?

9. The temperature on Monday was 0°C. The temperature on Tuesday was 14°C colder. What was the temperature on Tuesday?

NS7-9 Adding and Subtracting Multi-Digit Integers

1. Add 6,834 + 2,527 by using place value.

6, 8 3 4   _____ thousands + _____ hundreds + _____ tens + _____ ones

+ 2, 5 2 7   + _____ thousands + _____ hundreds + _____ tens + _____ ones

             = _____ thousands + _____ hundreds + _____ tens + _____ ones

after regrouping = _____ thousands + _____ hundreds + _____ tens + _____ ones

2. Add using the standard algorithm.

a)   3 7 4
   + 1 6 3

b)   9, 6 5 4
   +   8 2 4

c)   3 2 9, 7 8 4
   + 8 7 3, 1 0 6

d)   2 3 5, 2 7 5
   + 1 8 3, 7 4 6

3. a) Mark doesn't have enough ones to subtract 53 − 26. Help him by regrouping.

53 = 5 tens + 3 ones ——→   __4__ tens + __13__ ones
               regroup

                          − __2__ tens + __6__ ones

                          = _____ tens + _____ ones

b) Mark doesn't have enough tens to subtract 528 − 357. Help him by regrouping.

528 = 5 hundreds + 2 tens + 8 ones ——→   _____ hundreds + _____ tens + _____ ones

                                        − _____ hundreds + _____ tens + _____ ones

                                        = _____ hundreds + _____ tens + _____ ones

4. Subtract. Regroup where necessary.

a)
		7	14
	7	8̸	4̸
−	2	4	8

b)
5	3	7
− 4	6	1

c)
9	1	3
− 5	0	8

d)
4	0	9
− 1	4	0

e)
		12	
	5	2̸	14
	6̸	3̸	4̸
−	1	5	9

f)
5	1	2
− 1	6	4

g)
7	3	5
− 1	3	9

h)
9	4	3
− 6	4	7

5. Add.

a) − 342 − 875

	1		
	3	4	2
+	8	7	5
1	2	1	7

_−1,217_____

b) + 8,056 + 187

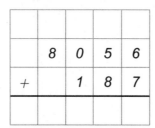

_____

c) − 516 − 843

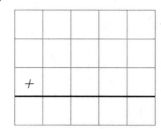

_____

d) − 7,218 − 95

e) + 174 + 292

f) − 1,854 − 277

g) + 342 + 3,987

h) − 50 − 95,000

i) − 803 − 6,000 − 87

6. Use the grid to subtract the absolute values. Then add the integers.

a) − 342 + 875

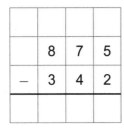

_____

b) + 304 − 587

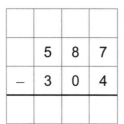

_____

c) − 63 + 874

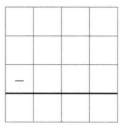

_____

d) − 3,201 + 954

e) + 190 − 450

f) − 2,308 + 2,803

7. Subtract by adding the opposite of the number you are subtracting.

a) −216 − (+154)

b) +183 − (−57)

c) +216 − (+53)

d) −814 − (−573)

e) +728 − (−943)

f) −573 − (+712)

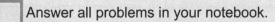 Answer all problems in your notebook.

8. Two nearby towns have populations of 442,680 and 564,943. What is the total population of both towns?

9. Anna, Sam, and Lily all ran for school president. Anna received 432 votes, Sam received 591 votes, and Lily received 1,246 votes. How many people voted in the election altogether?

10. The chart shows the population of each region on Earth in 2013. What was the total population of Earth in 2013?

Africa	1,110,635,000
Americas and Caribbean	972,005,000
Asia	4,298,723,000
Europe	742,452,000
Oceania	38,304,000

11. In the summer, the temperature at the South Pole is about −15°F. In the winter, it is about 57°F colder. What is the winter temperature at the South Pole?

12. The temperature on the Moon can reach as high as 253°F and as low as −243°F. How much hotter is the hottest temperature on the Moon than the coldest temperature?

13. The border the United States shares with Ontario, Canada, is 2,760 km long, and the border it shares with British Columbia, Canada, is 2,168 km long. How much longer is the US–Ontario border than the US–British Columbia border?

14. Backgammon was invented around 3000 BC, and introduced to the United States around 1920 AD. How many years later was that?

15. A red flame is burning at 980°F and a blue flame is burning at 2,793°F. How much hotter is the blue flame than the red flame?

16. A computer file with a size of 2,556 KB was separated into three files with the following sizes: 764 KB, 925 KB, and 928 KB. How much more space do the three files take up together than the single file did?

NS7-10 Factors

There are only three ways to write 4 as a product of two whole numbers:

$$1 \times 4 = 4 \qquad 2 \times 2 = 4 \qquad 4 \times 1 = 4$$

The numbers that appear in the products are called the **factors** of 4.
The factors of 4 are the numbers 1, 2, and 4.

1. Write the whole number that makes the equation true. If no whole number makes the equation true, write ✕ in the box.

   a) $3 \times \boxed{4} = 12$ b) $4 \times \boxed{✕} = 18$ c) $2 \times \boxed{} = 20$ d) $3 \times \boxed{} = 14$

2. Write "yes" or "no." Use your answers to Question 1 to explain your answer.

   a) Is 3 a factor of 12? _Yes_ because _4 makes the equation true_ .

   b) Is 4 a factor of 18? _No_ because _no number makes the equation true_ .

   c) Is 2 a factor of 20? _____ because _____ .

   d) Is 3 a factor of 14? _____ because _____ .

---

2 and 3 are a **factor pair** of 6 because $2 \times 3 = 6$.

---

3. List the factor pairs of each number. List each pair only once.

   a) 6   b) 8   c) 9

   ___1___ and ___6___   _____ and _____   _____ and _____

   ___2___ and ___3___   _____ and _____   _____ and _____

4. Alice lists the factor pairs of 12 by using a chart. When a number is not a factor, she writes an ✕ in the second column.

   a) Why didn't Alice list 13 as a first factor?

   _____

   b) Use Alice's chart to write the factors of 12.

   _____ , _____ , _____ , _____ , _____ , _____

   c) Use Alice's chart to write the factor pairs of 12.

   _____ and _____

   _____ and _____

   _____ and _____

First Factor	Second Factor
1	12
2	6
3	4
4	3
5	✕
6	2
7	✕
8	✕
9	✕
10	✕
11	✕
12	1

5. Use Alice's method to find all the factor pairs of each number.

a) 14   b) 15   c) 16   d) 18   e) 20   f) 24   g) 25

6. Use the top half of each chart to finish the bottom half.

a) 18

First Factor	Second Factor
1	18
2	9
3	6
6	3
	2
	1

b) 30

First Factor	Second Factor
1	30
2	15
3	10
5	6
	5
	3
	2
	1

c) 36

First Factor	Second Factor
1	36
2	18
3	12
4	9
6	6

To list all the factors of a given number, stop when you get a number that is already part of a factor pair.

7. Make a chart to find all the factor pairs. There might be more rows in the chart than you need.

a) 20

First Factor	Second Factor
1	20
2	10
4	5
5	STOP

b) 81

First Factor	Second Factor
1	81
3	27
9	9
STOP	

c) 32

First Factor	Second Factor

d) 35

First Factor	Second Factor

e) 44

First Factor	Second Factor

f) 56

First Factor	Second Factor

The **greatest common factor (GCF)** of two numbers is the greatest number that is a factor of both numbers.

8. a) Find and list all the factors of each number. You can make a chart if it helps.

   i) 36

   ii) 42

   iii) 99

   _____

   _____

   _____

   _____

   _____

   _____

   b) Use your answers from part a) to find the greatest common factor of …

   i) 36 and 42 _____

   ii) 36 and 99 _____

   iii) 42 and 99 _____

9. Make an equivalent fraction by dividing the numerator and denominator by the same number.

   a) $\dfrac{2 \div 2}{10 \div 2} = \dfrac{1}{5}$

   b) $\dfrac{12 \div 3}{18 \div 3} =$

   c) $\dfrac{812 \div 2}{826 \div 2} =$

Making an equivalent fraction with smaller numbers is called **reducing the fraction**.
A fraction is in **lowest terms** if it cannot be reduced further.

When a fraction is in lowest terms, the GCF of its numerator and denominator is 1.

Example: $\dfrac{6}{8}$ in lowest terms is $\dfrac{3}{4}$. The GCF of 3 and 4 is 1.

10. Find the GCF of the numerator and denominator. Is the fraction in lowest terms?

Fraction	$\dfrac{8}{10}$	$\dfrac{3}{8}$	$\dfrac{6}{9}$	$\dfrac{6}{5}$	$\dfrac{7}{8}$	$\dfrac{7}{4}$	$\dfrac{10}{8}$	$\dfrac{12}{9}$	$\dfrac{13}{8}$
GCF									
Lowest Terms									

11. Divide the numerator and denominator by their GCF.

   a) $\dfrac{6 \div 2}{10 \div 2} = \dfrac{3}{5}$

   b) $\dfrac{8}{12}$

   c) $\dfrac{5}{10}$

   d) $\dfrac{12}{16}$

   e) $\dfrac{9}{12}$

   f) $\dfrac{16}{18}$

   g) $\dfrac{25}{15}$

   h) $\dfrac{70}{80}$

   i) $\dfrac{85}{95}$

12. Are your answers to Question 11 in lowest terms? If not, find your mistake.

NS7-11 Adding and Subtracting Fractions with the Same Denominator

1. Imagine moving the shaded pieces from each pie onto the empty pie plate. Show how much of the empty pie plate would be filled, then write a fraction for the amount.

a)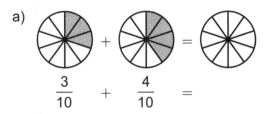

$$\frac{3}{10} + \frac{4}{10} =$$

b)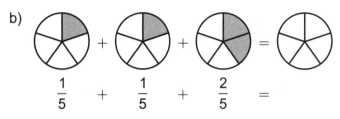

$$\frac{1}{5} + \frac{1}{5} + \frac{2}{5} =$$

2. Subtract by taking away the second amount.

a) $\dfrac{5}{8} - \dfrac{2}{8} =$

$$\frac{1}{8} + \frac{1}{8} + \frac{1}{8} + \boxed{\frac{1}{8} + \frac{1}{8}}$$

b) $\dfrac{6}{7} - \dfrac{4}{7} =$

$$\frac{1}{7} + \frac{1}{7} + \frac{1}{7} + \frac{1}{7} + \frac{1}{7} + \frac{1}{7}$$

3. Add or subtract.

a) $\dfrac{3}{5} + \dfrac{1}{5} =$ b) $\dfrac{3}{8} + \dfrac{3}{8} + \dfrac{1}{8} =$ c) $\dfrac{6}{5} - \dfrac{3}{5} =$ d) $\dfrac{9}{100} - \dfrac{2}{100} =$

4. Start at zero. Move right to add a positive number. Move left to add a negative number.

a) $+\dfrac{1}{5} + \dfrac{2}{5} = \boxed{}$

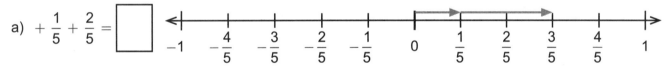

b) $+\dfrac{1}{5} - \dfrac{4}{5} = \boxed{}$

c) $-\dfrac{2}{5} + \dfrac{3}{5} = \boxed{}$

d) $-\dfrac{2}{5} - \dfrac{3}{5} = \boxed{}$

5. Evaluate by using opposites.

a) $+\dfrac{7}{5} - \dfrac{3}{5} = \boxed{}$

$-\dfrac{7}{5} + \dfrac{3}{5} = \boxed{}$

b) $+\dfrac{6}{4} + \dfrac{1}{4} = \boxed{}$

$-\dfrac{6}{4} - \dfrac{1}{4} = \boxed{}$

c) $+\dfrac{3}{1{,}000} + \dfrac{4}{1{,}000} = \boxed{}$

$-\dfrac{3}{1{,}000} - \dfrac{4}{1{,}000} = \boxed{}$

$$+1 - 4 = -3 \qquad \text{so} \qquad +1 \text{ fifth} - 4 \text{ fifths} = -3 \text{ fifths}$$

$$+\frac{1}{5} - \frac{4}{5} = -\frac{3}{5}$$

6. Write the addition without brackets. Then evaluate.

a) $\left(+\dfrac{3}{8}\right) + \left(-\dfrac{5}{8}\right) = +\dfrac{3}{8} - \dfrac{5}{8} = -\dfrac{2}{8}$

b) $\left(-\dfrac{4}{3}\right) + \left(-\dfrac{4}{3}\right) =$

c) $\left(+\dfrac{2}{7}\right) + \left(+\dfrac{4}{7}\right) =$

d) $\left(-\dfrac{5}{7}\right) + \left(+\dfrac{1}{7}\right) =$

e) $\left(+\dfrac{2}{5}\right) + \left(-\dfrac{6}{5}\right) =$

f) $\left(-\dfrac{3}{8}\right) + \left(-\dfrac{2}{8}\right) =$

g) $\left(-\dfrac{2}{9}\right) + \left(+\dfrac{5}{9}\right) =$

Bonus ▶ $\left(+\dfrac{4}{8}\right) + \left(-\dfrac{5}{8}\right) + \left(+\dfrac{1}{8}\right) =$

7. Subtract by adding the opposite number of what you are subtracting.

a) $\left(-\dfrac{7}{8}\right) - \left(-\dfrac{1}{8}\right) = \left(-\dfrac{7}{8}\right) + \left(+\dfrac{1}{8}\right)$

$\qquad = -\dfrac{7}{8} + \dfrac{1}{8}$

$\qquad = -\dfrac{6}{8}$

b) $\left(-\dfrac{1}{8}\right) - \left(+\dfrac{2}{8}\right) =$

c) $\left(+\dfrac{6}{4}\right) - \left(-\dfrac{3}{4}\right)$

d) $\left(-\dfrac{4}{9}\right) - \left(+\dfrac{7}{9}\right)$

e) $\left(-\dfrac{2}{5}\right) - \left(-\dfrac{7}{5}\right)$

f) $\left(+\dfrac{5}{11}\right) - \left(+\dfrac{7}{11}\right)$

NS7-12 Mixed Numbers and Improper Fractions

A **mixed number** is a mixture of a whole number and a fraction. An **improper fraction** has a numerator larger than the denominator.

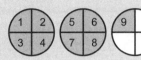

mixed number

improper fraction

1. Write these fractions as mixed numbers and as improper fractions

a)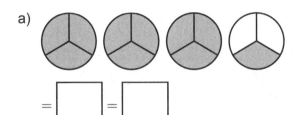

= ☐ = ☐

b)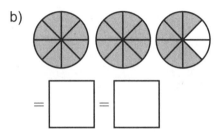

= ☐ = ☐

2. Shade the amount of pie given by the mixed number. Then write an improper fraction.

a) $3\frac{1}{2}$  _____

b) $2\frac{3}{4}$ 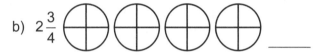 _____

c) $2\frac{2}{3}$  _____

d) $3\frac{2}{5}$  _____

3. Shade the area given by the improper fraction. Then write a mixed number.

a) $\frac{7}{3}$  _____

b) $\frac{17}{6}$  _____

c) $\frac{13}{5}$  _____

d) $\frac{21}{8}$  _____

4. Draw a picture to find out which is greater.

a) $3\frac{1}{2}$ or $\frac{5}{3}$

b) $1\frac{4}{5}$ or $\frac{11}{5}$

c) $\frac{15}{8}$ or $\frac{7}{3}$

d) $\frac{13}{4}$ or $2\frac{2}{3}$

5. Do you need to compare $\frac{1}{4}$ and $\frac{2}{9}$ to compare $6\frac{1}{4}$ and $5\frac{2}{9}$? Explain.

The Number System 7-12

How many quarter pieces are in $2\frac{3}{4}$ pies?

There are 4 quarter pieces in 1 pie.

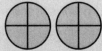

There are 2 × 4 quarters in 2 pies.

So there are 11 quarter pieces altogether.

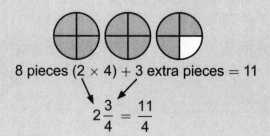

8 pieces (2 × 4) + 3 extra pieces = 11

$$2\frac{3}{4} = \frac{11}{4}$$

6. Find the number of **halves** in each amount.

   a) 1 pie = _____ halves

   b) 2 pies = _____ halves

   c) 3 pies = _____ halves

   d) $3\frac{1}{2}$ pies = _____ halves

   e) $4\frac{1}{2}$ pies = _____ halves

   f) $5\frac{1}{2}$ pies = _____ halves

7. Each pie has 3 pieces, so each piece is a third. Find the number of **thirds** in each amount.

   a) 1 pie = ___*3 thirds*___

   b) 2 pies = _____

   c) 5 pies = _____

   d) $5\frac{1}{3}$ pies = _____

   e) $2\frac{2}{3}$ pies = _____

   f) $4\frac{2}{3}$ pies = _____

8. A box holds 4 cans, so each can is a fourth. Find the number of cans each amount holds.

   a) 2 boxes hold _____ cans.

   b) $2\frac{1}{4}$ boxes hold _____ cans.

9. Write the mixed number as an improper fraction.

   a) $1\frac{4}{6} = \dfrac{}{6}$

   b) $5\frac{1}{2} = \dfrac{}{2}$

   c) $2\frac{3}{5} = \dfrac{}{}$

   d) $3\frac{2}{8} = \dfrac{}{}$

   e) $3\frac{1}{5} = \dfrac{}{}$

   f) $2\frac{6}{8} = \dfrac{}{}$

   g) $3\frac{6}{10} = \dfrac{}{}$

   h) $6\frac{3}{10} = \dfrac{}{}$

10. Look at your answers to Question 9. When the fraction part of the mixed number is in lowest terms, is the improper fraction also in lowest terms? _____

11. These pies are each cut into four pieces. There are 15 pieces of pie in total. How many whole pies are there and how many pieces are left over?

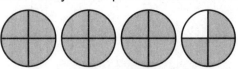

    15 ÷ 4 = _____ R _____

How many whole pies are in $\dfrac{13}{4}$ pies?

There are 13 pieces altogether, and each pie has 4 pieces: **13 ÷ 4 = 3 Remainder 1**

There are 3 whole pies and 1 quarter left over: 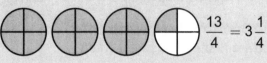 $\dfrac{13}{4} = 3\dfrac{1}{4}$

12. Find the number of whole pies in each amount by dividing.

a) $\dfrac{6}{2}$ pies = _____ whole pies   b) $\dfrac{12}{3}$ pies = _____ whole pies   c) $\dfrac{24}{4}$ pies = _____ whole pies

13. Find the number of whole pies and the number of pieces remaining by dividing.

a) $\dfrac{5}{2}$ pies = ___2___ whole pies and ___1___ half pie = $2\dfrac{1}{2}$ *pies*

b) $\dfrac{11}{2}$ pies = _____ whole pies and _____ half pie =

c) $\dfrac{7}{3}$ pies   d) $\dfrac{19}{4}$ pies   e) $\dfrac{17}{5}$ pies   f) $\dfrac{15}{8}$ pies   **Bonus ▶** $\dfrac{70}{9}$ pies

14. Divide the numerator by the denominator to write each improper fraction as a mixed number.

a) $\dfrac{16}{3}$ $16 \div 3 = $ ___5___ R ___1___   b) $\dfrac{19}{6}$ $19 \div 6 = $ ____ R ____   c) $\dfrac{18}{4}$ $18 \div 4 = $ ____ R ____

so $\dfrac{16}{3} = 5\dfrac{1}{3}$ so $\dfrac{19}{6} = $ so $\dfrac{18}{4} = $

d) $\dfrac{3}{2}$ e) $\dfrac{5}{4}$ f) $\dfrac{8}{3}$ g) $\dfrac{15}{4}$ h) $\dfrac{22}{5}$ i) $\dfrac{32}{5}$

15. Write a mixed number and an improper fraction for the total number of liters.

1 L

16. Write a mixed number and an improper fraction for the length of the rope.

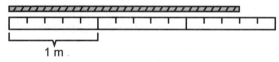

1 m

Since $\dfrac{7}{4} = 1\dfrac{3}{4}$, their opposites are equal too: $-\dfrac{7}{4} = -1\dfrac{3}{4}$.

17. Complete the chart.

Mixed Number	$-2\dfrac{3}{4}$	$-3\dfrac{2}{5}$		$-4\dfrac{1}{2}$				$-1\dfrac{3}{8}$
Improper Fraction	$-\dfrac{11}{4}$		$-\dfrac{7}{5}$		$-\dfrac{8}{3}$	$-\dfrac{9}{4}$	$-\dfrac{11}{3}$	

NS7-13 Adding and Subtracting Mixed Numbers

$1\frac{3}{8}$ $2\frac{4}{8}$ $1 + 2 = 3$ and $\frac{3}{8} + \frac{4}{8} = \frac{7}{8}$, so $1\frac{3}{8} + 2\frac{4}{8} = 3\frac{7}{8}$.

1. Add by adding the parts and the wholes separately.

a) $2\frac{1}{5} + 4\frac{3}{5} =$ b) $7\frac{1}{4} + 1\frac{2}{4} =$ c) $2\frac{1}{5} + 4\frac{3}{5} =$

d) $6\frac{2}{8} + 3\frac{5}{8} =$ e) $4\frac{3}{7} + 5\frac{2}{7} =$ f) $3\frac{1}{9} + 7\frac{4}{9} =$

You can add mixed numbers by changing them both to improper fractions.

Example: $1\frac{3}{5} + 2\frac{4}{5} \overset{1 \times 5 + 3}{=} \frac{8}{5} + \frac{14}{5} \overset{2 \times 5 + 4}{}$

$= \frac{22}{5}$

$= 4\frac{2}{5}$ because $22 \div 5 = 4$ R 2

Write your answer as a mixed number because the numbers you are adding are given in that form.

---

2. Write the mixed number as an improper fraction.

a) $5\frac{1}{8} = \frac{41}{8}$ b) $4\frac{1}{8} =$ c) $1\frac{3}{8} =$ d) $3\frac{5}{8} =$ e) $2\frac{7}{8} =$ f) $6\frac{4}{8} =$

3. Use your answers to Question 2 to add the mixed numbers. Write your answer as a mixed number.

a) $5\frac{1}{8} + 4\frac{1}{8} =$ b) $1\frac{3}{8} + 3\frac{5}{8} =$ c) $2\frac{7}{8} + 6\frac{4}{8} =$

d) $1\frac{3}{8} + 2\frac{7}{8}$ e) $6\frac{4}{8} + 4\frac{1}{8}$ f) $1\frac{3}{8} + 6\frac{4}{8}$

4. a) Raj adds $1\frac{3}{5} + 2\frac{4}{5}$ and gets $3\frac{7}{5}$, but $\frac{7}{5} > 1$, so he writes $3\frac{7}{5} = 3 + \frac{7}{5} = 3 + 1\frac{2}{5} = 4\frac{2}{5}$.

Is the answer correct?

b) Use Raj's method to add $2\frac{5}{9} + 1\frac{8}{9}$. Check by adding another way.

5. Add using Raj's method. You will need to change the improper fraction to a whole number.

$$1\frac{3}{5} + 2\frac{3}{5} + 3\frac{4}{5} =$$

To subtract $4\frac{5}{8} - 1\frac{3}{8}$, subtract the wholes and parts separately.

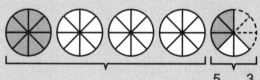

$$4 - 1 = 3 \qquad \frac{5}{8} - \frac{3}{8} = \frac{2}{8} \qquad \text{So } 4\frac{5}{8} - 1\frac{3}{8} = 3\frac{2}{8}.$$

6. Subtract the wholes and parts separately.

a) $7\frac{3}{5} - 4\frac{1}{5} =$ b) $5\frac{2}{4} - 2\frac{1}{4} =$ c) $8\frac{7}{9} - 4\frac{2}{9} =$

7. Write the mixed numbers or whole numbers as improper fractions, then subtract. Write your answer as a mixed number or whole number.

a) $6\frac{1}{3} - 2\frac{2}{3} = \frac{19}{3} - \frac{8}{3}$ b) $3\frac{2}{5} - 1\frac{4}{5} =$ c) $5\frac{7}{10} - 2\frac{7}{10} =$

$\qquad = \frac{11}{3}$

$\qquad = 3\frac{2}{3}$

8. Look at your answer to Question 7.c). How could you have predicted the answer?

_____

_____

9. Subtract $9\frac{1}{4} - 5\frac{3}{4}$ by writing $9\frac{1}{4}$ as $8 + 1\frac{1}{4} = 8 + \frac{5}{4}$. Then check your answer by subtracting another way.

10. Add the positive and negative numbers by first changing them to improper fractions

a) $+3\frac{4}{6} - 2\frac{5}{6}$ b) $-8 + 3\frac{5}{7}$ c) $-7\frac{5}{8} - 3\frac{6}{8}$

11. Subtract by first changing the mixed numbers to improper fractions.

a) $-2\dfrac{7}{8} - \left(-5\dfrac{3}{8}\right) = -2\dfrac{7}{8} + 5\dfrac{3}{8}$

$$= -\dfrac{23}{8} + \dfrac{43}{8}$$

$$= +\dfrac{20}{8} = 2\dfrac{4}{8} = 2\dfrac{1}{2}$$

b) $+2\dfrac{5}{9} - \left(-3\dfrac{4}{9}\right) =$

c) $-6\dfrac{1}{8} - \left(+2\dfrac{5}{8}\right)$

d) $+3\dfrac{4}{7} - \left(+5\dfrac{6}{7}\right)$

e) $-6\dfrac{1}{8} - \left(-4\dfrac{4}{8}\right)$

Bonus ▶ $-3\dfrac{2}{8} - 4\dfrac{5}{8} - 2\dfrac{5}{8} - 1\dfrac{7}{8}$

12. Subtract $\left(-2\dfrac{3}{4}\right) - \left(-5\dfrac{1}{4}\right)$ two ways.

a) Locate the numbers on the number line and use their distance apart.

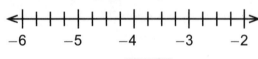

-6 -5 -4 -3 -2

$\left(-2\dfrac{3}{4}\right) - \left(-5\dfrac{1}{4}\right) = \boxed{}$

b) Add the opposite number.

$\left(-2\dfrac{3}{4}\right) - \left(-5\dfrac{1}{4}\right) = -2\dfrac{3}{4} + \boxed{}$

c) Did you get the same answer both ways? If not, find your mistake.

13. A viperfish is $\dfrac{7}{8}$ miles below sea level, a depth of $-\dfrac{7}{8}$ miles. A fangtooth is $1\dfrac{7}{8}$ miles below the viperfish. At what depth is the fangtooth?

     The Number System 7-13

NS7-14 Adding and Subtracting Fractions with Different Denominators

You can add or subtract fractions with different denominators.

Example: $\frac{1}{3} + \frac{2}{5}$

Step 1: Find the lowest common multiple of the denominators.

The LCM of 3 and 5 is 15.

Step 2: Create equivalent fractions with that denominator.

$\frac{1}{3} = \frac{5}{15}$ and $\frac{2}{5} = \frac{6}{15}$

So $\frac{1}{3} + \frac{2}{5}$ and $\frac{5}{15} + \frac{6}{15} = \frac{11}{15}$.

The **lowest common denominator** (**LCD**) of two fractions is the lowest common multiple (LCM) of the denominators.

1. Find the LCD of the pair of fractions. Then write what number you multiplied the numerator and denominator by.

   a) $\frac{2 \times 2}{2 \times 3} + \frac{1}{6}$

   LCD = _6_

   b) $\frac{1}{4} + \frac{5}{8}$

   LCD = _____

   c) $\frac{1}{6} + \frac{4}{9}$

   LCD = _____

2. Add or subtract the fractions by changing them to equivalent fractions. The denominators should be equal to the LCD of the fractions.

   a) $\frac{1}{5} + \frac{3}{4}$

   =

   =

   b) $\frac{5}{12} + \frac{2}{3}$

   =

   =

   c) $\frac{5}{6} - \frac{3}{10}$

   =

   =

3. Add or subtract. Write your answer in lowest terms.

   a) $\frac{3}{7} + \frac{1}{14}$

   b) $\frac{3}{5} - \frac{4}{15}$

   c) $\frac{15}{28} - \left(\frac{3}{4} - \frac{5}{7} \right)$

4. Do the first subtraction, then use opposites to do the second subtraction. Do your rough work in your notebook.

   a) $\frac{2}{5} - \frac{3}{10} = \boxed{}$

   $\frac{3}{10} - \frac{2}{5} = \boxed{}$

   b) $\frac{2}{3} - \frac{1}{4} = \boxed{}$

   $\frac{1}{4} - \frac{2}{3} = \boxed{}$

   c) $\frac{5}{8} + \frac{1}{4} = \boxed{}$

   $-\frac{5}{8} - \frac{1}{4} = \boxed{}$

same sign ——— To add two numbers ——— opposite sign

Add the absolute values. The sign is the same as for both numbers.

Subtract the absolute values. The sign is the same as for the number with the larger absolute value.

5. Add or subtract. Write your answer in lowest terms.

a) $-\dfrac{3}{4} - \dfrac{2}{8}$

$= -\dfrac{6}{8} - \dfrac{2}{8}$

$= -\dfrac{8}{8} = -1$

b) $+\dfrac{1}{6} - \dfrac{1}{3}$

c) $-\dfrac{4}{5} - \dfrac{2}{3}$

d) $-\dfrac{5}{8} + \dfrac{2}{8}$

e) $-2\dfrac{3}{4} - 3\dfrac{1}{6}$

f) $+4\dfrac{5}{6} + 2\dfrac{7}{10}$

g) $-\dfrac{2}{5} + \dfrac{1}{2}$

h) $-\dfrac{1}{6} - \dfrac{1}{2}$

i) $-5\dfrac{1}{6} + 2\dfrac{4}{9}$

j) $+1\dfrac{3}{5} + 1\dfrac{1}{4}$

k) $+3\dfrac{3}{8} - 1\dfrac{1}{8}$

l) $+2\dfrac{2}{5} - 1\dfrac{1}{8}$

6. Drop the brackets to subtract.

a) $-\dfrac{1}{8} - \left(+\dfrac{1}{4}\right)$

$= -\dfrac{1}{8} - \dfrac{1}{4}$

$= -\dfrac{1}{8} - \dfrac{2}{8}$

$= -\dfrac{3}{8}$

b) $-\dfrac{7}{8} - \left(-\dfrac{1}{8}\right)$

c) $+2\dfrac{2}{3} - \left(-3\dfrac{1}{4}\right)$

d) $-3\dfrac{5}{6} - \left(-2\dfrac{3}{8}\right)$

e) $-2\dfrac{1}{2} - \left(+2\dfrac{1}{3}\right)$

f) $+2\dfrac{3}{5} - \left(+3\dfrac{1}{8}\right)$

7. A dragonfish was found at a depth of $-1\dfrac{1}{4}$ miles. The deepest ever fish was found at a depth of $-4\dfrac{4}{5}$ miles. How much deeper is that?

The picture shows more than $\frac{1}{2}$ because more parts are shaded than are unshaded.

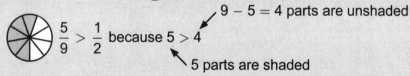

$9 - 5 = 4$ parts are unshaded

$\frac{5}{9} > \frac{1}{2}$ because $5 > 4$

5 parts are shaded

1. Imagine a picture of the fraction. How many parts are shaded? How many are unshaded? Is more of the picture shaded or unshaded?

   a) $\frac{7}{12}$ ___7___ shaded

      ___5___ unshaded

      more is ___shaded___

   b) $\frac{5}{8}$ _____ shaded

      _____ unshaded

      more is _____

   c) $\frac{49}{100}$ _____ shaded

      _____ unshaded

      more is _____

2. Write $>$ or $<$ in the box.

   a) $\frac{3}{7}$ ☐ $\frac{1}{2}$

   b) $\frac{6}{11}$ ☐ $\frac{1}{2}$

   c) $\frac{53}{100}$ ☐ $\frac{1}{2}$

Round a mixed number up if the fraction part is equal to or more than $\frac{1}{2}$. Round down if the fraction part is less than $\frac{1}{2}$. Example: $3\frac{4}{5} \approx 4$ because $\frac{4}{5} > \frac{1}{2}$, but $3\frac{2}{5} \approx 3$ because $\frac{2}{5} < \frac{1}{2}$.

3. Round the mixed number to the nearest whole number.

   a) $2\frac{7}{9} \approx$ _____

   b) $13\frac{3}{8} \approx$ _____

   c) $8\frac{47}{100} \approx$ _____

   d) $19\frac{2}{3} \approx$ _____

   e) $8\frac{1}{2} \approx$ _____

   f) $12\frac{51}{1,000} \approx$ _____

4. Change the improper fraction to a mixed number. Then round to the nearest whole number.

   a) $\frac{7}{2} =$ ☐ $\approx$ _____

   b) $\frac{9}{5} =$ ☐ $\approx$ _____

   c) $\frac{13}{4} =$ ☐ $\approx$ _____

   d) $\frac{8}{5} =$ ☐ $\approx$ _____

   e) $\frac{7}{3} =$ ☐ $\approx$ _____

   f) $\frac{13}{5} =$ ☐ $\approx$ _____

   g) $\frac{13}{2} =$ ☐ $\approx$ _____

   h) $\frac{15}{7} =$ ☐ $\approx$ _____

   i) $\frac{100}{9} =$ ☐ $\approx$ _____

You can round negative numbers the same way you round positive numbers.

Example: $-2\frac{3}{4} \approx -3$ because $2\frac{3}{4} \approx 3$

5. Round to the nearest integer.

a) $-5\frac{2}{3} \approx$ _____

b) $-2\frac{1}{5} \approx$ _____

c) $-8\frac{12}{25} \approx$ _____

d) $-\frac{11}{2} = \boxed{-5\frac{1}{2}} \approx$ ____

e) $-\frac{10}{3} = \boxed{} \approx$ ____

f) $-\frac{90}{25} = \boxed{} \approx$ ____

6. Estimate the sum or difference by rounding both numbers to the nearest integer.

a) $8\frac{1}{5} - \left(-5\frac{3}{5}\right)$

$\approx 8 - (-6)$

$= 8 + 6 = 14$

b) $-3\frac{4}{9} + 2\frac{5}{11}$

$\approx$

$=$

c) $-7\frac{7}{9} - \left(-3\frac{1}{8}\right)$

$\approx$

$=$

7. Calculate the actual sums and differences in Question 6. Were your estimates close?

8. a) Do you expect $9 - 2\frac{3}{8}$ to be more or less than $9 - 2 = 7$? Why? _____

_____

_____

b) Check your prediction by doing the subtraction.

9. John biked $3\frac{1}{2}$ miles to school, $2\frac{1}{4}$ miles to the library, and then $1\frac{2}{5}$ miles back home. About how far did he bike altogether?

10. Mona is making muffins using the ingredients below:

$1\frac{3}{4}$ cups of flour

$\frac{1}{3}$ cup of sugar

$\frac{1}{2}$ cup of berries

$\frac{3}{8}$ cups butter

$1\frac{1}{4}$ cups milk

2 eggs ($\frac{1}{5}$ cup each)

Estimate the total amount of ingredients. Do you think a 5-cup bowl is large enough?

NS7-16 Multiplying a Fraction and a Whole Number

1. The picture shows 15 dots divided into 5 equal groups. Fill in the blank.

   a) $\frac{1}{5}$ of 15 = _____   b) $\frac{2}{5}$ of 15 = _____   c) $\frac{3}{5}$ of 15 = _____   d) $\frac{4}{5}$ of 15 = _____

2. Draw the correct number of dots in each group. Then circle the amount, and fill in the blank.

   a) $\frac{2}{3}$ of 15

   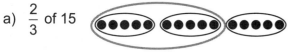

   so $\frac{2}{3}$ of 15 = _____

   b) $\frac{3}{4}$ of 12 ⬭ ⬭ ⬭ ⬭

   so $\frac{3}{4}$ of 12 = _____

   c) $\frac{5}{6}$ of 24 ⬭ ⬭ ⬭ / ⬭ ⬭ ⬭

   so $\frac{5}{6}$ of 24 = _____

   d) $\frac{3}{8}$ of 24 ⬭ ⬭ ⬭ ⬭ / ⬭ ⬭ ⬭ ⬭

   so $\frac{3}{8}$ of 24 = _____

3. Draw a picture to find $\frac{3}{5}$ of 10.

   $\frac{3}{5}$ of 10 = _____

Andy finds $\frac{2}{3}$ of 12 as follows:

Step 1: He finds $\frac{1}{3}$ of 12 by dividing 12 by 3.

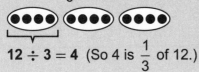

$12 \div 3 = 4$ (So 4 is $\frac{1}{3}$ of 12.)

Step 2: Then he multiplies the result by 2.

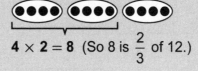

$4 \times 2 = 8$ (So 8 is $\frac{2}{3}$ of 12.)

---

4. Find the following amounts using Andy's method.

   a) $\frac{1}{3}$ of 6 = _____ so $\frac{2}{3}$ of 6 = _____   b) $\frac{1}{4}$ of 8 = _____ so $\frac{3}{4}$ of 8 = _____

   c) $\frac{2}{3}$ of 15 = _____   d) $\frac{3}{5}$ of 25 = _____

   e) $\frac{4}{5}$ of 20 = _____   f) $\frac{5}{7}$ of 21 = _____

In mathematics, the word "of" can mean multiply.

"2 groups of 4" means 2×4

$2 \times 4 = 8$

"$\frac{1}{2}$ of a group of 6" means $\frac{1}{2} \times 6$

$\frac{1}{2} \times 6 = 3$

5. Calculate the product by calculating the fraction of the whole number.

a) $\frac{2}{3} \times 9 = \frac{2}{3}$ of $9 = \underline{\ 6\ }$ ← $(2 \times 9) \div 3$

b) $\frac{1}{2} \times 10 = \frac{1}{2}$ of $10 = \underline{\ \ \ \ }$

c) $\frac{2}{5} \times 10$

d) $\frac{3}{4} \times 12$

e) $\frac{1}{3} \times 15$

f) $\frac{2}{3} \times 12$

6. How can you tell from your answers to Question 5 that $\frac{1}{2} > \frac{2}{5}$?

REMINDER: Multiplication by a whole number is a short form for repeated addition.

Example: $5 \times 7 = 7 + 7 + 7 + 7 + 7$

7. Imagine moving the shaded pieces from each pie onto the empty pie plate. Show how much of the empty pie plate would be filled. Then write a fraction for that amount.

a)
$\frac{3}{10} + \frac{3}{10} =$

b)
$\frac{1}{5} + \frac{1}{5} + \frac{1}{5} =$

c)
$5 \times \frac{1}{6} =$

d)
$4 \times \frac{2}{9} =$

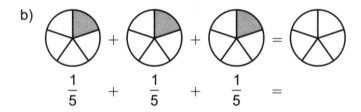

$4 \times \frac{3}{5} = \frac{4 \times 3}{5} = \frac{12}{5}$

8. Multiply.

a) $10 \times \frac{4}{9} =$

b) $3 \times \frac{4}{5} =$

c) $7 \times \frac{7}{10} =$

d) $8 \times \frac{1}{3} =$

e) $8 \times \frac{3}{5} =$

f) $9 \times \frac{2}{5} =$

g) $5 \times \frac{4}{3} =$

h) $6 \times \frac{7}{2} =$

9. Multiply the same numbers, but in a different order.

$\dfrac{2}{3} \times 9 = \dfrac{2}{3}$ of $9 =$ 　　　　　　　　　　　　　　$9 \times \dfrac{2}{3} =$

Did you get the same answer both times? If not, find your mistake.

10. Find the product. Write your answer in lowest terms.

a) $3 \times \dfrac{5}{6} = \dfrac{15}{6} = \dfrac{5}{2}$ 　　　b) $6 \times \dfrac{2}{3} = \dfrac{12}{3} = 4$ 　　　c) $4 \times \dfrac{3}{10} =$

d) $\dfrac{3}{4} \times 2 =$ 　　　　　　　　e) $\dfrac{7}{6} \times 10 =$ 　　　　　　　f) $\dfrac{5}{8} \times 4 =$

You can multiply whole numbers by negative fractions, too!

$3 \times (-4) = (-4) + (-4) + (-4)$ 　　　　　$3 \times \left(-\dfrac{1}{2}\right) = \left(-\dfrac{1}{2}\right) + \left(-\dfrac{1}{2}\right) + \left(-\dfrac{1}{2}\right)$

$\qquad\qquad = -4 - 4 - 4$ 　　　　　　　　　　$= -\dfrac{1}{2} - \dfrac{1}{2} - \dfrac{1}{2}$

$\qquad\qquad = -12$ 　　　　　　　　　　　　　　$= -\dfrac{3}{2}$

---

11. Multiply by using repeated addition.

a) $5 \times (-3) = \underline{(-3) + (-3) + (-3) + (-3) + (-3)}$ 　b) $4 \times (-2) = \underline{\qquad\qquad\qquad\qquad}$

$\qquad = \underline{-3 - 3 - 3 - 3 - 3} = \underline{\quad}$ 　　　　　$= \underline{\qquad\qquad} = \underline{\quad}$

c) $3 \times \left(-\dfrac{5}{8}\right) = \left(-\dfrac{5}{8}\right) + \left(-\dfrac{5}{8}\right) + \left(-\dfrac{5}{8}\right)$ 　　d) $2 \times \left(-\dfrac{3}{5}\right) = \underline{\qquad\qquad\qquad}$

$\qquad = \underline{\qquad\qquad} = \underline{\quad}$ 　　　　　　$= \underline{\qquad\qquad} = \underline{\quad}$

12. Multiply.

a) $4 \times 5 = 20$ 　　　　　　b) $5 \times 3 = 15$ 　　　　　　c) $6 \times 4 = 24$

so $4 \times (-5) =$ 　　　　　　so $5 \times (-3) =$ 　　　　　so $(-6) \times 4 =$

d) $\left(-\dfrac{2}{5}\right) \times 3 =$ 　　　　e) $\left(-\dfrac{4}{3}\right) \times 5 =$ 　　　f) $10 \times \left(-\dfrac{3}{5}\right) =$

13. Grace gets 1 point for every correct answer on a test, and $-\dfrac{3}{4}$ points for every incorrect answer. She got 15 correct answers and 5 incorrect answers. How many points did she get in total?

NS7-17 Problems and Puzzles

1. Eddy is playing football. Add Eddy's team's gains and losses from its turn, then subtract the other team's gains and losses from its turn. How did Eddy's team do overall?

Eddy's Team	Other Team	Integer Subtraction	Eddy's Team's Overall Result
gains 7 yards	gains 3 yards	$+7 - (+3) = +4$	gains 4 yards
loses 7 yards	gains 3 yards		
gains 7 yards	loses 3 yards		
loses 7 yards	loses 3 yards		

2. At the South Pole, the average daily high temperature is $-26°C$ in January and $-56°C$ in July. How much warmer is the South Pole in January than in July?

3. Use pictures to show that $-2 + 1 = -2 - (-1)$.

$-2 = \ominus \ominus$ 　　　　　 $-2 + 1 =$ 　　　　　 $-2 - (-1) =$

4. Kate spins the spinner twice and adds the two results.

   a) What is the highest total she could score? _____

   b) What is the lowest total she could score? _____

   c) What is the largest possible difference between the two scores?

   _____

   d) How could she score zero? _____

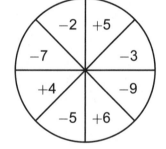

5. a) Find $2 \times \dfrac{4}{5}$ and $3 \times \dfrac{4}{5}$. Show your answer on the number line.

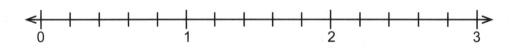

   b) Use $2 \times \dfrac{4}{5}$ and $3 \times \dfrac{4}{5}$ to predict $2\dfrac{1}{2} \times \dfrac{4}{5}$. _____

   Show your answer on the number line in part a).

Answer all problems in your notebook.

6. Jane lives in time zone +5 (that is, 5 hours ahead of London time). Bob is in time zone −4 (that is, 4 hours behind London time). How many hours ahead of Bob is Jane?

7. Mount Lamlam on the island of Guam is one of the tallest mountains in the world. Its peak is 406 m above sea level. It extends to 10,911 m below sea level. How tall is Mount Lamlam?

8. Do you expect the answer to $3\frac{1}{2} - 5\frac{3}{5}$ to be more than or less than −2? Explain your prediction, and then check it by doing the subtraction.

9. Find two fractions with different denominators and different signs (+ or −) that add to $\frac{11}{12}$.

10. Jin wants to center a picture on a wall. The picture is $3\frac{1}{3}$ feet wide. The wall is $10\frac{1}{2}$ feet wide. How far from each edge of the wall should he place the picture? Fill in the dimensions on the diagram to help you.

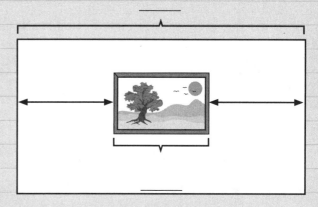

11. On a test, Tasha gets 1 point for each correct answer, $-\frac{1}{4}$ points for every incorrect answer, and $-\frac{1}{2}$ points for every question left blank. Tasha answered 12 questions correctly, 5 questions incorrectly, and left 3 questions blank.

How many points did she get altogether?

12. a) Group the fractions that have the same denominators. Then add or subtract.

i) $\frac{3}{4} + \frac{2}{5} - \frac{1}{4}$

ii) $-\frac{7}{2} + \frac{3}{5} + \frac{3}{2}$

iii) $-2\frac{3}{4} + 3\frac{1}{8} - 1\frac{1}{4}$

b) Do part ii) of Question 12.a) without grouping the fractions first. Was it more work? Explain why or why not.

EE7-1 Order of Operations

Add and subtract in the order you read: from left to right.

1. Add or subtract from left to right.

   a) $8 + 2 - 1$

   $= 10 - 1$

   $= 9$

   b) $8 - 2 + 1$

   c) $8 + 2 + 1$

   d) $8 - 2 - 1$

Multiplication and division are also done from left to right.

2. Multiply or divide from left to right.

   a) $3 \times 4 \div 6$

   b) $10 \div 2 \times 4$

   c) $10 \times 3 \times 2$

   d) $24 \div 3 \div 2$

First do all multiplications and divisions from left to right. Then do all additions and subtractions from left to right.

3. Circle the operation you would do first.

   a) $3 + \boxed{4 \times 5}$

   b) $9 - 5 + 6$

   c) $9 + 3 \div 3$

   d) $20 - 10 \div 5$

   e) $10 \div 5 \times 2$

   f) $15 - 3 \times 4$

   g) $8 + 2 - 4$

   h) $8 \times 9 \div 3$

4. Which operation is done first? Do the operation, then rewrite the rest of the expression.

   a) $5 + 6 - 3 = \underline{\;11 - 3\;}$

   b) $4 + 6 \div 2 = \underline{\;4 + 3\;}$

   c) $30 \div 5 + 3 = \underline{}$

   d) $10 - 2 \times 4 = \underline{}$

   e) $14 - 8 - 5 = \underline{}$

   f) $4 \times 6 \div 3 = \underline{}$

A **numerical expression** is a combination of numbers, operation signs, and sometimes brackets that represents a quantity. If there are brackets in an expression, do the operations in brackets first.

Example: $8 - 3 + 2 = 5 + 2 = 7$ but $8 - (3 + 2) = 8 - 5 = 3$

5. Do the operation in brackets first. Then write the answer.

   a) $10 + (4 \times 2)$

   $= 10 + 8$

   $= 18$

   b) $(10 + 4) \times 2$

   c) $(10 + 4) \div 2$

   d) $10 \times (4 + 2)$

Expressions and Equations 7-1

6. Evaluate.

a) $10 + (4 \div 2)$

b) $10 - (4 \times 2)$

c) $(10 - 4) \times 2$

d) $(10 - 4) \div 2$

e) $10 - (4 \div 2)$

f) $10 \div (4 - 2)$

To avoid writing brackets all the time, use the **standard order of operations**:

Step 1: Do operations in brackets.

Step 2: Do all multiplications and divisions from left to right.

Step 3: Do all additions and subtractions from left to right.

---

7. Do the operations one at a time, in the standard order.

a) $8 \div 4 \times (12 - 5)$

= _____

= _____

= _____

b) $3 \times 7 - 6 \div 2$

= _____

= _____

= _____

c) $4 + 3 \times (7 - 5)$

= _____

= _____

= _____

d) $(8 - 3) \times 2 + 5$

= _____

= _____

= _____

e) $8 - 3 \times 2 + 5$

= _____

= _____

= _____

f) $8 + 12 \div 2 \times 3$

= _____

= _____

= _____

REMINDER: $\dfrac{2}{5} \times 8 = \dfrac{2 \times 8}{5} = \dfrac{16}{5} = 3\dfrac{1}{5}$

---

g) $\dfrac{3}{5} + \dfrac{1}{5} \times 7$

h) $\dfrac{2}{3} + \dfrac{1}{2} \times 4$

i) $\left(\dfrac{2}{5} + \dfrac{1}{5}\right) \times 4$

j) $3 \times \dfrac{1}{4} + \dfrac{1}{2}$

k) $3 \times \left(\dfrac{1}{4} + \dfrac{1}{2}\right)$

l) $\dfrac{2}{3} + \dfrac{3}{4} \times 5$

If there is more than one set of brackets, you can do those operations all in one step.

Example: $10 - (2 + 3) + (4 - 2) \times 6$

$$= 10 - 5 + 2 \times 6$$
$$= 10 - 5 + 12$$
$$= 5 + 12 = 17$$

8. Evaluate.

a) $(7 - 4) + 8 \div (6 - 2) + 5$

= _____

= _____

= _____

= _____

b) $7 + (5 - 1) \div (8 - 6) - 1$

= _____

= _____

= _____

= _____

c) $8 - (1 + 3) + (6 \div 2) - 5$

d) $9 - (5 - 3) + (7 - 4) \times 2$

e) $(2 \times 8) \div (1 + 3) - (6 - 3)$

f) $15 \div (3 + 2) + (4 - 3) \times (1 + 3)$

Sometimes, brackets include more than one operation. Do those operations in the standard order, too.

Example: $(20 - 3 \times 4) \div 2$

$$= (20 - 12) \div 2$$
$$= 8 \div 2$$
$$= 4$$

When there are brackets within brackets, do the inside brackets first.

Example: $24 \div (8 - (2 \times 3) + 10)$

$$= 24 \div (8 - 6 + 10)$$
$$= 24 \div (2 + 10)$$
$$= 24 \div 12 = 2$$

---

9. Do the operations in the standard order.

a) $(3 + 12 \div 2) \times 3$

= _____

= _____

= _____

= _____

b) $4 \times 5 - (40 \div (8 + 2) \times 3)$

= _____

= _____

= _____

= _____

c) $(70 - 5 \times 7) \div (8 + 2 - 3)$

d) $(24 - 2 \times 6) \div (12 \div 3)$

e) $3 \times (28 \div (3 + 4))$

f) $16 \div (3 + (15 - (7 \times 2)))$

EE7-2 The Associative and Commutative Properties

Addition is **commutative** because the order you write the numbers you are adding does not affect the answer. Example: $1 + 3$ and $3 + 1$ are equal.

1. Write two additions for the picture.

a) ● ● ○ ○ ○

$$\underset{\text{shaded}}{\underline{\quad 2 \quad}} + \underset{\text{unshaded}}{\underline{\quad 3 \quad}} = \underset{\text{total}}{\underline{\quad 5 \quad}}$$

$$\underset{\text{unshaded}}{\underline{\qquad\qquad}} + \underset{\text{shaded}}{\underline{\qquad\qquad}} = \underset{\text{total}}{\underline{\qquad\qquad}}$$

b) ● ● ● ● ○ ○ ○ ○ ○

$$\underset{\text{shaded}}{\underline{\qquad\qquad}} + \underset{\text{unshaded}}{\underline{\qquad\qquad}} = \underset{\text{total}}{\underline{\qquad\qquad}}$$

$$\underset{\text{unshaded}}{\underline{\qquad\qquad}} + \underset{\text{shaded}}{\underline{\qquad\qquad}} = \underset{\text{total}}{\underline{\qquad\qquad}}$$

2. a) Write two multiplications for the picture.

● ● ● ●
● ● ● ●
● ● ● ●

$$\underset{\text{rows}}{\underline{\qquad\qquad}} \times \underset{\text{in each row}}{\underline{\qquad\qquad}} = \underset{\text{total}}{\underline{\qquad\qquad}}$$

$$\underset{\text{columns}}{\underline{\qquad\qquad}} \times \underset{\text{in each column}}{\underline{\qquad\qquad}} = \underset{\text{total}}{\underline{\qquad\qquad}}$$

  b) Is multiplication commutative? How do you know? _____

  _____

  _____

3. Is subtraction commutative? _____ Use the subtractions to check.

  a) $5 - 3 =$ _____ $3 - 5 =$ _____   b) $6 - 1 =$ _____ $1 - 6 =$ _____

  c) $(+5) - (-3)$ $(-3) - (+5)$ d) $(-2) - (-5)$ $(-5) - (-2)$

  = _____   = _____   = _____   = _____

  = _____   = _____   = _____   = _____

Addition is **associative** because the addition you do first does not affect the answer.

Example: $(1 + 3) + 2 = 4 + 2$ and $1 + (3 + 2) = 1 + 5$ are both equal to 6.

4. Is subtraction associative? _____ Use the subtractions to check.

  a) $(7 - 5) - 2$ $7 - (5 - 2)$ b) $(8 - 5) - 6$ $8 - (5 - 6)$

  = _____   = _____   = _____   = _____

  = _____   = _____   = _____   = _____

Multiplication is associative because the multiplication you do first does not affect the answer.

The picture shows that $(2 \times 4) \times 3 = 2 \times (4 \times 3)$.

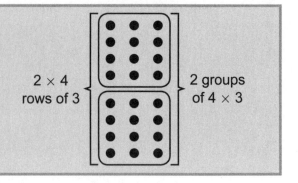

2×4
rows of 3

2 groups
of 4×3

5. Is division associative? _____ Use the divisions to check.

   a) $(18 \div 6) \div 3$ $18 \div (6 \div 3)$ b) $(20 \div 4) \div 2$ $20 \div (4 \div 2)$

6. Which property does the equation show?

   A. the commutative property   **B.** the associative property

   a) $2 \times 6 = 6 \times 2$ _____

   b) $3 \times (4 \times 5) = (3 \times 4) \times 5$ _____

   c) $(4 + 6) + 7 = 4 + (6 + 7)$ _____

   d) $5 + 3 = 3 + 5$ _____

The equation $(3 + 2) \times 7 = 7 \times (3 + 2)$ shows the commutative property because the two numbers being multiplied, $3 + 2$ and 7, are being interchanged.

7. Use the commutative property to finish the equation.

   a) $(3 + 4) \times 5 = $ _____ $\times (3 + 4)$

   b) $2 \times (5 - 4) = (5 - 4) \times$ _____

   c) $(2 + 3 + 4) \times 9 = $ _____ $\times (2 + 3 + 4)$

   d) $(8 + 5 - 2) \times 6 = 6 \times ($ _____ $)$

   e) $(8 \div 2) \times 3 = 3 \times ($ _____ $)$

   f) $(5 + 4 \div 2) \times 7 = 7 \times ($ _____ $)$

   g) $(7 + 3) \times 4 = $ _____ $\times$ _____

   h) $9 \times (8 - 3) = $ _____

You can use the commutative property on part of an expression.

Example: $(3 + 2) \times 7 = (2 + 3) \times 7$ because $3 + 2 = 2 + 3$.

8. Use the commutative property of addition to finish the equation.

   a) $(2 + 8) \times 3 = $ _____

   b) $8 \times (3 + 6) = $ _____

   c) $9 \times (5 + 3) = $ _____

   d) $(6 + 5) \times 19 = $ _____

9. Jayden writes these equations and justifies them by the commutative property.

a) Evaluate both sides. Write ✓ if the answer is right and ✗ if it is wrong.

    i) $(3 + 4) \times 5 = 5 \times (3 + 4)$ _____

    ii) $5 \times (8 - 2) = (8 - 2) \times 5$ _____

    iii) $8 - 3 = 3 - 8$ _____

    iv) $(7 + (-4)) \times 5 = ((-4) + 7) \times 5$ _____

    v) $4 \times (5 - 3) = 5 \times (4 - 3)$ _____

    vi) $4 \times 5 - 3 = 5 \times 4 - 3$ _____

b) Each correct answer is worth 1 mark. So, Jayden's work gets _____ out of 6 marks.

10. Look at what changes from each expression to the next. What property is being used?

    A. the commutative property   **B.** the associative property

a) $2 \times (19 \times 5) = 2 \times (5 \times 19)$ __*A*__

    $= (2 \times 5) \times 19$ __*B*__

b) $(4 + 8) + 26 = (8 + 4) + 26$ _____

    $= 8 + (4 + 26)$ _____

c) $74 + (17 + 6) = 74 + (6 + 17)$ _____

    $= (74 + 6) + 17$ _____

d) $(25 \times 7) \times 4 = (7 \times 25) \times 4$ _____

    $= 7 \times (25 \times 4)$ _____

Multiples of 10 are easy to multiply by and easy to add.

Example: $14 + (32 + 26)$

    $= 14 + (26 + 32)$

    $= (14 + 26) + 32$

    $= 40 + 32 = 72$

---

11. Which property is being used in the calculation below? Circle where it is used.

_____

    $34 \times 20 = 34 \times (2 \times 10)$

    $= (34 \times 2) \times 10$

    $= 68 \times 10 = 680$

12. The two expressions have the same answer. Circle the expression that is easier to evaluate, then evaluate it.

a) $8 \times (5 \times 7)$ $(8 \times 5) \times 7$

b) $(19 + 25) + 31$ $25 + (19 + 31)$

13. Calculate the product or sum by first changing it to an easier problem. Justify each step by saying what property you used.

a) $(27 \times 5) \times 2$

b) $(27 + 36) + 43$

EE7-3 The Distributive Property

The picture shows that $2 \times (3 + 4) = 2 \times 3 + 2 \times 4$.

$3 + 4$	$2 \times (3 + 4)$	$2 \times 3 + 2 \times 4$

● ● ● ○ ○ ○ ○   ● ● ● ○ ○ ○ ○   =   ● ● ● + ○ ○ ○ ○
                      ● ● ● ○ ○ ○ ○   ● ● ●   ○ ○ ○ ○

This is called the **distributive property of multiplication over addition**.

1. Evaluate both expressions. Are they equal? If not, find your mistake.

   a) $5 \times (3 + 4)$ and $5 \times 3 + 5 \times 4$

   b) $8 \times (5 + 2)$ and $8 \times 5 + 8 \times 2$

   c) $(3 + 2) \times 6$ and $3 \times 6 + 2 \times 6$

   d) $(10 + 4) \times 6$ and $10 \times 6 + 4 \times 6$

The picture shows that $2 \times (7 - 3) = 2 \times 7 - 2 \times 3$.

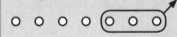
$7 - 3$

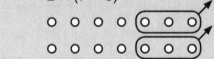
$2 \times (7 - 3)$

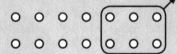
$2 \times 7 - 2 \times 3$

This is called the **distributive property of multiplication over subtraction**.

2. Evaluate both expressions. Are they equal? If not, find your mistake.

   a) $3 \times (9 - 5)$ and $3 \times 9 - 3 \times 5$

   b) $4 \times (7 - 2)$ and $4 \times 7 - 4 \times 2$

   c) $(9 - 4) \times 3$ and $9 \times 3 - 4 \times 3$

   d) $(12 - 2) \times 3$ and $12 \times 3 - 2 \times 3$

3. a) Evaluate both expressions. Are they equal?

   i) $(35 + 15) \div 5$ and $35 \div 5 + 15 \div 5$ 　　　　ii) $24 \div (4 + 2)$ and $24 \div 4 + 24 \div 2$

   iii) $(35 - 15) \div 5$ and $35 \div 5 - 15 \div 5$ 　　　iv) $24 \div (6 - 2)$ and $24 \div 6 - 24 \div 2$

   b) Look at your answers to part a). When does division distribute over addition and subtraction?

   _____

4. Which property does the equation show?

   A. the commutative property 　　**B.** the associative property 　　**C.** the distributive property

   a) $3 \times 5 = 5 \times 3$ _____ 　　　　　　　　　　b) $3 \times (4 + 5) = 3 \times 4 + 3 \times 5$ _____

   c) $2 + (3 + 7) = (2 + 3) + 7$ _____ 　　　　　d) $285 + 3 = 3 + 285$ _____

   e) $(3 + 3) \times 4 = 3 \times 4 + 3 \times 4$ _____ 　　f) $2 \times (5 \times 7) = (2 \times 5) \times 7$ _____

   g) $274 \times 39 = 39 \times 274$ _____ 　　　　　h) $(8 + 8) \times 8 = 8 \times 8 + 8 \times 8$ _____

5. Use the given property to finish the equation.

   a) $(2 + 5) \times 8 =$ _____ (the commutative property of addition)

   b) $(2 + 5) \times 8 =$ _____ (the commutative property of multiplication)

   c) $(2 + 5) \times 8 =$ _____ (the distributive property of multiplication over addition)

Multiplication is sometimes written using brackets instead of the $\times$ sign.

Example: $2(3) = 2 \times 3 = 6$

---

6. Multiply.

   a) $3(4) = 12$ 　　　b) $2(5)$ 　　　　c) $5(8)$ 　　　　d) $4(7)$

   e) $8(6 \div 3)$ 　　　f) $9(5 - 4)$ 　　　g) $(2 + 3)(5 - 2)$ 　　h) $(3 + 1)(3 - 1)$

---

7. Which property is being used?

    A. the commutative property   **B.** the associative property   **C.** the distributive property

a) $3(2 + 4) = 3(2) + 3(4)$ _____

b) $2(3(4)) = (2(3))4$ _____

c) $9(3) + 17(9) = 9(3) + 9(17)$ _____

              $= 9(3 + 17)$ _____

d) $2(9(5)) = 2(5(9))$ _____

          $= (2(5))9$ _____

8. The distributive property shows that $7(32) + 7(18) = 7(32 + 18)$. Which expression is easier to calculate? Explain your choice.

_____ because _____

_____

_____

9. Circle the expression that is easier to evaluate, then evaluate it.

a) $7 \times 83 - 7 \times 81$ $7 \times (83 - 81)$

b) $9 \times 24 + 9 \times 36$ $9 \times (24 + 36)$

10. Use the distributive property to make an expression that is easier to evaluate. Then evaluate it.

a) $8(13) + 8(27)$ b) $8(10 + 7)$ c) $9(81) - 9(76)$ d) $8(63) - 8(43)$

REMINDER: Multiplying by a whole number is repeated addition.

Example: $3 \times (-4) = \overset{\displaystyle -(3 \times 4)}{-4 - 4 - 4} = -12$

$3 \times \left(-\dfrac{2}{5}\right) = -\dfrac{2}{5} - \dfrac{2}{5} - \dfrac{2}{5} = \overset{\displaystyle -\left(3 \times \frac{2}{5}\right)}{-\dfrac{6}{5}}$

---

11. Multiply.

a) $3(-2)$ b) $4(-5)$ c) $5(-7)$ d) $100(-3,000)$

e) $2\left(-\dfrac{3}{5}\right)$ f) $5\left(-\dfrac{5}{8}\right)$ g) $3\left(-\dfrac{2}{3}\right)$ h) $4\left(-\dfrac{7}{8}\right)$

EE7-4 More Properties of Operations

12 dots ÷ 3 groups = 4 dots in each group   (12 × 2) dots ÷ (3 × 2) groups = 4 dots in each group

1. Evaluate all expressions. Are your answers equal? If not, find your mistake(s).

   a) $10 \div 2 = $ _____

   $(10 \times 2) \div (2 \times 2) = $ _____ $\div$ _____ $=$ _____

   $(10 \times 3) \div (2 \times 3) = $ _____ $\div$ _____ $=$ _____

   $(10 \times 4) \div (2 \times 4) = $ _____ $\div$ _____ $=$ _____

   b) $24 \div 12 = $ _____

   $(24 \div 2) \div (12 \div 2) = $ _____ $\div$ _____ $=$ _____

   $(24 \div 3) \div (12 \div 3) = $ _____ $\div$ _____ $=$ _____

   $(24 \div 4) \div (12 \div 4) = $ _____ $\div$ _____ $=$ _____

2. Use dividing by 10 to make an easier problem. Then solve.

   a) $240 \div 5 = $ _480_ $\div 10$

   $= $ _48_

   b) $135 \div 5 = $ _____ $\div 10$

   $= $ _____

   c) $430 \div 5 = $ _____ $\div 10$

   $= $ _____

   d) $285 \div 5 = $ _____ $\div 10$

   $= $ _____

   e) $645 \div 5 = $ _____ $\div 10$

   $= $ _____

   f) $375 \div 5 = $ _____ $\div 10$

   $= $ _____

3. Circle the greater product. Do not calculate the products.

   a) 6×35 5×35

   b) 34×5 36×8

Remember: $5 \times 3 = 15$, so $15 \div 3 = 5$. But $\boxed{} \times 0 = 7$ has no answer, so $7 \div 0$ has **no answer**.

Does $0 \div 0$ have an answer? Emma uses $1 \times 0 = 0$ and says $0 \div 0 = 1$. Ken uses $2 \times 0 = 0$ and says $0 \div 0 = 2$. But $0 \div 0$ cannot have two answers, so it does not have an answer at all!

4. Write the answer or ✗ (when there is no answer) in the box.

   a) $\boxed{} \times 7 = 7$

   b) $0 \times 1 = \boxed{}$

   c) $0 \times \boxed{} = 1$

   d) $0 \div 8 = \boxed{}$

   e) $8 \div 0 = \boxed{}$

   f) $8 \div 8 = \boxed{}$

   g) $0 \times 1 = \boxed{}$

   h) $\boxed{} \times 0 = 9$

   i) $\boxed{} \div 0 = 0$

   j) $7 \div \boxed{} = 1$

   k) $7 \div \boxed{} = 0$

   l) $0 \div 0 = \boxed{}$

5. What is the only number that cannot be written in the box? Explain.

   $0 \div \boxed{} = 0$

Subtracting 1 more makes the answer 1 less. Example: $10 - (3 + 1)$ and $10 - 3 - 1$

$$= 10 - 4 \qquad = 7 - 1$$
$$= 6 \qquad\qquad = 6$$

The expressions $10 - (3 + 1)$ and $10 - 3 - 1$ are **equivalent** because they have the same value.

6. Evaluate both expressions. Are your answers the same? If not, find your mistake.

   a) $9 - (5 + 1)$ and $9 - 5 - 1$

   b) $20 - (10 + 1)$ and $20 - 10 - 1$

   c) $10 - (1 + 2 + 3)$ and $10 - 1 - 2 - 3$

   d) $20 - (8 + 3 + 4)$ and $20 - 8 - 3 - 4$

7. Write an equivalent expression without brackets that uses all the same numbers.

   a) $15 - (10 + 2) = $ _____

   b) $15 - (5 + 3 + 6) = $ _____

Subtracting 1 less makes the answer 1 more. Example: $10 - (3 - 1)$ and $10 - 3 + 1$ are equivalent because $10 - (3 - 1) = 10 - 2 = 8$ and $10 - 3 + 1 = 7 + 1 = 8$.

8. Write an expression without brackets that uses all the same numbers and has the same answer.

   a) $10 - (7 - 2) = $ _____

   b) $15 - (10 - 3) = $ _____

   c) $18 - (4 - 3) = $ _____

   d) $10 - (3 - 1) = $ _____

   Bonus ▶ $20 - (5 - 2 + 1) = $ _____

9. Check your answers to Questions 7 and 8 by evaluating both expressions.

10. Evaluate both expressions. Are the two expressions equivalent?

	Expression 1	Expression 2	Equivalent?
a)	$42 \div (3 \times 2) = 42 \div 6 = 7$	$42 \div 3 \div 2$	
b)	$32 \div (8 \div 4)$	$32 \div 8 \times 4$	
c)	$24 \div (4 \times 3 \div 6)$	$24 \div 4 \div 3 \times 6$	

11. Use all the same numbers to write an equivalent expression without brackets.

   $60 \div (4 \times 5 \div 2 \times 3) = $ _____

12. Explain how you can know, without calculating, that $8 \times 74 < 740$.

EE7-5 The Standard Method for Multiplication

How to solve $3 \times 42 = 3 \times 40 + 3 \times 2$

$$= 3 \times 4 \text{ tens} + 3 \times 2 \text{ ones}$$

Step 1

Multiply the ones digit by 3
(3×2 ones $= 6$ ones).

```
    4  2
×      3
       6
```
↑
ones

Step 2

Multiply the tens digit by 3
(3×4 tens $= 12$ tens).

Regroup 10 tens as 1 hundred.

```
    4  2
×      3
 1  2  6
```
↑   ↑
hundreds tens

1. Use **Steps 1** and **2** to find the product.

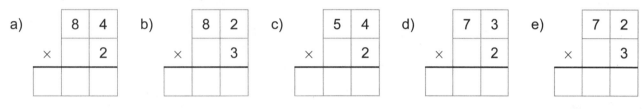

a)
```
  8  4
×    2
```

b)
```
  8  2
×    3
```

c)
```
  5  4
×    2
```

d)
```
  7  3
×    2
```

e)
```
  7  2
×    3
```

How to solve $7 \times 53 = 7 \times 50 + 7 \times 3$

$$= 7 \times 5 \text{ tens} + 7 \times 3 \text{ ones}$$

Step 1

Multiply 3 ones by 7
($7 \times 3 = 21$).

```
    2
  5  3
×    7
     1
```

Step 2

Regroup 20 ones as 2 tens.

2. Complete **Steps 1** and **2** of the multiplication.

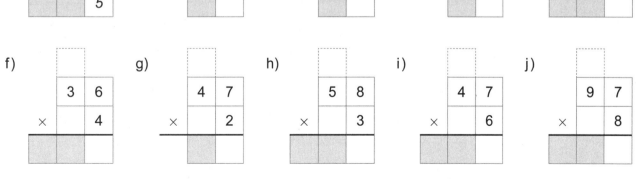

a)
```
  3
  2  7
×    5
     5
```

b)
```
  1  4
×    6
```

c)
```
  2  6
×    3
```

d)
```
  1  7
×    3
```

e)
```
  5  9
×    5
```

f)
```
  3  6
×    4
```

g)
```
  4  7
×    2
```

h)
```
  5  8
×    3
```

i)
```
  4  7
×    6
```

j)
```
  9  7
×    8
```

Step 3

Multiply 5 tens by 7
(7×5 tens = 35 tens).

Step 4

Add 2 tens to the result
($35 + 2 = 37$ tens).

3. Complete **Steps 3** and **4** of the multiplication.

a)
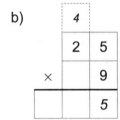

	1	
	2	4
×		3
	7	2

b)

	4	
	2	5
×		9
		5

c)

	3	
	1	7
×		5
		5

d)

	1	
	8	3
×		5
		5

e)

	4	
	7	9
×		5
		5

4. Complete **all steps** of the multiplication.

a)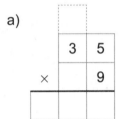

	3	5
×		9

b)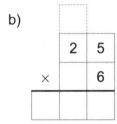

	2	5
×		6

c)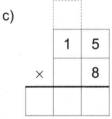

	1	5
×		8

d)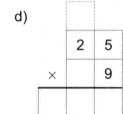

	2	5
×		9

e)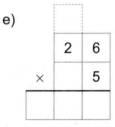

	2	6
×		5

5. Multiply by regrouping ones as tens.

a)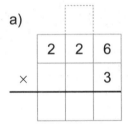

	2	2	6
×			3

b)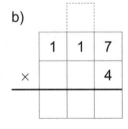

	1	1	7
×			4

c)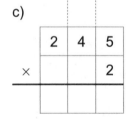

	2	4	5
×			2

d)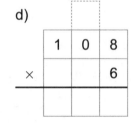

	1	0	8
×			6

e)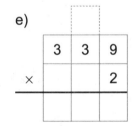

	3	3	9
×			2

6. Multiply by regrouping when you need to.

a)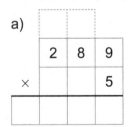

	2	8	9
×			5

b)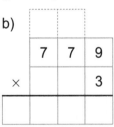

	7	7	9
×			3

c)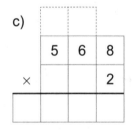

	5	6	8
×			2

d)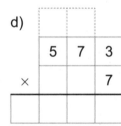

	5	7	3
×			7

e)

	2	4	2
×			8

7. A dog is 16 years old. Multiply that by 7 to estimate the dog's age in dog years.

8. Anna has borrowed a library book for 21 days. She reads 8 pages each day. If the book is 165 pages long, will she need to renew the book?

To multiply 37 × 20, first multiply 37 × 2, then multiply by 10.

This is how to record your answer on a grid:

9. Multiply.

a)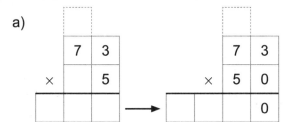

b)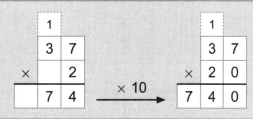

c) 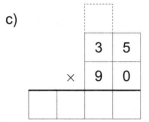   d) 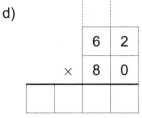   e) 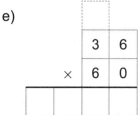   f)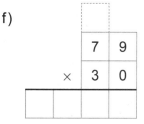

To multiply 37 × 25, split 25 into two numbers that are easier to multiply by. The picture shows why this works.

a multiple of 10   a 1-digit number

$37 × 25 = 37 × \mathbf{20} + 37 × \mathbf{5}$

$= 740 + 185$

$= 925$

$37 × 25$ ┤ $37 × 20$ / $37 × 5$

10. Multiply. Do your rough work in your notebook.

a) 11 × 57

11 × 50 = _____

11 × 7 = _____

so 11 × 57 = _____

b) 76 × 43

76 × 40 = _____

76 × 3 = _____

so 76 × 43 = _____

c) 95 × 16

95 × 10 = _____

95 × 6 = _____

so 95 × 16 = _____

d) 58 × 35

58 × 30 = _____

58 × 5 = _____

so 58 × 35 = _____

11. Multiply.

a) 58 × 70

b) 71 × 62

c) 84 × 23

d) 94 × 57

12. Is your answer to Question 11.a) double your answer to Question 10.d)?
If not, find your mistake.

Expressions and Equations 7-5

You can record the steps in multiplying 2-digit numbers on a grid.

Example: Find 37 × 25.

Step 1: Calculate 37 × 5.

Step 2: Calculate 37 × 20.

Step 3: Add the results.

1	3	
	3	7
×	2	5
1	8	5	← 37 × 5
7	4	0	← 37 × 20
9	2	5

13. Practice Step 1.

a)

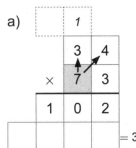

= 24 × 3

b)

c)

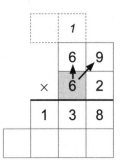

d)

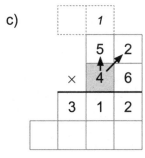

14. Practice Step 2.

a)

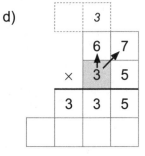

= 34 × 70

b)

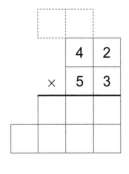

c)

d)

15. Practice Steps 1 and 2.

Regrouping 35 × 20 →   ← Regrouping for 35 × 6

a)

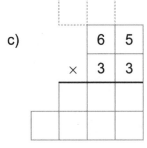

= 35 × 6

0 = 35 × 20

b)

c)

d)

16. Multiply.

a)

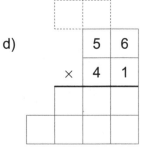

+   0

b)

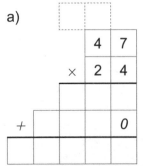

+   0

c)

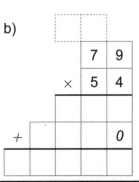

d)

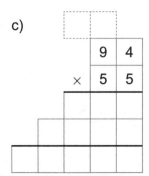

EE7-6 Variables and Expressions

1. There are 5 people in one family. Write an addition expression for the number of chairs needed if the family has …

   a) 2 guests   b) 3 guests   c) 7 guests   d) n guests

      __$5 + 2$__   _____   _____   _____

A **variable** is a letter or symbol that represents a number.

---

2. Evaluate the expression when $n = 5$.

   a) $n + 2 = 5 + 2$ b) $8 - n = 8 - 5$ c) $6 + n =$ d) $n - 4 =$

       $= 7$ $=$ $=$ $=$

3. Evaluate the expression when n is the given value.

   a) $n + 3,\quad n = 7$ b) $n - 5,\quad n = 2$ c) $8 + n,\quad n = -3$ d) $-7 - n,\quad n = -2$

    $7 + 3 = 10$ $2 - 5 =$

4. The nth row of a theater has $n + 4$ seats. How many seats are in the 21st row? _____

5. The nth person in line waited for $10 + n$ minutes. How long did the 50th person wait in line? _____

6. It costs \$3 to rent skates for an hour. Write a multiplication expression for the cost of renting skates for …

   a) 2 hours _____   b) 5 hours _____   c) 6 hours _____   d) n hours _____

7. Write an expression for the distance a car would travel at the given speed for the given amount of time.

   a) 60 miles per hour for 2 hours   b) 80 miles per hour for 3 hours

   _____   _____

   c) 50 miles per hour for h hours   d) m miles per hour for 4 hours

   _____   _____

In a product of a number and a variable, the multiplication sign is usually dropped.

Examples: $3 \times T$ can be written as $3T$ and $5 \times z$ can be written as $5z$.

---

8. Write the expression without multiplication signs.

   a) $8 \times r =$ __$8r$__   b) $2 \times s =$ _____   c) $4 \times P =$ _____   **Bonus ▶** $r \times s =$ _____

9. Write the expression with multiplication signs.

Bonus ▶

a) $3w = \underline{\quad 3 \times w \quad}$ b) $5r = \underline{\qquad\qquad}$ c) $6W = \underline{\qquad\qquad}$ $8rT = \underline{\qquad\qquad\qquad}$

10. Renting skis cost $5 an hour. Write two expressions for the cost of renting skis for …

a) h hours: $\underline{\quad 5 \times h \quad}$ or $\underline{\quad 5h \quad}$

b) t hours: $\underline{\qquad\qquad}$ or $\underline{\qquad}$

c) x hours: $\underline{\qquad\qquad}$ or $\underline{\qquad}$

d) n hours: $\underline{\qquad\qquad}$ or $\underline{\qquad}$

To evaluate $3h$ at $h = 5$, use brackets: $3h = 3(5)$—not 35!

---

11. Evaluate the expression for $n = 2$.

a) $5n = 5(2)$

$\quad = 10$

b) $7n = 7(2)$

c) $11n$

d) $30,000n$

12. Evaluate the expression at the given value of n.

a) $3n, \quad n = 7$ b) $10n, \quad n = 14$ c) $8n, \quad n = 100$ d) $500n, \quad n = 6,000$

13. The nth figure uses $5n$ squares. How many squares does the 10th figure use? $\underline{\qquad}$

14. Renting a boat for n hours costs $6n$. How much does renting the boat for 4 hours cost? $\underline{\qquad}$

15. Draw a rectangle when x is the given value.

	$2x$	$x + 2$
	$x \;\square$	$x \;\square$
a) $x = 1$ cm		
b) $x = 2$ cm		
c) $x = 3$ cm		

Expressions and Equations 7-6

EE7-7 Expressions with Two Operations

REMINDER: When brackets don't tell you which operation to do first, do multiplication before addition.

Example: $2 + 3(5) = 2 + 3 \times 5$

$$= 2 + 15 = 17$$

1. Evaluate the expression for $n = 4$.

a) $3n + 5$

$= 3(4) + 5$

$= 12 + 5$

$= 17$

b) $15 - 2n$

c) $9 + 4n$

d) $3n - 20$

e) $8 - 7n$

f) $-3 + 2n$

REMINDER: Multiplication by a whole number is repeated addition.

$$\overset{-(3 \times 5)}{\text{Example: } 5 \times (-3) = -3 - 3 - 3 - 3 - 3 = -15}$$

2. Evaluate the expression for $x = -1$.

a) $2x + 6$

b) $3x + 4$

c) $9x - 4$

d) $2x - 5$

e) $3 - 7x$

f) $-5 - 2x$

REMINDER: $\dfrac{3}{8} \times 5 = \dfrac{3 \times 5}{8} = \dfrac{15}{8} = 1\dfrac{7}{8}$

3. Evaluate the expression for the given number.

a) $5h + 2$, $h = 3$

b) $2n - 3$, $n = 6$

c) $3 - 5t$, $t = -4$

d) $3m + 2$, $m = -\dfrac{1}{2}$

e) $5t - \dfrac{3}{4}$, $t = \dfrac{5}{8}$

f) $\dfrac{7}{5} - 2t$, $t = -\dfrac{3}{4}$

g) $\dfrac{3}{2}w + 5$, $w = 3$

h) $\dfrac{5}{8}r - 7$, $r = 8$

i) $-3 + \dfrac{2}{5}s$, $s = 7$

Expressions and Equations 7-7

> A **flat fee** is a fixed charge that does not depend on how long you rent an item.
>
> Example: It costs a flat fee of $7 to rent a boat, plus $3 for each hour you use the boat.

4. Write an expression for the amount you would pay to rent a boat for …

a) 2 hours

Flat fee: $9

Hourly rate: $5 per hour

_____2 × 5 + 9_____

b) 3 hours

Flat fee: $4

Hourly rate: $6 per hour

_____

c) 7 hours

Flat fee: $5

Hourly rate: $4 per hour

_____

d) *h* hours

Flat fee: $5

Hourly rate: $4 per hour

_____4h + 5_____

e) *t* hours

Flat fee: $8

Hourly rate: $3 per hour

_____

f) *w* hours

Flat fee: $6

Hourly rate: $5 per hour

_____

5. Match the fee (left) for renting a windsurfing board to the correct algebraic expression (right).

A $15 flat fee and $7 for each hour $15h + 7$

$15 for each hour, no flat fee $7h + 15$

A $7 flat fee and $15 for each hour $15h$

6. Write an expression for the cost. Use *n* for the variable.

a) Umbrellas are on sale for $2 each. _____

b) A copy shop charges $0.79 for each copy. _____

c) A bus company charges a $10 flat fee, plus $5 per passenger. _____

d) A boat company charges a $20 flat fee, plus $7 per passenger. _____

7. A company charges a $6 flat fee to rent a pair of skis, plus $3 for each hour you use the skis. The total is given by the expression $3h + 6$. Find the cost of renting a pair of skis for …

a) 4 hours

$3(4) + 6$

$= 12 + 6$

$= 18$

b) 2 hours

c) 5 hours

8. Socks cost $2 per pair. The cost of *n* pairs is $2n. Kyle says that the cost of 6 pairs is $26 and the cost of 7 pairs is $27. Explain how the mistakes were made.

_____

_____

Expressions and Equations 7-7

A triangle has a mass of *t* kg and a circle has a mass of 1 kg.

The mass of △△ (with *t*) is 2*t* kg and the mass of ①①① is 3 kg.

9. Write the mass of the set.

a) △△△①   b) ①①   c) △△①①①   d) △①①①

    __3*t* + 1__ kg   _____ kg   _____ kg   _____ kg

An **algebraic expression** is an expression with at least one variable. Two algebraic expressions are equivalent if they have the same value for every value of the variable.

---

10. a) Write the mass as an expression.

    i) ①①△ has a mass of _____ kg   ii) △①① has a mass of _____ kg

   b) Will the two pictures always have the same mass for the same value of *t*? _____

      Are the expressions $t + 2$ and $2 + t$ equivalent? _____

   c) Evaluate the expressions $t + 2$ and $2 + t$ when …

    i) $t = 0$ _____   ii) $t = 1$ _____   iii) $t = 5$ _____   **Bonus** ▶ $t = -3$ _____

   d) The expressions $t + 2$ and $2 + t$ are equivalent. Circle the property that shows this.

      the associative property   the commutative property

11. a) Draw a picture beside each expression, using circles and triangles to show the mass.

    $1 + 2t$ $2t + 1$

   b) Are $1 + 2t$ and $2t + 1$ equivalent? _____ How do you know? _____

    _____

   c) Evaluate the expressions from part a) when …

    i) $t = 0$ _____   ii) $t = 1$ _____   iii) $t = 5$ _____   **Bonus** ▶ $t = -3$ _____

12. a) Draw a picture to show the masses of $3(4t)$ and $(3 \times 4)t$.

   b) Are the expressions equivalent? How do you know?

   c) Evaluate the expressions $3(4t)$ and $(3 \times 4)t$ when …

    i) $t = 0$ ii) $t = 1$ iii) $t = 5$ **Bonus** ▶ $t = -3$

   d) The expressions $3(4t)$ and $(3 \times 4)t$ are equivalent. Does this show the associative property, the commutative property, or the distributive property?

Expressions and Equations 7-7

EE7-8 Adding and Subtracting Expressions

> Remember: 3×2 is short for $2 + 2 + 2$. Similarly, $3x$ is short for $x + x + x$.

1. Write the sum as a product of a number and a variable.

   a) $x + x + x + x =$ _____

   b) $y + y + y =$ _____

2. Write the product as a sum.

   a) $4w =$ _____

   b) $5r =$ _____

3. Add by writing how many x's there are altogether.

   a) $3x$ $+$ $2x$

      $= x + x + x \;+\; x + x = \underline{\quad 5x \quad}$

   b) $4x$ $+$ $3x$

      $= x + x + x + x \;+\; x + x + x = \underline{\qquad}$

   c) x $+$ $6x$

      $= \underline{\hspace{5cm}} = \underline{\qquad}$

   d) $2x$ $+$ $2x$

      $= \underline{\hspace{5cm}} = \underline{\qquad}$

4. Write two equivalent expressions for $6x$.

   $6x = x + x \;+\; x + x + x + x$

   $= \underline{\quad} + \underline{\quad}$

   $6x = x + x + x \;+\; x + x + x$

   $= \underline{\quad} + \underline{\quad}$

> By the distributive property …
>
> $2 \times 4 \;+\; 3 \times 4 \;=\; (2 + 3) \times 4$
>
> $4 + 4 \;+\; 4 + 4 + 4 = 4 + 4 + 4 + 4 + 4$
>
> And for any number x …
>
> $2x \;+\; 3x \;=\; (2 + 3)x$
>
> $x + x \;+\; x + x + x = x + x + x + x + x$

5. Add by adding the numbers in front of the variable.

   a) $3x + 4x = (3 + 4)x =$ _____

   b) $8x + x = (8 + 1)x =$ _____

   c) $4x + 4x = ($ _____ $)x =$ _____

   d) $3x + 8x + 9x = ($ _____ $)x =$ _____

6. Evaluate both expressions. Are your answers the same? If not, find your mistake.

	$2x + 5x$	$7x$
a) $x = 3$	$2(3) + 5(3) = 6 + 15 = 21$	$7(3) = 21$
b) $x = 5$		
c) $x = \dfrac{3}{5}$		

$5x - 3x = 2x$ $x + x + \boxed{x + x + x}$ ↗

7. Subtract by taking away x's.

   a) $6x - 2x = $ _____

      $x + x + x + x + \boxed{x + x}$ ↗

   b) $9x - 4x = $ _____

      $x + x + x + x + x + x + x + x + x$

   c) $7x - 5x = $ _____

      $x + x + x + x + x + x + x$

   d) $10x - 6x = $ _____

      $x + x + x + x + x + x + x + x + x + x$

8. Draw x's and take some away to subtract.

   a) $5x - 3x = $ _____

   b) $8x - 5x = $ _____

9. Add and subtract. Hint: Circle the x's being added and evaluate those first.

   a) $\boxed{7x} - 4x + \boxed{3x} + \boxed{2x} - x$

      $= 12x - 5x = 7x$

   b) $6x - x - x - x - x - x$

   c) $-2x + 3x - 5x - x + 4x$

   d) $7x - 2x + 4x - 8x - 2x + x$

REMINDER: $+(+) = +$ $+(-) = -$ $-(+) = -$ $-(-) = +$

10. Add and subtract.

   a) $3x + (-2x) - (-6x) - (+4x) + (+7x) - (-3x)$

      $= 3x - 2x + 6x - 4x + 7x + 3x$

      $= 19x - 6x$

      $= 13x$

   b) $7x - (-2x) + (-3x) - (+5x) + (+4x)$

   c) $-5x - (+3x) - (-2x) + (-7x) + (+4x) - (-8x)$

   d) $-x + (-x) + (+x) - (-x) - (+x)$

EE7-9 Like Terms

Terms with the same variable are called **like** terms. Constant terms are also like terms.

To **simplify** expressions like the ones below, you can start by putting like terms together. Then add or subtract the like terms.

Examples: $7 + 8x + 2 + 5x = 8x + 5x + 7 + 2$

$\qquad\qquad\qquad = 13x + 9$

$7x + 2 - 5x + 3 = 7x - 5x + 2 + 3$

$\qquad\qquad\qquad\quad = 2x + 5$

1. Simplify the expression. Start by putting like terms together.

   a) $2x + 5 + 3x$

   b) $3 + 4x + 7$

   c) $8x + 5 + 3x + 2$

   d) $3x + 4 + 7 + 6x$

   e) $5x + 1 - 4 - 3x + 5$

   f) $8x + 2 - 5x + 7 - 4 + x$

2. Find the perimeter (the distance around the shape). Then simplify the expression.

   a)

   $\underline{\quad x + x + x + x = 4x \quad}$

   b)

   _____

   c)

   _____

   d)

   _____

   e)

   _____

   f)

   _____

3. Put like terms together to add the expressions.

   a) $(10x + 3) + (5x - 4)$

   b) $(3x + 7) + (5x - 3)$

   $= 10x + 3 + 5x - 4$

   $= 10x + 5x + 3 - 4$

   $= 15x - 1$

   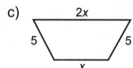 c) $(7x + 6) + (-8x - 9)$

    d) $(2x + 5) + (-3x + 1)$

$$7 - (2 + 1) = 7 - 2 - 1$$
$$7 - (3 + 1) = 7 - 3 - 1$$
$$7 - (4 + 1) = 7 - 4 - 1$$
For any x,
$$7 - (x + 1) = 7 - x - 1$$

$$7 - (5 - 3) = 7 - 5 + 3$$
$$7 - (6 - 3) = 7 - 6 + 3$$
$$7 - (7 - 3) = 7 - 7 + 3$$
For any x,
$$7 - (x - 3) = 7 - x + 3$$

4. Write the subtraction without brackets, then combine like terms to simplify.

a) $5 - (x + 1)$

b) $8 - (x - 1)$

c) $6 - (3x - 2)$

d) $7x - (x + 2)$

e) $2x + 3 - (2x - 3)$

f) $2x + 5 - (3x + 7)$

g) $3x + (5x - 4)$

h) $3x - (5x - 4)$

i) $(3x + 2) - (3x - 5)$

j) $(2 - 7x) + (3 - 5x)$

k) $(2 - 7x) - (3 - 5x)$

l) $(3x - 7) - (5 - 3x)$

5. Check your answer to Question 4 part e) for $x = 10$, $x = 11$, and one other value.

6. Ray hired Sun and Peter to help him move. Sun charged a $20 flat fee and $30 per hour. Peter charged $25 per hour.

a) Write an expression for Ray's total cost if Sun and Peter each work h hours.

_____

b) Write an expression for the difference in pay if Sun and Peter each work h hours.

_____

7. Tessa has nine children and hires two babysitters at a time. Tim charges $15 per hour with the first hour free, and Yu charges $10 per hour plus a flat fee of $20. Write an expression for Tessa's total cost, and say what the variable represents.

EE7-10 Coefficients and Constant Terms

An **equation** shows two expressions that are equal.

1. Circle the equations.

$5n - 3$ $n + 6 = 7$ $2 - x = 4$

          $7 - 5x$ $9 = 8 + 3x + 4x$

$9 = 5 + 4$ $9 \times 3 + (8 - 4) \times 5$ $5(6x - 3)$

In an expression, the **coefficient** is the number of times that the variable is added.

Examples:

- $5x + 2 = x + x + x + x + x + 2$ has coefficient 5 because x is being added 5 times.
- $w - 7 = 1w - 7$ has coefficient 1 because w is being added once.

2. Write the coefficient.

a) $3a + 2$ _____   b) $m - 3$ _____   c) $3 + 8w$ _____

d) $2 + 6r$ _____   e) $9 + p$ _____   f) $s - 4$ _____

When the variable is subtracted, the coefficient is written as a negative number.

Examples:

- $3 - 4y$ has coefficient -4.
- $-5 - x$ has coefficient -1.

3. Write the coefficient.

a) $3 - m$ _____   b) $5 - 7w$ _____   c) $-6r - 3$ _____

In the expression $3a + 7b + 5$, the **coefficient of a** is 3 and the **coefficient of b** is 7.

4. Write the coefficient of x.

a) $3x + 4y + 7$ _____   b) $8x - y + 9$ _____   c) $2u + 4x - 5$ _____

d) $3u - 7x - 8$ _____   e) $9w + 3x + 8y$ _____   f) $-5 + 4w - 3x$ _____

5. The cost in dollars of s sandwiches and d drinks is $3s + 2d$.

a) Find the cost of 5 sandwiches and 4 drinks.

b) What does the coefficient of s tell you?

6. Evaluate the expression at the given values for the variables.

	$x = 1, y = 2$	$x = 2, y = 1$
a) $3x + y$	$3(1) + 2 = 3 + 2 = 5$	$3(2) + 1 = 6 + 1 = 7$
b) $5x - 2y$		
c) $2x - 3y$		

7. Simplify by combining like terms.

a) $2x + 3y + 4 + x + 5y + 7$ b) $7x - 5y + 2 - x + 2y + 6$ c) $-2x + 3 + 4y - 5x + 6y$

$= \underline{\ 2x + x + 3y + 5y + 4 + 7\ }$ $= \underline{\hspace{3cm}}$ $= \underline{\hspace{3cm}}$

$= \underline{\ 3x + 8y + 11\ }$ $= \underline{\hspace{3cm}}$ $= \underline{\hspace{3cm}}$

In an expression, the quantity without the variable is called the **constant term**.

Examples: • $3x + 4$ has constant term 4.
   • $5x = 5x + 0$ has constant term 0.
   • $7x - 5$ has constant term -5.

---

8. Write the constant term.

a) $3x + 4y + 7$ _____   b) $8x - y + 9$ _____   c) $2u + 4x - 5$ _____

d) $3u - 7x - 8$ _____   e) $9w + 3x + 8y$ _____   **Bonus ▶** $8 - y - 3$ _____

9. What is -4, the coefficient or the constant term?

a) $4 - 4x$ b) $x - 4$ c) $-4 - x$

_____   _____   _____

10. It costs \$3 per hour to use the ski hill and \$10 to rent skis.

a) Write an expression for the cost of renting skis to go skiing for h hours. _____

b) In the expression, the coefficient is _____ and the constant term is _____.

11. The cost of renting a bike for h hours is $\$5h + 4$. Match each term to the correct item.

a) flat fee   5   b) flat fee   constant term

   hourly rate h hourly rate   variable

   hours rented   4   hours rented   coefficient

12. Evaluate the expression $7x - 4$ at $x = 0$. Is your answer the coefficient or the constant term?

Expressions and Equations 7-10

EE7-11 Equivalent Expressions

> REMINDER: A triangle has a mass of t kg and a circle has a mass of 1 kg.
>
> The mass of △ △ is $2t$ kg and the mass of ○○○ is 3 kg.

1. Write the mass of the set.

   a)    b)    c) △△△○   d) △○○○

   _____4t_____ kg   _____ kg   _____ kg   _____ kg

2. Draw triangles and circles to show each mass (given in kg).

   a) $t + 2$ ⟶ $3(t + 2)$

   △○○
   △○○
   △○○

   b) $2t + 1$ ⟶ $2(2t + 1)$
   △△○

   c) $2t + 3$ ⟶ $3(2t + 3)$

   d) $3t + 1$ ⟶ $4(3t + 1)$

3. Draw a picture for the expression. Write a new equivalent expression without brackets.

   a) $2(t + 4)$ b) $2(3t + 2)$ c) $3(2t + 1)$ d) $3(4t + 1)$

   △○○○○
   △○○○○

   _____2t + 8_____   _____   _____   _____

   e) $3(t + 2)$ f) $2(5t + 1)$ g) $4(3t + 4)$ h) $5(2t + 1)$

REMINDER: By the associative property, $3(5w) = (3 \times 5)w = 15w$.

4. Multiply.

a) $4(3r)$

= _____

b) $6(5s)$

= _____

c) $3(7w)$

= _____

d) $8(9x)$

= _____

By the distributive property, $3(2w + 5) = 3(2w) + 3(5)$
$$= 6w + 15.$$

5. To multiply an expression by 4, multiply each term by 4.

a) $4(x + 1)$

$4x + 4$

b) $4(x + 2)$

_____

c) $4(2x + 1)$

_____

d) $4(2x + 5)$

_____

e) $4(-x + 2)$

_____

f) $4(3x - 2)$

_____

g) $4(7 - 5x)$

_____

h) $4(-3x - 4)$

_____

You can simplify sums and differences of expressions.
$$7 - 2(3x + 4) = 7 - (6x + 8)$$
$$= 7 - 6x - 8$$
$$= -1 - 6x$$

6. Simplify.

a) $9x - 3(x + 4)$

$= 9x - (3x + 12)$

=

b) $9x - (3x + 4)$

c) $9 - 3(2x + 4)$

d) $9 - 3(2x - 4)$

e) $7 - 2(3 - 8x)$

f) $8x - 3(4 - 5x)$

g) $2 - 4(3 - 2x)$

h) $4x - 3(-7 + 3x)$

i) $(8x + 2) - 4(3 - 2x) + (3x - 5)$

j) $(5 + 4x) + (9 - 4x) - 3(-7 + 3x)$

Bonus ▶ Write the expression without brackets, then simplify.
$$2(x + 2) + 3(x + 7) - 5(2x - 4)$$

EE7-12 Using Pictures to Make Equivalent Expressions

By grouping the dots differently, you can write two equivalent expressions.

$$8 + 12 = 4 \times (2 + 3)$$

1. Write two equivalent expressions for the picture.

a)

$$\underline{\hspace{1.5cm}} + \underline{\hspace{1.5cm}} = 3 \times (\underline{\hspace{1cm}} + \underline{\hspace{1cm}})$$

b)

$$\underline{\hspace{1.5cm}} + \underline{\hspace{1.5cm}} = 2 \times (\underline{\hspace{1cm}} + \underline{\hspace{1cm}})$$

2. Imagine the picture to fill in the blanks.

a) $10 + 6 = 2 \times (\underline{\hspace{1.5cm}} + \underline{\hspace{1.5cm}})$

b) $9 + 15 = 3 \times (\underline{\hspace{1.5cm}} + \underline{\hspace{1.5cm}})$

c) $18 + 45 = 9 \times (\underline{\hspace{1.5cm}} + \underline{\hspace{1.5cm}})$

d) $21 + 49 = 7 \times (\underline{\hspace{1.5cm}} + \underline{\hspace{1.5cm}})$

Bonus ▶ $18 + 24 + 33 = 3 \times (\underline{\hspace{1.5cm}} + \underline{\hspace{1.5cm}} + \underline{\hspace{1.5cm}})$

REMINDER: The GCF of two numbers is the greatest number that is a factor of both numbers.

Example: To find the GCF of 42 and 56, start by listing the factors of each number.

The factors of 42 are 1, 2, 3, 6, 7, **14**, 21, and 42. ⎤ The GCF is 14—the largest number
The factors of 56 are 1, 2, 4, 7, 8, **14**, 28, and 56. ⎦ on both lists.

---

3. Find the GCF of the two numbers. Then rewrite the sum using the GCF as one factor.

a) $18 + 24 = \underset{\text{GCF}}{\underline{\hspace{1.5cm}}} \times (\underline{\hspace{1.5cm}} + \underline{\hspace{1.5cm}})$

b) $25 + 35 = \underset{\text{GCF}}{\underline{\hspace{1.5cm}}} \times (\underline{\hspace{1.5cm}} + \underline{\hspace{1.5cm}})$

c) $6 + 30 = \underset{\text{GCF}}{\underline{\hspace{1.5cm}}} \times (\underline{\hspace{1.5cm}} + \underline{\hspace{1.5cm}})$

d) $9 + 30 = \underset{\text{GCF}}{\underline{\hspace{1.5cm}}} \times (\underline{\hspace{1.5cm}} + \underline{\hspace{1.5cm}})$

e) $28 + 35 = \underset{\text{GCF}}{\underline{\hspace{1.5cm}}} \times (\underline{\hspace{1.5cm}} + \underline{\hspace{1.5cm}})$

f) $42 + 60 = \underset{\text{GCF}}{\underline{\hspace{1.5cm}}} \times (\underline{\hspace{1.5cm}} + \underline{\hspace{1.5cm}})$

4. The pictures below each use some unshaded dots and an unknown number (x) of shaded dots. Write two equivalent expressions for each picture.

a)

$$\boxed{\begin{array}{c} x \\ x \end{array}} \boxed{\begin{array}{ccc} \circ & \circ & \circ \\ \circ & \circ & \circ \end{array}} = \begin{array}{c} \boxed{x \; \circ \; \circ \; \circ} \\ \boxed{x \; \circ \; \circ \; \circ} \end{array}$$

<u>   2x + 6   </u> = <u> 2(x + 3) </u>

b)

$$\boxed{\begin{array}{c} x \\ x \\ x \end{array}} \boxed{\begin{array}{c} \circ \\ \circ \\ \circ \end{array}} = \begin{array}{c} \boxed{x \; \circ} \\ \boxed{x \; \circ} \\ \boxed{x \; \circ} \end{array}$$

_____ = _____

c)

$$\boxed{\begin{array}{c} x \\ x \end{array}} \boxed{\begin{array}{cc} \circ & \circ \\ \circ & \circ \end{array}} = \begin{array}{c} \boxed{x \; \circ \; \circ} \\ \boxed{x \; \circ \; \circ} \end{array}$$

_____ = _____

d)

$$\boxed{\begin{array}{ccc} x & x & x \\ x & x & x \end{array}} \boxed{\begin{array}{cc} \circ & \circ \\ \circ & \circ \end{array}} = \begin{array}{c} \boxed{x \; x \; x \; \circ \; \circ} \\ \boxed{x \; x \; x \; \circ \; \circ} \end{array}$$

_____ = _____

e)

$$\boxed{\begin{array}{cc} x & x \\ x & x \\ x & x \end{array}} \boxed{\begin{array}{c} \circ \\ \circ \\ \circ \end{array}} = \begin{array}{c} \boxed{x \; x \; \circ} \\ \boxed{x \; x \; \circ} \\ \boxed{x \; x \; \circ} \end{array}$$

_____ = _____

f)

$$\boxed{\begin{array}{cc} x & x \\ x & x \\ x & x \end{array}} \boxed{\begin{array}{cccc} \circ & \circ & \circ & \circ \\ \circ & \circ & \circ & \circ \\ \circ & \circ & \circ & \circ \end{array}} = \begin{array}{c} \boxed{x \; x \; \circ \; \circ \; \circ \; \circ} \\ \boxed{x \; x \; \circ \; \circ \; \circ \; \circ} \\ \boxed{x \; x \; \circ \; \circ \; \circ \; \circ} \end{array}$$

_____ = _____

5. Find the GCF of the two numbers. Then rewrite the sum using the GCF as one factor.

a) $12x + 14 =$ <u> 2 </u> $\times ($ <u> 6x + 7 </u> $)$ b) $6x + 15 =$ _____ $\times ($ _____ $)$

c) $18x + 30 =$ _____ $\times ($ _____ $)$ d) $40x + 64 =$ _____ $\times ($ _____ $)$

e) $16x + 40 =$ _____ $\times ($ _____ $)$ f) $5x + 20 =$ _____ $\times ($ _____ $)$

You can write $4x + 6$ as $2(2x + 3)$. This is called **factoring** $4x + 6$.

You can write $2(2x + 3)$ as $4x + 6$. This is called **expanding** $2(2x + 3)$.

---

6. Factor the expression.

a) $6x + 9$ b) $6x + 4$ c) $12x - 18$ d) $15 - 10x$

= _____   = _____   = _____   = _____

Bonus ▶ $6x + 3y + 15 =$ _____

7. Expand the expression.

a) $3(x + 5)$ b) $4(2x + 7)$ c) $3(4 - 2x)$ d) $5(3x - 8)$

= _____   = _____   = _____   = _____

Bonus ▶ $2(x + 3y + 8p + 4w + 11) =$ _____

8. Use the picture to write an equivalent expression.

a)

	s	1
2	_2s_	_2_

$2(s + 1) =$ ___2s___ + ___2___

b)

	s	2
3	_____	_____

$3(s + 2) =$ _____ + _____

c)

	3w	5
4	_12w_	_____

$4(3w + 5) =$ _____ + _____

d)

	8	2r
7	_____	_____

$7(8 + 2r) =$ _____ + _____

9. Find the area of the shaded part in three different ways.

a)

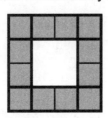

$4 \times$ ___3___ $=$ $4 \times$ ___2___ $+ 4$ $=$ $2 \times$ _____ $+ 2 \times$ _____

b)

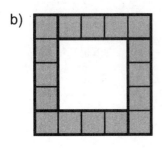   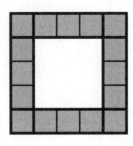   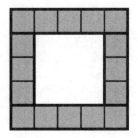

$4 \times$ _____ $=$ $4 \times$ _____ $+ 4$ $=$ $2 \times$ _____ $+ 2 \times$ _____

Bonus ▶

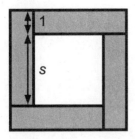   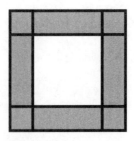   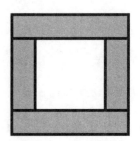

$4 \times ($ _____ $)$ $=$ $4 \times ($ _____ $) + 4$ $=$ $2 \times ($ _____ $) + 2 \times$ _____

Expressions and Equations 7-12

NS7-18 Decimal Fractions

In a **decimal fraction**, the denominator is a power of ten.

10, 100, 1,000, 10,000, … are **powers of 10**.	5, 26, 111, 700, … are **not powers of 10**.
Example: $\dfrac{8}{100}$ is a decimal fraction.	Example: $\dfrac{8}{700}$ is not a decimal fraction.

1. Circle the decimal fractions.

   $\dfrac{3}{10}$ $\dfrac{3}{21}$ $\dfrac{53}{100}$ $\dfrac{9}{26}$ $\dfrac{7}{100}$ $\dfrac{5}{35}$ $\dfrac{63}{1,000}$ $\dfrac{100}{15}$ $\dfrac{125}{600}$ $\dfrac{100}{52}$

Entire grid $= \dfrac{100}{100} = 1$ one

1 column $= \dfrac{10}{100} = \dfrac{1}{10} = 1$ tenth

1 square $= \dfrac{1}{100} = 1$ hundredth

1 one

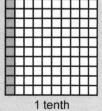
1 tenth

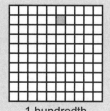
1 hundredth

---

2. Write two equivalent fractions for the shaded part of the grid.

   a) $=$

   $\dfrac{3}{10} = \dfrac{}{100}$

   b) $=$

   $\dfrac{}{10} = \dfrac{}{100}$

   c) $=$

   $\dfrac{}{10} = \dfrac{}{100}$

3. Write an equivalent fraction with denominator 100.

   a) $\dfrac{8 \times 10}{10 \times 10} = \dfrac{}{100}$

   b) $\dfrac{3 \times 10}{10 \times 10} = \dfrac{}{100}$

   c) $\dfrac{5}{10} = \dfrac{}{100}$

   d) $\dfrac{4}{10} = \dfrac{}{}$

   e) $\dfrac{9}{10} = \dfrac{}{}$

   f) $\dfrac{6}{10} = \dfrac{}{}$

4. Write an equivalent fraction with denominator 1,000.

   a) $\dfrac{9 \times 10}{100 \times 10} = \dfrac{}{1,000}$

   b) $\dfrac{3}{100} = \dfrac{}{1,000}$

   c) $\dfrac{4}{100} = \dfrac{}{1,000}$

   d) $\dfrac{8 \times 100}{10 \times 100} = \dfrac{}{1,000}$

   e) $\dfrac{3}{10} = \dfrac{}{1,000}$

   f) $\dfrac{5}{10} = \dfrac{}{1,000}$

   g) $\dfrac{6}{10} = \dfrac{}{}$

   h) $\dfrac{6}{100} = \dfrac{}{}$

   i) $\dfrac{1}{100} = \dfrac{}{}$

5. Write the equivalent hundredths and thousandths.

Tenths	$\dfrac{7}{10}$	$\dfrac{3}{10}$	$\dfrac{8}{10}$	$\dfrac{2}{10}$	$\dfrac{9}{10}$	$\dfrac{10}{10}$
Hundredths						
Thousandths						

Notice the pattern:

6. How many more zeros are in the second denominator? Add the same number of zeros to the numerator.

a) $\dfrac{9}{10} = \dfrac{}{100}$ 　　b) $\dfrac{80}{100} = \dfrac{}{1,000}$ 　　c) $\dfrac{4}{100} = \dfrac{}{1,000}$ 　　d) $\dfrac{4}{10} = \dfrac{}{1,000}$

e) $\dfrac{6}{10} = \dfrac{}{1,000}$ 　　f) $\dfrac{2}{10} = \dfrac{}{100}$ 　　**Bonus ▶** $\dfrac{30}{1,000} = \dfrac{}{10,000,000}$

7. Write the decimal fraction shown by the shaded part of the grid in four ways.

		$\dfrac{}{100}$	$\dfrac{}{10} + \dfrac{}{100}$	_____ hundredths	_____ tenths _____ hundredths
a)		$\dfrac{32}{100}$	$\dfrac{3}{10} + \dfrac{2}{100}$	__32__ hundredths	__3__ tenths __2__ hundredths
b)		$\dfrac{}{100}$	$\dfrac{}{10} + \dfrac{}{100}$	_____ hundredths	_____ tenths _____ hundredths
c)				_____ hundredths	_____ tenths _____ hundredths

To add $\dfrac{9}{10} + \dfrac{4}{100} + \dfrac{8}{1{,}000}$, change all fractions to thousandths.

$$\dfrac{9 \times 100}{10 \times 100} + \dfrac{4 \times 10}{100 \times 10} + \dfrac{8}{1{,}000} = \dfrac{900}{1{,}000} + \dfrac{40}{1{,}000} + \dfrac{8}{1{,}000} = \dfrac{948}{1{,}000}$$

8. Add. Show your work.

a) $\dfrac{5 \times 100}{10 \times 100} + \dfrac{3 \times 10}{100 \times 10} + \dfrac{7}{1{,}000}$

b) $\dfrac{2 \times 100}{10 \times 100} + \dfrac{8 \times 10}{100 \times 10} + \dfrac{6}{1{,}000}$

$= \dfrac{500}{1{,}000} + \dfrac{30}{1{,}000} + \dfrac{7}{1{,}000} = \dfrac{537}{1{,}000}$

$= \dfrac{}{1{,}000} + \dfrac{}{1{,}000} + \dfrac{}{1{,}000} = \dfrac{}{1{,}000}$

c) $\dfrac{3 \times}{10 \times} + \dfrac{9 \times}{100 \times} + \dfrac{4}{1{,}000}$

d) $\dfrac{3}{10} + \dfrac{3}{100} + \dfrac{3}{1{,}000}$

$= \dfrac{}{1{,}000} + \dfrac{}{1{,}000} + \dfrac{}{1{,}000} = \dfrac{}{1{,}000}$

$= \dfrac{}{1{,}000} + \dfrac{}{1{,}000} + \dfrac{}{1{,}000} = \dfrac{}{1{,}000}$

9. Write the sum as a sum of fractions with the same denominator.

a) $\dfrac{1}{10} + \dfrac{6}{100} + \dfrac{2}{1{,}000} = \dfrac{100}{1{,}000} + \dfrac{60}{1{,}000} + \dfrac{2}{1{,}000} = \dfrac{162}{1{,}000}$

b) $\dfrac{6}{10} + \dfrac{7}{100} + \dfrac{5}{1{,}000} =$

c) $\dfrac{2}{10} + \dfrac{3}{100} + \dfrac{4}{1{,}000} =$

10. Add the tenths and hundredths.

a) $\dfrac{1}{10} + \dfrac{9}{100} = \underline{}$

b) $\dfrac{6}{10} + \dfrac{7}{100} = \underline{}$

c) $\dfrac{2}{10} + \dfrac{7}{100} = \underline{}$

d) $\dfrac{3}{10} + \dfrac{1}{100} = \underline{}$

11. Add.

a) $\dfrac{9}{10} + \dfrac{6}{100} + \dfrac{7}{1{,}000} =$

b) $\dfrac{8}{10} + \dfrac{8}{100} + \dfrac{8}{1{,}000} =$

c) $\dfrac{9}{10} + \dfrac{4}{1{,}000} =$

d) $\dfrac{7}{100} + \dfrac{9}{1{,}000} =$

e) $\dfrac{5}{100} + \dfrac{3}{1{,}000} =$

f) $\dfrac{4}{10} + \dfrac{4}{1{,}000} =$

NS7-19 Place Value and Decimals

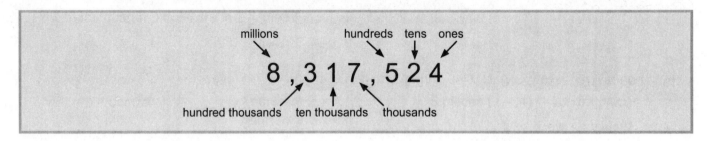

1. Write the place value of the underlined digit.

    a) 56,236 _____hundreds_____

    b) 1,956,336 _____

    c) 8,256,601 _____

    d) 7,103,256 _____

    e) 2,589,143 _____

    f) 3,921,052 _____

    g) 903,746 _____

    h) 2,605,416 _____

    i) 3,459,012 _____

    j) 7,018,762 _____

2. Write the place value of the digit 6 in each of the numbers below.
   Hint: First underline the 6 in each number.

    a) 36,589 _____thousands_____

    b) 6,308,503 _____

    c) 35,906 _____

    d) 612 _____

    e) 2,642 _____

    f) 3,461,528 _____

    g) 43,261 _____

    h) 162,775 _____

    i) 1,643,001 _____

    j) 6,704,021 _____

    k) 7,306 _____

    l) 9,596,000 _____

3. Write the number in the place value chart.

	Millions	Hundred Thousands	Ten Thousands	Thousands	Hundreds	Tens	Ones
a) 8,413,712							
b) 83,406							
c) 7,503,219							
d) 2,499							
e) 23							
f) 775,206							
g) 8,003,005							

Decimals are a way to record place values based on decimal fractions.

3 hundreds + 6 tens + 5 ones

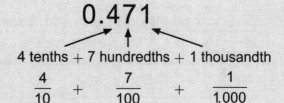

4 tenths + 7 hundredths + 1 thousandth

$$\frac{4}{10} + \frac{7}{100} + \frac{1}{1,000}$$

4. Write the decimal as the sum of a whole number and decimal fractions.

a) $2.17 = \underline{\ 2\ } + \frac{1}{10} + \frac{7}{100}$

b) $3.24 = \underline{\hspace{1cm}} + \frac{}{10} + \frac{}{100}$

c) $8.31 = \underline{\hspace{1cm}} + \frac{}{10} + \frac{}{100}$

d) $5.02 = \underline{\hspace{1cm}} + \frac{}{10} + \frac{}{100}$

e) $0.46 = \underline{\hspace{1cm}} + \frac{}{10} + \frac{}{100}$

f) $9.15 = \underline{\hspace{1cm}} + \frac{}{10} + \frac{}{100}$

g) $3.206 = \underline{\hspace{1cm}} + \frac{}{10} + \frac{}{100} + \frac{}{1,000}$

h) $3.104 = \underline{\hspace{1cm}} + \frac{}{10} + \frac{}{100} + \frac{}{1,000}$

i) $6.521 = \underline{\hspace{1cm}} + \frac{}{10} + \frac{}{100} + \frac{}{1,000}$

j) $7.602 = \underline{\hspace{1cm}} + \frac{}{10} + \frac{}{100} + \frac{}{1,000}$

5. Write the decimal as a sum of a whole number and decimal fractions.
Do not write the fractions with a numerator of 0.

a) $4.017 = \underline{\ 4\ } + \frac{1}{100} + \frac{7}{1,000}$

b) $8.305 = \underline{\hspace{1cm}} + \frac{}{10} + \frac{}{1,000}$

c) $0.801 =$

d) $9.058 =$

e) $0.005 =$

f) $6.003 =$

6. What is the value of the 9 in each decimal? Write the answer two ways.

a) $0.497 \quad \dfrac{9}{100}$ or _9 hundredths_

b) $8.439 \quad \dfrac{9}{\quad}$ or _9_____

c) $1.923 \quad \dfrac{9}{\quad}$ or _____

d) $0.907 \quad \dfrac{9}{\quad}$ or _____

e) $0.749 \quad \underline{\quad}$ or _____

f) $7.591 \quad \underline{\quad}$ or _____

g) $4.903 \quad \underline{\quad}$ or _____

h) $3.809 \quad \underline{\quad}$ or _____

7. Write the decimal fraction in the place value chart, then write the number as a decimal.

a) $\frac{3}{10} = 0.\underline{3}$

Ones	Tenths
0	3

b) $\frac{7}{10} = 0.\underline{}$

Ones	Tenths

c) $\frac{7}{10} + \frac{3}{100} = \underline{0}.\underline{}\,\underline{}$

Ones	Tenths	Hundredths
0		

d) $\frac{3}{10} + \frac{8}{100} = \underline{}.\underline{}\,\underline{}$

Ones	Tenths	Hundredths

e) $\frac{2}{10} + \frac{4}{100} = \underline{}.\underline{}\,\underline{}$

Ones	Tenths	Hundredths
0		

f) $\frac{1}{10} + \frac{9}{100} + \frac{3}{1,000} = \underline{}.\underline{}\,\underline{}\,\underline{}$

Ones	Tenths	Hundredths	Thousandths
0	1	9	3

g) $\frac{1}{10} + \frac{3}{100} + \frac{8}{1,000} = \underline{}.\underline{}\,\underline{}\,\underline{}$

Ones	Tenths	Hundredths	Thousandths
0			

h) $5 + \frac{2}{10} + \frac{4}{100} = \underline{5}.\underline{}\,\underline{}$

Ones	Tenths	Hundredths
5		

i) $7 + \frac{5}{100} + \frac{3}{1,000} = \underline{}.\underline{}\,\underline{}\,\underline{}$

Ones	Tenths	Hundredths	Thousandths

j) $50 + 8 + \frac{1}{100} = \underline{}\,\underline{}.\underline{}\,\underline{}$

Tens	Ones	Tenths	Hundredths

8. The decimal point is between the _____ and _____ place values.

9. Write the decimal in the place value chart.

	Ones	Tenths	Hundredths	Thousandths	
a) 0.51	0	5	1		← leave this blank because there are no thousandths in 0.51
b) 0.6	0	6			
c) 0.5					
d) 1.354					
e) 7.482					
f) 0.9					
g) 7.53					

NS7-20 Positive and Negative Decimals

> The whole-number part of a decimal is the part **to the left** of the decimal point.
>
> decimal point
>
> 17.348
>
> whole-number part   fractional part

1. Underline the whole-number part of the decimal.

   a) <u>36</u>.497   b) 807.3   c) 16.54   d) 9.051   e) 0.92

2. Write the number as a decimal.

   a) 3 tens + 6 ones + 2 tenths + 5 hundredths + 3 thousandths = ____ ____.____ ____ ____

   b) 8 ones + 6 tenths + 1 hundredth + 4 thousandths = _____

   c) 6 tens + 9 ones + 7 tenths + 3 hundredths = _____

3. Write the decimal in the place value chart.

	Hundreds	Tens	Ones	Tenths	Hundredths	Thousandths
a) 17.34		1	7	3	4	
b) 9.213						
c) 630.54						
d) 87.006						

4. Write the whole number and how many hundredths or thousandths.

   a) 6.45 ____six____ and _____forty-five_____ hundredths

   b) 2.46 _____ and _____ hundredths

   c) 93.005 _____ and _____ thousandths

   d) 5.083 _____ and _____ thousandths

   e) 70.201 _____ and _____ thousandths

5. Write the decimal in words.

   a) 6.8 ___six and eight tenths_____

   b) 6.03 _____

   c) 15.84 _____

   d) 72.359 _____

A decimal can be written as a mixed number. Example: $3.75 = 3\dfrac{75}{100}$

6. Write the number represented on the grids in three ways.

a)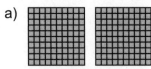

  _2_ ones _35_ hundredths   _2_ . _3_ _5_ $2\dfrac{35}{100}$

b)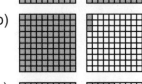

  ____ one ____ hundredths   ____ . ____ ____ $\dfrac{}{100}$

c)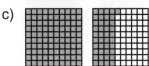

  ____ one ____ hundredths   ____ . ____ ____ $\dfrac{}{100}$

7. Write a mixed number for the decimal.

a) $5.3 =$ b) $7.05 =$ c) $6.034 =$

When two numbers are equal, so are their opposites!

Example: $7.4 = 7\dfrac{4}{10}$ so $-7.4 = -7\dfrac{4}{10}$

---

8. Write a negative mixed number for the negative decimal.

a) -3.21 b) -3.85 c) -6.8 d) -1.973 e) -13.67 f) -28.404

    $-3\dfrac{21}{100}$

9. Write a decimal for the mixed number.

a) $+2\dfrac{13}{100}$ b) $-1\dfrac{53}{100}$ c) $+76\dfrac{5}{10}$ d) $-5\dfrac{304}{1,000}$ e) $-2\dfrac{9}{10}$ f) $27\dfrac{9}{1,000}$

When the whole-number part of the decimal is zero, you don't have to write the 0.

Example: 0.25 can be written as .25.

---

10. Circle the numbers that are equal to five tenths.

a) $\dfrac{5}{1,000}$ $\dfrac{5}{10}$ $\dfrac{5}{100}$ five hundredths   five tens

    .05   0.5   0.05   .5   50   500

b) Write four tenths in at least three ways.

To write an improper fraction as a decimal:

$$\frac{43,725}{10} = 4,372.5$$

1 zero → 1 digit

$$\frac{43,725}{100} = 437.25$$

2 zeros → 2 digits

$$\frac{43,725}{1,000} = 43.725$$

3 zeros → 3 digits

11. Change the improper fraction into a mixed number by shading the correct number of pieces.

a) $\frac{23}{10}$

Mixed number: _____

b) $\frac{34}{10}$

Mixed number: _____

12. Fill in the blanks. Then write the mixed number.

a) $48 \div 10 =$ _____ R _____ so $\frac{48}{10} = 4\frac{8}{10}$

b) $87 \div 10 =$ _____ R _____ so $\frac{87}{10} =$

c) $99 \div 10 =$ _____ R _____ so $\frac{99}{10} =$

d) $342 \div 100 =$ _____ R _____ so $\frac{342}{100} =$

13. Write the improper fraction as a mixed number and then as a decimal.

a) $\frac{23}{10} = \boxed{2\frac{3}{10}} =$ _2.3_

b) $\frac{64}{10} = \boxed{} =$ _____

c) $\frac{838}{100} = \boxed{} =$ _____

d) $\frac{9,547}{100} = \boxed{} =$ _____

To write the improper fraction $\frac{43,725}{100}$ as a decimal:

Step 1: Write the numerator without the commas.

Step 2: Place the decimal point to match the denominator of the fraction.

$$\frac{43,\underset{2 \text{ zeros}}{725}}{\underset{}{100}} = 437.\underset{2 \text{ digits}}{25}$$

14. Write the improper fraction as a decimal.

a) $\frac{74}{10} =$ _7.4_

b) $\frac{536}{100} =$ _____

c) $\frac{712}{100} =$ _____

d) $\frac{6,347}{10} =$ _____

e) $\frac{2,804}{100} =$ _____

Bonus ▶ $\frac{714,295}{10,000} =$ _____

15. Write the negative improper fraction as a negative decimal.

a) $-\frac{89}{10} =$ _−8.9_

b) $-\frac{341}{10} =$ _____

c) $-\frac{512}{100} =$ _____

d) $-\frac{608}{10} =$ _____

e) $-\frac{5,903}{100} =$ _____

Bonus ▶ $-\frac{643,081}{10,000} =$ _____

NS7-21 Comparing Fractions and Decimals

Point A is at $\frac{8}{10} = 0.8$. Point B is at $-\frac{8}{10} = -0.8$.

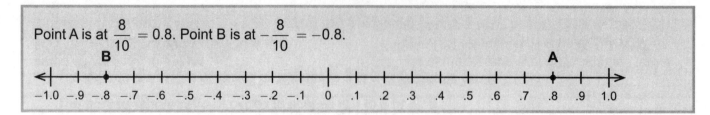

1. Write a decimal and a fraction for each point on the number line.

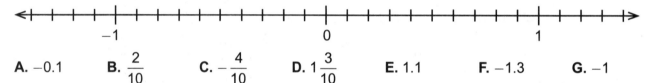

	A	B	C	D	E	F
Decimal	−1.4					
Fraction	$-1\frac{4}{10}$					

2. a) Mark each point with a dot and the correct letter.

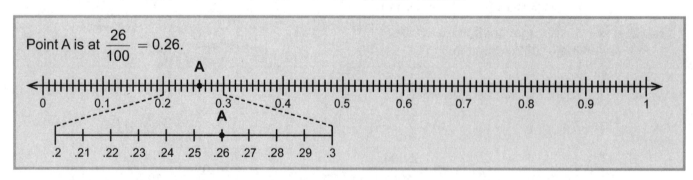

A. −0.1   **B.** $\frac{2}{10}$ **C.** $-\frac{4}{10}$ **D.** $1\frac{3}{10}$ **E.** 1.1   **F.** −1.3   **G.** −1

   b) Write the numbers from part a) from least to greatest.

   _____ < _____ < _____ < _____ < _____ < _____ < _____

Point A is at $\frac{26}{100} = 0.26$.

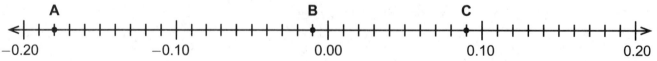

3. Write a decimal fraction and a decimal for each point on the number line.

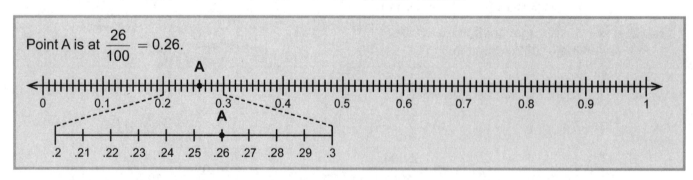

   A. _____ _____   B. _____ _____   C. _____ _____

4. a) Write a decimal for each mark on the number line.

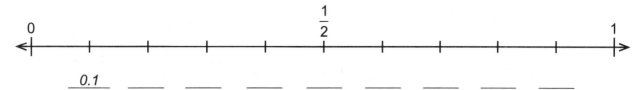

<u> 0.1 </u> ____ ____ ____ ____ ____ ____ ____ ____ ____

b) Which decimal is equal to one half? _____

c) Use the number line to compare the pair of numbers. Write < (less than),
 > (greater than), or = (equal to).

i) 0.9 $\boxed{>}$ $\dfrac{1}{2}$

ii) $\dfrac{1}{2}$ $\boxed{}$ 0.3

iii) 0.1 $\boxed{}$ $\dfrac{1}{2}$

iv) $\dfrac{1}{2}$ $\boxed{}$ 0.8

v) 0.5 $\boxed{}$ $\dfrac{1}{2}$

vi) $\dfrac{1}{2}$ $\boxed{}$ 0.7

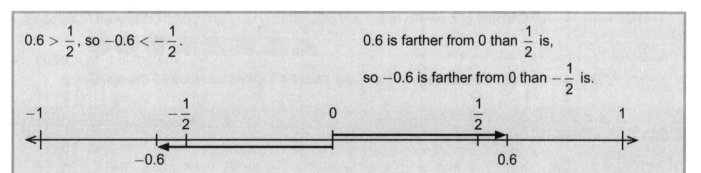

$0.6 > \dfrac{1}{2}$, so $-0.6 < -\dfrac{1}{2}$.

0.6 is farther from 0 than $\dfrac{1}{2}$ is,

so -0.6 is farther from 0 than $-\dfrac{1}{2}$ is.

5. Write < , >, or =.

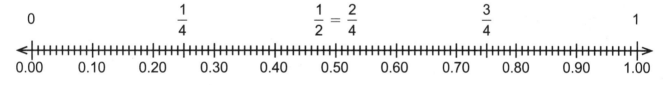

a) $\dfrac{3}{4}$ $\boxed{}$ 0.72

so $-\dfrac{3}{4}$ $\boxed{}$ -0.72

b) 0.38 $\boxed{}$ $\dfrac{1}{4}$

so -0.38 $\boxed{}$ $-\dfrac{1}{4}$

c) 0.44 $\boxed{}$ $\dfrac{1}{2}$

so -0.44 $\boxed{}$ $-\dfrac{1}{2}$

d) $-\dfrac{2}{4}$ $\boxed{}$ -0.53

e) $-\dfrac{3}{4}$ $\boxed{}$ -0.81

f) -0.23 $\boxed{}$ $-\dfrac{1}{4}$

6. Change both numbers to fractions with denominator 100. Then write < or >.

a) $\dfrac{3}{4} = \dfrac{}{100}$ $\boxed{}$ $0.73 = \dfrac{}{100}$

so $-\dfrac{3}{4}$ $\boxed{}$ -0.73

b) $0.19 = \dfrac{}{100}$ $\boxed{}$ $\dfrac{1}{4} = \dfrac{}{100}$

so -0.19 $\boxed{}$ $-\dfrac{1}{4}$

c) $\dfrac{3}{5} = \dfrac{}{100}$ $\boxed{}$ $0.81 = \dfrac{}{100}$

so $-\dfrac{3}{5}$ $\boxed{}$ -0.81

The Number System 7-21

NS7-22 Adding and Subtracting Multi-Digit Decimals

1. Add the decimals by adding each place value, then regroup.

   a) $0.72 + 4.5$

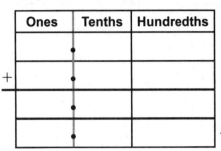

   b) $60.8 + 8.94$

   ← after regrouping →

2. Add the decimals by lining up the decimal points.

   a) $0.32 + 0.57$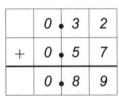

   b) $0.61 + 0.03$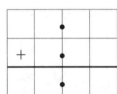

   c) $0.6 + 0.27$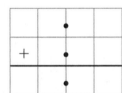

   d) $0.31 + 0.48$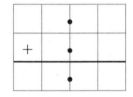

You can show regrouping on a grid.

Example: $6.9 + 2.3$

9 tenths + 3 tenths = 12 tenths were regrouped as **1** one and **2** tenths

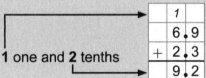

---

3. Add the decimals by lining up the decimal points. You will need to regroup.

   a) $0.9 + 0.47$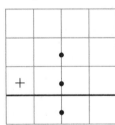

   b) $0.68 + 0.37$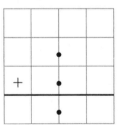

   c) $0.91 + 0.59$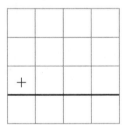

   d) $0.35 + 0.23 + 2.47$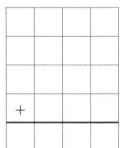

4. Line up the decimal points and add the following numbers.

   a) $5.34 + 2.19$

   b) $3.68 + 5.43$

   c) $4.972 + 3.287$

   d) $0.678 + 0.73$

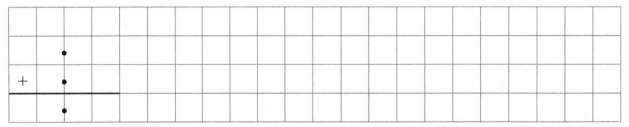

5. Subtract the decimals by lining up the decimal points.

a) 0.53 − 0.21

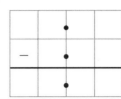

b) 0.77 − 0.43

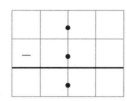

c) 0.58 − 0.21

d) 0.57 − 0.12

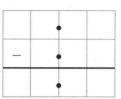

6. Subtract the decimals. You will need to regroup.

a) 0.35 − 0.17

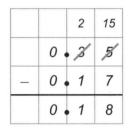

b) 0.84 − 0.58

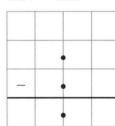

c) 0.82 − 0.49

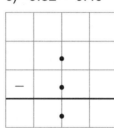

d) 0.73 − 0.49

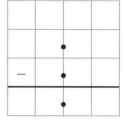

e) 1.00 − 0.73   f) 1.00 − 0.39   g) 1.00 − 0.55   h) 1.00 − 0.92

7. Subtract the decimals.

a) .91 − .45   b) .97 − .59   c) .72 − .57   d) .31 − .24

e) .58 − .2   f) .73 − .7   g) .876 − .014   h) .630 − .182

> To add two numbers with the same sign (+ or −), add the absolute values. The sum has the same sign as both numbers.
>
> Example: To add − 3.2 − 4.6, first add 3.2 + 4.6 = 7.8. So − 3.2 − 4.6 = −7.8.

8. Use the grid to add the absolute values. Then write the answer with the correct sign.

a) − 3.25 − 18.5

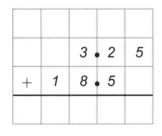

_____

b) + 16.9 + 7.85

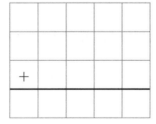

_____

c) − 17.04 − 18.37

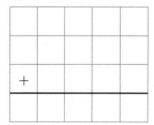

_____

d) + 17.41 + 3.894   e) − 493.1 − 18.4   f) + 3.47 + 1.62

g) − 182.3 − 18.23   h) − 15.3 − 37.49   i) − 5.84 − 71.2 − 18.35

To add two numbers with different signs, subtract their absolute values. The sum has the same sign as the number with the greater absolute value.

Example: To add $-5.2 + 4.6$, subtract $5.2 - 4.6 = 0.6$. Since $|-5.2| > |4.6|$, the sum is negative.
So $-5.2 + 4.6 = -0.6$.

9. Add the numbers by subtracting the absolute values.

a) $-5.8 + 18.93$

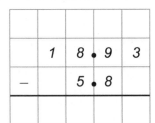

b) $+21.4 - 58.63$

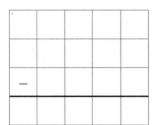

c) $-7.43 + 26.28$

_____

_____

_____

d) $-15.4 + 6.83$

e) $+70.4 - 107.2$

f) $-5.46 + 17.4$

REMINDER: $+(+) = +$ $+(-) = -$ $-(+) = -$ $-(-) = +$

10. Rewrite the question. Then add or subtract.

a) $-5.4 - (+3.61)$

= _____ $-5.4 - 3.61$ _____

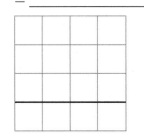

b) $+18.5 + (-4.8)$

= _____

c) $+74.21 - (+8.5)$

= _____

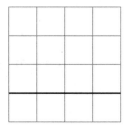

_____

_____

_____

d) $-32.18 - (-5.714)$

e) $+13.61 - (-7.4)$

f) $-5.2 + (+17.63)$

11. A bank statement shows a credit when money is put in and a debit when money is taken out.

a) Complete the balance column.

b) The first debit shown was a mistake by the bank and is cancelled. What is the new bank account balance?

Debit (−)	Credit (+)	Balance
		$0
$15.34		−$15.34
	$27.81	
$23.42		
	$5.41	

The Number System 7-22

NS7-23 Division with Fractional and Decimal Answers

Three people share 5 pancakes. How much does each person get?

Divide each pancake into thirds. Give each person one piece from each pancake.
The shaded parts show how much one person gets.

Each person gets $\dfrac{1}{3} + \dfrac{1}{3} + \dfrac{1}{3} + \dfrac{1}{3} + \dfrac{1}{3} = 5 \times \dfrac{1}{3} = \dfrac{5}{3}$ pancakes.

1. Shade one person's share of the pancakes. How much does each person get?

   a) 5 people share 4 pancakes.

   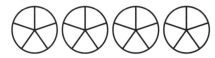

   _____ × _____ = _____ pancakes

   b) 4 people share 3 pancakes.

   _____ × _____ = _____ pancakes

2. Draw a picture to solve the problem: 4 people share 7 oranges.

   How many oranges does each person get? _____

The division sign (÷) can be used for equal sharing, whether the answer is a whole number or not.

Example: When 3 people share 5 pancakes equally, each person gets $\dfrac{5}{3}$ pancakes. So, $5 \div 3 = \dfrac{5}{3}$.

---

3. Draw a picture to show how much one person gets. Write the division equation.

   a) Two people share 9 pancakes.

   _____ ÷ _____ = _____

   b) Four people share 5 pancakes.

   _____ ÷ _____ = _____

REMINDER: You can write tenths, hundredths, and thousandths as decimals. The number of digits
after the decimal point is equal to the number of zeros in the denominator.

Examples: $\dfrac{7}{10} = 0.7$ $\dfrac{382}{100} = 3.82$ $\dfrac{17}{1,000} = 0.017$

4. Divide. Write the answer as a fraction and a decimal.

a) $3 \div 10$

$= \dfrac{3}{10}$

$= 0.3$

b) $38 \div 100$

$=$

$=$

c) $53 \div 10$

$=$

$=$

d) $7 \div 1,000$

$=$

$=$

e) $912 \div 10$

$=$

$=$

f) $638 \div 100$

$=$

$=$

g) $49 \div 1,000$

$=$

$=$

h) $30,408 \div 1,000$

$=$

$=$

REMINDER: You can change a fraction to a decimal by first changing the fraction to a decimal fraction,
where the denominator is a power of 10. The powers of 10 are 10, 100, 1,000, …

Example: $\dfrac{5}{4} = \dfrac{5 \times 25}{4 \times 25} = \dfrac{125}{100} = 1.25$

5. Divide. Write your answer as a decimal.

a) $3 \div 5$

$\dfrac{3}{5} = \dfrac{}{10} = \underline{\hspace{1cm}}$

b) $7 \div 5$

$\dfrac{7}{5} = \dfrac{}{10} = \underline{\hspace{1cm}}$

c) $9 \div 20$

$\dfrac{9}{20} = \dfrac{}{100} = \underline{\hspace{1cm}}$

d) $10 \div 4$

e) $3 \div 4$

f) $28 \div 20$

g) $33 \div 20$

h) $21 \div 25$

i) $7 \div 4$

Bonus ▶ $11 \div 8$

6. Compare your answers to Question 5, parts b) and f). What do you notice?
Why is that the case?

NS7-24 Long Division

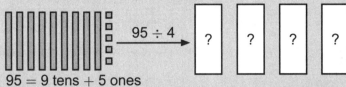

Divide 95 objects into 4 groups (95 ÷ 4) using long division and a base ten model:

95 = 9 tens + 5 ones

Step 1: Write the number like this:

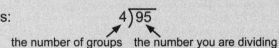

the number of groups   the number you are dividing

Step 2: How can you divide 9 tens blocks equally into the 4 groups?
You can divide 8 of the 9 tens blocks into 4 equal groups of size 2:

There are 2 tens blocks in each group. →
There are 4 groups.
2 × 4 = 8 tens blocks placed →

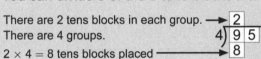

1. How many groups are you going to make? How many tens blocks can you put in each group?

a) 4)91

b) 3)84

c) 6)75

d) 2)93

groups _____

groups _____

groups _____

groups _____

number of tens
in each group _____

number of tens
in each group _____

number of tens
in each group _____

number of tens
in each group _____

2. Find out how many tens can be placed in each group. Then multiply to find out how many tens have been placed.

a) 5)9 1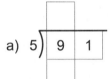

b) 3)8 2

c) 4)9 8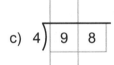

d) 5)9 9

e) 9)9 3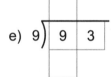

Step 3: How many tens blocks are left?

Subtract to find out. →

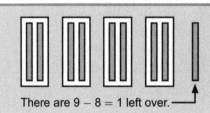

There are 9 − 8 = 1 left over. →

3. For each question, carry out the first three steps of long division.

a) 7)8 7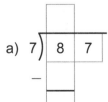

b) 3)8 4

c) 2)8 3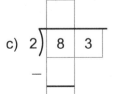

d) 4)6 3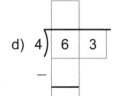

e) 6)9 9

Step 4: There is 1 tens block left over, and there are 5 ones in 95. So there are 15 ones left in total. Write the 5 beside the 1 to show this.

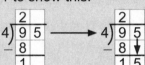 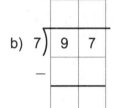

There are still this many ones to place.

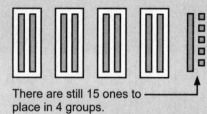

There are still 15 ones to place in 4 groups.

4. Carry out the first four steps of long division.

a) 5$\overline{)85}$ b) 7$\overline{)97}$ c) 4$\overline{)92}$ d) 2$\overline{)75}$ e) 2$\overline{)73}$

Step 5: How many ones can you put in each group?

Divide to find out:
$$4\overline{)95} \quad 2\,3 \leftarrow 15 \div 4 = 3\,R\ \underline{?}$$
$$-8$$
$$15$$

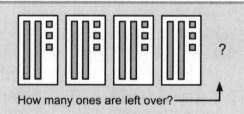

How many ones are left over? ?

5. Carry out the first five steps of long division.

a) 5$\overline{)61}$ b) 4$\overline{)47}$ c) 2$\overline{)86}$ d) 3$\overline{)63}$ e) 5$\overline{)81}$

Step 6 and 7: Find the number of ones left over.

$$4\overline{)95} \quad 2\,3$$
$$-8$$
$$15$$
$$-12 \leftarrow \text{There are } 3 \times 4 = 12 \text{ ones placed.}$$
$$3 \leftarrow \text{There are } 15 - 12 = 3 \text{ ones left over.}$$

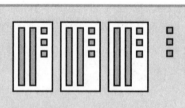

Long division and the model both show that **95 ÷ 4 = 23 with 3 left over**.

6. Carry out all the steps of long division on grid paper.

a) 6$\overline{)81}$ b) 4$\overline{)52}$ c) 3$\overline{)95}$ d) 3$\overline{)82}$ e) 4$\overline{)64}$

f) 7$\overline{)87}$ g) 6$\overline{)92}$ h) 8$\overline{)90}$ i) 9$\overline{)84}$ j) 9$\overline{)71}$

To divide 334 objects into 2 groups using long division:

Step 1: Divide the hundreds into 2 groups.

```
    1
2)3 3 4
 −2
  1
```

Step 2: Regroup the remaining hundreds as tens.

```
    1
2)3 3 4
 −2
  1 3
```

Step 3: Divide the tens into 2 groups.

```
    1 6
2)3 3 4
 −2
  1 3
 −1 2
    1
```

Step 4: Regroup the remaining tens as ones and divide.

```
    1 6 7
2)3 3 4
 −2
  1 3
 −1 2
    1 4
   −1 4
      0
```

7. Divide.

a) 5)8 1 2

b) 2)3 2 7

c) 4)5 3 1

d) 4)9 8 9

REMINDER: You can write division answers as decimals instead of with a remainder.

Example: $16 \div 5 = 3 \text{ R } 1$, so $16 \div 5 = 3\frac{1}{5} = 3\frac{2}{10} = 3.2$

---

8. Write your answers to Question 7 as decimals.

a) $812 \div 5 = $ _____

b) $327 \div 2 = $ _____

c) $531 \div 4 = $ _____

d) $989 \div 4 = $ _____

9. Divide using long division. Write your answers as decimals.

a) $917 \div 5$

b) $577 \div 2$

c) $794 \div 4$

d) $895 \div 4$

e) $811 \div 2$

f) $614 \div 4$

g) $836 \div 5$

h) $981 \div 8$

10. In each question below, there are not enough tens to divide into the groups. Write a "0" in the tens place to show that no tens can be placed, then continue the division, regrouping tens as ones.

a)
```
        2   0 ← 8   — 0 tens in each group
    3 ) 6   2   5
      - 6
        0   2   — 2 tens to place in 3 groups
      -     0   — 0 tens placed
            2   5
          - 2   4
                1
```

b) 4) 8 1 7

c) 2) 6 1 7

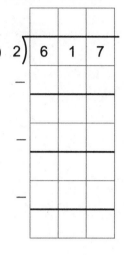

d) 7) 7 6 1

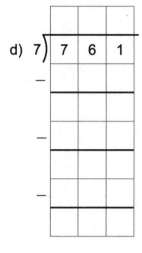

11. In each question below, there are fewer hundreds than the number of groups. Write a "0" in the hundreds place to show that no hundreds can be placed in equal groups. Then perform the division as if the hundreds had been exchanged for tens.

a)
```
        0   4 ← 3   — 4 tens in each group
    8 ) 3   4   6
      - 3   2   — 32 tens placed
            2 ← 6   — 2 tens are left over
          - 2   4
                2
```

b) 5) 3 9 5

c) 9) 6 9 6

d) 7) 5 1 8

e) 3) 121

f) 4) 214

g) 8) 641

h) 6) 584

i) 9) 365

12. In each question below, say how many tens or hundreds can be placed in 5 groups. Underline the place values you will divide by 5.

a) 5) 3̲1̲5   b) 5) 7̲26   c) 5) 623   d) 5) 321

   ___31 tens___   ___7 hundreds___   _____   _____

e) 5) 892   f) 5) 240   g) 5) 987   h) 5) 412

   _____   _____   _____   _____

13. Divide. Write your answer as a decimal.

a) 2) 136   b) 4) 263   c) 5) 584   d) 5) 407

e) 2) 7,913   f) 4) 9,807   g) 5) 2,764   h) 8) 4,012

The Number System 7-24

RP7-12 Rounding

1. For the circled number, draw an arrow to show which multiple of ten you would round to.
   Then round the number to the nearest ten.

a)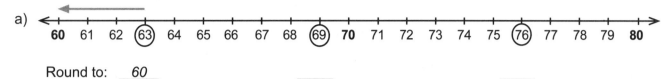

   Round to: _60_   ____   ____

b)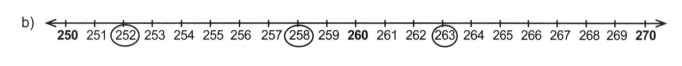

   Round to: ____   ____   ____

> To round to a given place value, underline the digit you want to round to.
>
> If the digit to the right of it is 0, 1, 2, 3, or 4, round down. If the digit is 5, 6, 7, 8, or 9, round up.

2. Underline the digit you wish to round to. Then say whether you would round up or down.

a) thousands

| 2 | <u>7</u> | 3 | 2 | 5 |

   round up   (round down)

b) ten thousands

| 8 | 7 | 5 | 2 | 3 |

   round up   round down

c) hundreds

| 9 | 7 | 5 | 1 | 3 |

   round up   round down

d) tens

| 2 | 7 | 5 | 3 | 2 | 3 |

   round up   round down

e) thousands

| 1 | 9 | 6 | 7 | 8 | 2 |

   round up   round down

f) thousands

| 3 | 0 | 0 | 5 | 2 | 7 |

   round up   round down

> Round the underlined digit up or down.
> • To round up, add 1 to the digit.
> • To round down, keep the digit the same.
>
>
>
> The digits to the right of the rounded digit become zeros.
> The digits to the left remain the same.
>
>

3. Round the number to the given digit.

a) thousands

| 7 | 3 | 2 | 0 | 1 | ru |
| | | | | | rd |

b) ten thousands

| 3 | 5 | 8 | 3 | 5 | ru |
| | | | | | rd |

c) hundreds

| 9 | 4 | 2 | 1 | 7 | ru |
| | | | | | rd |

d) hundreds

| 2 | 8 | 6 | 8 | 1 | ru |
| | | | | | rd |

e) tens

| 5 | 2 | 3 | 7 | 2 | ru |
| | | | | | rd |

f) ten thousands

| 8 | 3 | 9 | 2 | 1 | ru |
| | | | | | rd |

Sometimes when rounding, you have to regroup.

Example: Round 37,952 to the nearest hundred.

3	7	9	5	2
		10		

9 hundreds rounds to
10 hundreds.

		1		
3	7	9	5	2
	8	0		

Regroup the 10 hundreds
as 1 thousand. Add it to the
7 thousands to make 8 thousands.

3	7	9	5	2
3	8	0	0	0

Complete the rounding.

4. Round the number to the given digit, regrouping if necessary.

a) 2,195   tens

_____

b) 3,942   hundreds

_____

c) 9,851   thousands

_____

d) 4,921   hundreds

_____

e) 12,291   tens

_____

f) 6,973   hundreds

_____

The symbol ≈ means "approximately equal to."

5. What is the length, to the nearest centimeter?

a)

2.7 cm ≈ _____ cm

b)

0.8 cm ≈ _____ cm

c)

3.3 cm ≈ _____ cm

To round 23.586 to the nearest hundredth:

Step 1: Underline the digit you want to round to: 23.5_8_6.

Step 2: The digit to the right is **5 or more**, so round up: 23.586 ≈ 23.59.
You don't need to write 0s after the digit you rounded to because 23.59 = 23.590.

6. Follow the steps above to round the decimal to the given digit.

a) tenths

2	.	4	8	5

b) hundredths

3	.	1	9	4

c) tenths

4	2	.	3	9	5

d) ones

9	6	.	7	2

e) tens

5	2	.	0	8

f) ones

1	.	1

Ratios and Proportional Relationships 7-12

7. Round the decimal to the given digit.

a) tenths

3	.	3	1

b) hundredths

4	2	.	7	3	1

c) thousandths

3	.	2	7	0	6

d) tenths

9	2	.	1	5	7

e) hundredths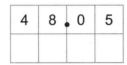

3	6	.	2	8	3

f) ones

1	.	5	3	2

g) ones

7	.	6	2

h) tens

4	8	.	0	5

i) hundredths

5	.	2	9	9

8. Calculate using a calculator. Then round your answer to the nearest hundredth.

a) $1 \div 3 \approx 0.$_____ _____

b) $22 \div 7 \approx 3.$_____ _____

c) $46 \div 13 \approx 3.$_____ _____

d) $5 \div 8 \approx 0.$_____ _____

e) $5 \div 6 \approx 0.$_____ _____

f) $17 \div 9 \approx 1.$_____ _____

9. The decimal hundredths that could be rounded to 5.3 are from 5.25 to 5.34. Which decimal hundredths could be rounded to 7.2? Explain.

10. Round each decimal to the nearest tenth, hundredth, and thousandth.

		Nearest Tenth	**Nearest Hundredth**	**Nearest Thousandth**
a)	0.1234			
b)	4.6789			
c)	0.6327			

11. To round 4.649 to the nearest tenth, Ivan rounded to the nearest hundredth first, then rounded the result to the nearest tenth. Is the answer correct? Explain.

12. The Olympic women's high jump gold medal was earned with a jump of 2.06 m. The silver medal jump was 2.02 m.

a) Round both jumps to the nearest tenth.

b) Make up two jumps that would round to the same number when rounded to the tenths.

c) Why are Olympic high jumps measured to such small place values?

RP7-13 Upper Bounds and Lower Bounds

> Rounding to the ones place is called **rounding to the nearest whole number**.

1. a) Estimate the sum by rounding each number to the nearest whole number.

  i) $32.7 + 4.16$

  ii) $25.3 + 10.657$

  iii) $97.2 + 0.9$

  i) $\approx$ __33__ + __4__

     $=$ __37__

  ii) $\approx$ _____ + _____

     $=$ _____

  iii) $\approx$ _____ + _____

     $=$ _____

  b) Use a calculator to check your estimates from part a).

> When adding two numbers, you can round both numbers up to get an **upper bound**, which is a number that is equal to or greater than the answer.
>
> Example: $3.45 + 6.89 < 4 + 7 = 11$
>
> You can round both numbers down to get a **lower bound**, which is a number that is equal to or less than the answer.
>
> Example: $3.45 + 6.89 > 3 + 6 = 9$
>
> The actual sum (in this case, 10.34) is between the lower and upper bounds.

2. Complete the chart. To find the lower and upper bounds, round each number to the nearest whole number. Make sure the actual sum is between your lower and upper bounds.

		Lower Bound	Upper Bound	Actual Sum Using a Calculator
a)	$4.8 + 5.3$			
b)	$3.7 + 5.2$			
c)	$16.37 + 13.89$			
d)	$21.35 + 41.98$			
e)	$26.58 + 13.4$			
f)	$37.5 + 64.91$			

3. A T-shirt costs $5.80 and pants cost $13.42.

  a) Use a calculator to find the total cost of the shirt and pants. _____

  b) Tina estimated the cost by rounding to the nearest whole number.

    i) How much did Tina estimate the total cost to be? _____

    ii) If she brought that much money, would she have enough? _____

  c) How should Tina estimate the total cost? Should she use an upper bound or a lower bound? Why?

4. a) Estimate the product by rounding each number to the nearest whole number.

    i) 2.7×4.16 ii) 5.3×10.871 iii) 97.2×0.9

        $\approx \underline{\ \ 3\ \ } \times \underline{\ \ 4\ \ }$ $\approx \underline{\ \ \ \ \ } \times \underline{\ \ \ \ \ }$ $\approx \underline{\ \ \ \ \ } \times \underline{\ \ \ \ \ }$

        $= \underline{\ \ 12\ \ }$ $= \underline{\ \ \ \ \ }$ $= \underline{\ \ \ \ \ }$

b) Use a calculator to check your estimates from part a).

> When multiplying two numbers, you can round both numbers up to get an upper bound for the answer.
>
> Example: $3.45 \times 6.89 < 4 \times 7 = 28$
>
> You can round both numbers down to get a lower bound for the answer.
>
> Example: $3.45 \times 6.89 > 3 \times 6 = 18$
>
> The actual product (in this case, 23.7705) is between the lower and upper bounds.

5. Complete the chart. To find the lower and upper bounds, round each number to the nearest whole number. Make sure the actual product is between your lower and upper bounds.

		Lower Bound	Upper Bound	Actual Product Using a Calculator
a)	4.9×5.1			
b)	6.5×7.5			
c)	2.7×5.4			
d)	11.7×8.9			
e)	9.51×9.42			
f)	1.35×4.68			
g)	2.1×3.429			

Note: When estimating in the questions below, round to the nearest whole number.

6. A wedding party dinner will cost $23.49 per guest. Estimate the cost for 500 guests. Do you think the bride and groom will be more interested in an upper or lower bound for the cost? Why?

7. Roy is planning a 300-mile trip. He needs 2.6 gallons of gas for every 100 miles. Estimate how much gas he should get for the trip. Did you use a lower or upper bound? Why?

8. 12 people shared a $302.84 restaurant bill. If each person paid $24.50, did they pay enough? Use an upper-bound estimation to justify your answer.

9. A 13-year-old boy said he climbed 12,000 feet in 6.5 hours. If the world record for speed climbing is 1,388 feet per hour, is the boy's statement reasonable?

RP7-14 Multiplying Decimals by Powers of 10

REMINDER: Each place value is 10 times greater than the place value to its right.

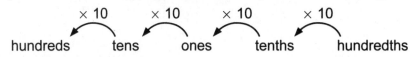

$\times$ 10 $\times$ 10 $\times$ 10 $\times$ 10

hundreds   tens   ones   tenths   hundredths

1. Use place value to multiply by 10.

a) 3 tens $\times$ 10

= ___3 hundreds___

b) 5 hundredths $\times$ 10

= _____

c) 8 tenths $\times$ 10

= _____

2. Use expanded form to multiply by 10.

a) 24.7 = ___$20 + 4 + 0.7$___ so 24.7 $\times$ 10 = ___$200 + 40 + 7$___ = __247__

b) 7.12 = _____ so 7.12 $\times$ 10 = _____ = _____

c) 0.345 = _____ so 0.345 $\times$ 10 = _____ = _____

d) 16.4 = _____ so 16.4 $\times$ 10 = _____ = _____

e) 0.803 = _____ so 0.803 $\times$ 10 = _____ = _____

f) 54.03 = _____ so 54.03 $\times$ 10 = _____ = _____

To multiply by 10, shift the decimal point one place to the right.

To multiply by 100, shift the decimal point two places to the right.

3. Multiply by 10 or 100. Do your rough work in the grid.

a)   100 $\times$ 0.7   = ___70___

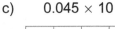

b)   10 $\times$ 3.6   = _____

c)   0.045 $\times$ 10   = _____

d)   8.9 $\times$ 100   = _____

e)   0.704 $\times$ 100   = _____

f)   6.84 $\times$ 10   = _____

g)   3.081 $\times$ 10   = _____

h)   0.051 $\times$ 100   = _____

4. Change the fraction equation to a decimal equation and write how many places the decimal point moved.

a) $1,000 \times \dfrac{1}{1,000} = 1$

so $\underline{\quad 1,000 \quad} \times \underline{\quad 0.001 \quad} = \underline{\quad 1 \quad}$

The decimal point moved $\underline{\quad 3 \quad}$ places right.

b) $100,000 \times \dfrac{1}{100,000} = 1$

so $\underline{\qquad\qquad} \times \underline{\qquad\qquad} = \underline{\qquad\qquad}$

The decimal point moved $\underline{\qquad}$ places right.

c) $10,000 \times \dfrac{1}{10,000} = 1$

so $\underline{\qquad\qquad} \times \underline{\qquad\qquad} = \underline{\qquad\qquad}$

The decimal point moved $\underline{\qquad}$ places right.

d) $10,000,000 \times \dfrac{1}{10,000,000} = 1$

so $\underline{\qquad\qquad} \times \underline{\qquad\qquad} = \underline{\qquad\qquad}$

The decimal point moved $\underline{\qquad}$ places right.

5. To multiply by a power of 10 (such as 10, 100, 1,000, and so on), shift the decimal point the correct number of places to the right.

a) $1,000 \times 0.076 = $ _____

b) $1,000 \times 5.03 = $ _____

c) $3.8 \times 100 = $ _____

d) $0.07 \times 10,000 = $ _____

e) $100,000 \times 0.00004 = $ _____

f) $0.0081 \times 1,000,000 = $ _____

6. To change from centimeters to millimeters, you multiply by 10. There are 10 mm in 1 cm. Convert the centimeters to millimeters.

a) 5.3 cm = _____ mm   b) 0.16 cm = _____ mm   c) 80 cm = _____ mm

7. A quarter is 0.175 cm thick. How tall would a stack of 100 quarters be? _____

8. To multiply by 10,000,000,000, move the decimal point _____ places to the right.

9. Skip count by 0.4s to multiply 10×0.4.

RP7-15 Multiplying and Dividing by Powers of 10

Division can be used to "undo" multiplication.

1. How do you undo multiplying by 10, 100, or 1,000?

   a) To multiply by 10, I move the decimal point _____ place to the _____.

      So, to divide by 10, I move the decimal point _____ place to the _____.

   b) To multiply by 100, I move the decimal point _____ places to the _____.

      So, to divide by 100, I move the decimal point _____ places to the _____.

   c) To multiply by 1,000, I move the decimal point _____ places to the _____.

      So, to divide by 1,000, I move the decimal point _____ places to the _____.

2. Divide by shifting the decimal point one, two, or three places to the left.

   a) $0.7 \div 10$ = _____

   b) $52.3 \div 1,000$ = _____

   c) $7.5 \div 1,000$ = _____

   d) $8.9 \div 100$ = _____

   e) $36,543.26 \div 1,000$ = _____

   If there is no decimal point, add one to the right of the number first.

   f) $80 \div 100$ = _____

8	0	.	0

   g) $9 \div 10$ = _____

   h) $2,543,700 \div 1,000$ = _____

3. Explain why $1.00 \div 100 = 0.01$. Use a dollar bill as the whole.

4. A 3.6 m wide wall is painted with 100 stripes of equal width. How wide is each strip?

Ratios and Proportional Relationships 7-15

5. a) To multiply by 10, move the decimal point ____1____ place(s) to the _____.

b) To divide by 1,000, move the decimal point _____ place(s) to the _____.

c) To multiply by 100, move the decimal point _____ place(s) to the _____.

d) To _____ by 10, move the decimal point _____ place(s) to the left.

e) To _____ by 1,000, move the decimal point _____ place(s) to the right.

f) To divide by _____, move the decimal point 2 places to the _____.

g) To multiply by _____, move the decimal point 4 places to the _____.

h) To multiply by 100,000, move the decimal point _____ place(s) to the _____.

i) To divide by 10,000,000, move the decimal point _____ place(s) to the _____.

6. Fill in the blanks. Next, draw arrows to show how you would shift the decimal point. Then write your final answer in the grid.

a) $7.845 \times 1,000$

Move the decimal point _____ places _____.

b) $5.4 \div 100$

Move the decimal point _____ places _____.

c) $247.567 \times 10,000$

Move the decimal point _____ places _____.

d) $100.45 \div 10,000$

Move the decimal point _____ places _____.

e) $0.602 \times 100,000$ f) $24.682 \div 10,000$ g) $0.07 \times 100,000$ h) $36.07 \div 1,000$

7. a) Multiply the fraction by 10. Write your answer in lowest terms.

i) $10 \times \dfrac{2}{10}$ ii) $10 \times \dfrac{3}{100}$ iii) $10 \times \dfrac{16}{10}$ iv) $10 \times \dfrac{7}{1,000}$

b) Multiply the decimal by 10.

i) 10×0.2 ii) 10×0.03 iii) 10×1.6 iv) 10×0.007

c) Are your answers to parts a) and b) the same? Why is this the case?

RP7-16 Multiplying Decimals by Whole Numbers

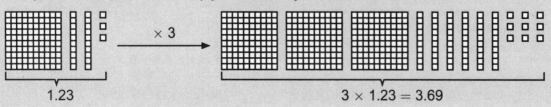

The picture shows how to multiply a decimal by a whole number.

1.23   × 3 →   3 × 1.23 = 3.69

1. Multiply mentally. Multiply each digit separately.

a) 3 × 2.13 = _____   b) 2 × 4.2 = _____   c) 8 × 1.01 = _____   d) 3 × 2.3 = _____

e) 4 × 2.21 = _____   f) 3 × 1.3 = _____   g) 3 × 4.21 = _____   h) 8 × 4.11 = _____

2. Multiply by exchanging tenths for ones.

a) 7 × 1.3 = __7__ ones + __21__ tenths   b) 3 × 3.6 = _____ ones + _____ tenths

   = __9__ ones + __1__ tenth   = _____ ones + _____ tenths

   = __9.1__   = _____

c) 11 × 1.2 = __11__ ones + __22__ tenths   d) 12 × 4.2 = _____ ones + _____ tenths

   = _____ ones + _____ tenths   = _____ ones + _____ tenths

   = _____   = _____

3. Multiply by exchanging tenths for ones or hundredths for tenths.

a) 3 × 3.15 = _____ ones + _____ tenths + _____ hundredths

   = _____ ones + _____ tenths + _____ hundredths = _____

b) 4 × 2.41 = _____ ones + _____ tenths + _____ hundredths

   = _____ ones + _____ tenths + _____ hundredths = _____

You may need to regroup twice.

c) 4 × 1.34 = _____ ones + _____ tenths + _____ hundredths

   = _____ ones + _____ tenths + _____ hundredths

   = _____ ones + _____ tenths + _____ hundredths = _____

d) 11 × 2.13 = _____ ones + _____ tenths + _____ hundredths

   = _____ ones + _____ tenths + _____ hundredths

   = _____ ones + _____ tenths + _____ hundredths = _____

To multiply a decimal and a whole number:

Step 1: Multiply as though both numbers are whole numbers.

Step 2: In the product of the whole numbers, put as many digits after the decimal point as the decimal has. Remove any final 0s.

Example: 3.42×15

$342 \times 15 = 5{,}130$

$3.42 \times 15 = 51.30$

$= 51.3$

This works because 342×15 is 100 times greater than 3.42×15.

4. Multiply. In some questions you will have to regroup twice.

a)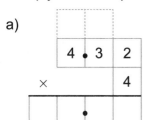

b)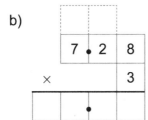

c)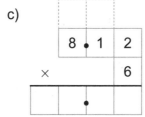

d)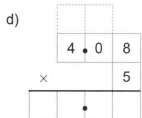

e)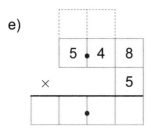

f)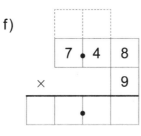

g)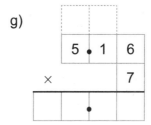

h)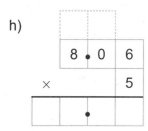

i) 5×3.6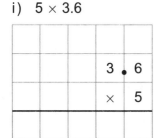

j) 3×0.4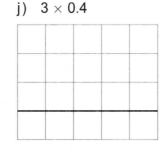

k) 4.2×6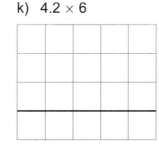

l) 3×46.92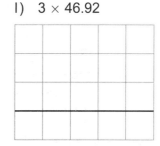

5. Multiply.

a)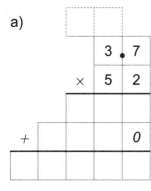

b)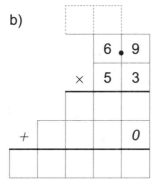

c)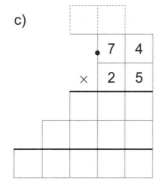

d)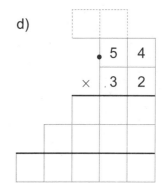

e) 13×2.3

f) 4.2×15

g) 4×36.75

h) 21×18.04

REMINDER: Multiplying by a whole number is repeated addition.

Examples: $3 \times 2.1 = 2.1 + 2.1 + 2.1 = 6.3$ and $3 \times (-2.1) = -2.1 - 2.1 - 2.1 = -6.3$

6. Multiply by using repeated addition.

a) $2 \times 0.8 = $ _____ = _____   b) $3 \times (-0.6) = $ _____ = _____

c) $3 \times 1.3 = $ _____ = _____   d) $2 \times (-1.8) = $ _____ = _____

e) $7 \times (-2.1) = $ _____ = _____

7. Use $\frac{1}{5} = 0.2$ to write $\frac{4}{5}$ as a decimal.

$$\frac{4}{5} = \frac{1}{5} + \frac{1}{5} + \frac{1}{5} + \frac{1}{5} = \underline{\ 0.2\ } + \underline{\hspace{1cm}} + \underline{\hspace{1cm}} + \underline{\hspace{1cm}} = \underline{\hspace{1cm}}$$

8. Use $\frac{1}{4} = 0.25$ to write $-\frac{3}{4}$ as a decimal.

$$-\frac{3}{4} = -\frac{1}{4} - \frac{1}{4} - \frac{1}{4} = -\underline{\hspace{1cm}} - \underline{\hspace{1cm}} - \underline{\hspace{1cm}} = \underline{\hspace{1cm}}$$

9. Use multiplication to write the fraction as a decimal.

a) $\frac{3}{2} = 3 \times \frac{1}{2} = 3 \times \underline{\hspace{1cm}} = \underline{\hspace{1cm}}$ b) $-\frac{5}{4} = 5 \times \left(-\frac{1}{4}\right) = 5 \times (\underline{\hspace{1cm}}) = \underline{\hspace{1cm}}$

Bonus ▶ Check your answers to Questions 7 to 9 by converting the fractions
to decimals another way.

10. a) Continue the pattern to write $\frac{7}{20}$ as a decimal.

$\frac{1}{20}$	$\frac{2}{20}$	$\frac{3}{20}$	$\frac{4}{20}$	$\frac{5}{20}$	$\frac{6}{20}$	$\frac{7}{20}$
0.05	0.10	0.15	0.20	_____	_____	_____

b) If you know $\frac{1}{20}$ as a decimal, how can you use multiplication to write $\frac{11}{20}$
as a decimal? How can you write $-\frac{11}{20}$ as a decimal?

c) What is $\frac{17}{20}$ written as a decimal? How does your answer compare to $\frac{7}{20}$
as a decimal? Why does this make sense?

Ratios and Proportional Relationships 7-16

RP7-17 Percentages

A **percentage** is a ratio that compares a number to 100.

The term *percent* means "per 100" or "for every 100" or "out of 100." For example, 84% on a test means 84 out of 100.

You can think of a percentage as a short form for a fraction with denominator 100. Example: $45\% = \dfrac{45}{100}$

1. Write the percentage as a fraction.

   a) 3%   b) 87%   c) 6%   d) 35%

   e) 50%   f) 100%   g) 9%   h) 13%

2. Write the fraction as a percentage.

   a) $\dfrac{2}{100}$ b) $\dfrac{13}{100}$ c) $\dfrac{27}{100}$ d) $\dfrac{100}{100}$

   e) $\dfrac{19}{100}$ f) $\dfrac{66}{100}$ g) $\dfrac{8}{100}$ h) $\dfrac{1}{100}$

3. Write the decimal as a fraction and then a percentage.

   a) $0.72 = \dfrac{72}{100} = 72\%$ b) 0.34   c) 0.05

4. Write the fraction as a percentage by first changing it to a fraction with denominator 100.

   a) $\dfrac{3 \times 20}{5 \times 20} = \dfrac{60}{100} = 60\%$ b) $\dfrac{2}{5}$

   c) $\dfrac{4}{5}$ d) $\dfrac{1}{4}$

   e) $\dfrac{3}{4}$ f) $\dfrac{1}{2}$

   g) $\dfrac{1}{10}$ h) $\dfrac{9}{10}$

   i) $\dfrac{19}{25}$ j) $\dfrac{13}{20}$

   k) $\dfrac{7}{25}$ l) $\dfrac{15}{20}$

   m) $\dfrac{43}{50}$ n) $\dfrac{27}{50}$

5. Write the decimal as a percentage.

a) $0.2 = \dfrac{2 \times 10}{10 \times 10} = \dfrac{20}{100} = 20\%$

b) 0.5

c) 0.7

d) 0.9

6. Write the percentage as a fraction, then as a decimal.

a) $32\% = \dfrac{32}{100} = 0.32$

b) 8%

c) 51%

d) 4%

7. What percent of the figure is shaded?

a)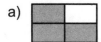

b)

c)

d)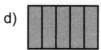

8. Change the fraction to a percentage by first reducing it to lowest terms.

a) $\dfrac{9 \div 3}{15 \div 3} = \dfrac{3}{5} = \dfrac{3 \times 20}{5 \times 20} = \dfrac{60}{100} = 60\%$

b) $\dfrac{12}{15}$

c) $\dfrac{3}{6}$

d) $\dfrac{14}{35}$

e) $\dfrac{21}{28}$

f) $\dfrac{11}{44}$

g) $\dfrac{24}{30}$

h) $\dfrac{8}{16}$

i) $\dfrac{30}{40}$

j) $\dfrac{8}{40}$

k) $\dfrac{90}{150}$

l) $\dfrac{45}{75}$

Ratios and Proportional Relationships 7-17

RP7-18 Decimals, Fractions, and Percentages

1. Fill in the chart. The first column has been done for you.

Drawing				
Fraction	$\dfrac{23}{100}$	$\dfrac{}{100}$	$\dfrac{54}{100}$	$\dfrac{}{100}$
Decimal	0.23	0.____	0.____	0.87
Percent	23%	36%	____%	____%

2. Use a centimeter ruler. Color 50% of the rectangle blue, $\dfrac{4}{10}$ red, and 0.1 green.

3. Write the shaded part in three ways.

Fraction: _____   Percent: _____   Decimal: _____

4. Write a fraction and a percentage for each division of the number line.

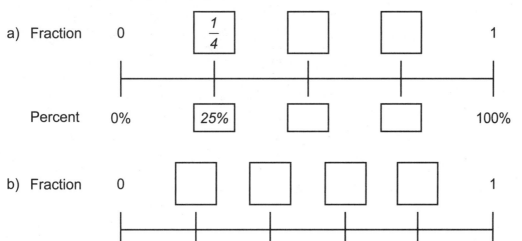

a) Fraction   0 $\boxed{\dfrac{1}{4}}$ □   □   1

Percent   0% $\boxed{25\%}$ □   □   100%

b) Fraction   0   □   □   □   □   1

Percent   0%   □   □   □   □   100%

5. Complete the chart.

Fraction	$\frac{1}{4}$		$\frac{3}{20}$			$\frac{6}{15}$	$\frac{23}{25}$		
Decimal		0.35			0.60				0.55
Percent				30%				75%	

6. Write $<$, $>$, or $=$ between each pair of numbers. Change the numbers in each pair to fractions with the same denominator first.

a) $\frac{1}{2}$ ☐ 47%

$\dfrac{50 \times 1}{50 \times 2}$ ☐ $\dfrac{47}{100}$

$\dfrac{50}{100}$ $\boxed{>}$ $\dfrac{47}{100}$

b) $\frac{1}{2}$ ☐ 49%

☐

☐

c) $\frac{3}{4}$ ☐ 78%

☐

☐

d) $\frac{2}{5}$ ☐ 35%

☐

☐

e) $\frac{2}{3}$ ☐ 60%

$\dfrac{100 \times 2}{100 \times 3}$ ☐ $\dfrac{60 \times 3}{100 \times 3}$

$\dfrac{200}{300}$ $\boxed{>}$ $\dfrac{180}{300}$

f) 0.9 ☐ $\frac{8}{9}$

☐

☐

g) 11% ☐ $\frac{1}{9}$

☐

☐

h) $\frac{1}{11}$ ☐ 0.09

☐

☐

i) 0.76 ☐ 93%

☐

☐

j) $\frac{4}{7}$ ☐ 53%

☐

☐

k) 0.7 ☐ 7%

☐

☐

l) 0.9 ☐ 10%

☐

☐

7. Write the set of numbers in order from least to greatest by first changing each number to a fraction.

a) $\frac{3}{5}$, 42%, 0.73

b) $\frac{1}{2}$, 0.74, 80%

c) $\frac{1}{4}$, 0.09, 15%

d) $\frac{2}{3}$, 57%, 0.62

8. 20 m² of a 50 m² field is used for growing potatoes. What fraction and what percent of the field is this?

9. In Sandy's class, 41% of the students like pop music best, 19% like rock music, and $\frac{2}{5}$ like rap music. Which type of music do more students like best?

RP7-19 Finding Percentages (Introduction)

If you use a thousands cube to represent 1 whole, you can see that taking $\frac{1}{10}$ of a number is the same as dividing the number by 10—the decimal shifts one place left.

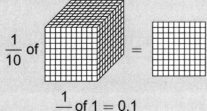

$\frac{1}{10}$ of $\boxed{}$ = $\boxed{}$

$\frac{1}{10}$ of 1 = 0.1

$\frac{1}{10}$ of $\boxed{}$ = $|$

$\frac{1}{10}$ of 0.1 = 0.01

$\frac{1}{10}$ of $|$ = $\square$

$\frac{1}{10}$ of 0.01 = 0.001

1. Find $\frac{1}{10}$ of the number by shifting the decimal. Write your answer in the box.

   a) 4 (= 4.0)   b) 9   c) 23   d) 210   e) 8.3   f) 5.2

       ☐   ☐   ☐   ☐   ☐

2. 10% is short for $\frac{10}{100}$ or $\frac{1}{10}$. Find 10% of the number.

   a) 8   b) 7.5   c) 3.06   d) 6.45   e) 0.09   f) 12.2

   ☐   ☐   ☐   ☐   ☐   ☐

You can find percentages that are multiples of 10.

Example: To find 30% of 21, find 10% of 21 and multiply the result by 3.

Step 1: 10% of 21 = $\boxed{2.1}$

Step 2: 3 × $\boxed{2.1}$ = 6.3 ⟶ 30% of 21 = 6.3

---

3. Find the percentage using the method above.

   a) 60% of 15

      10% of _15_ = ☐

      _6_ × ☐ = _____

   b) 80% of 25

      10% of _____ = ☐

      _____ × ☐ = _____

   c) 90% of 2.3

      10% of _____ = ☐

      _____ × ☐ = _____

   d) 70% of 35

      10% of _____ = ☐

      _____ × ☐ = _____

   e) 20% of 24

      10% of _____ = ☐

      _____ × ☐ = _____

   f) 30% of 1.3

      10% of _____ = ☐

      _____ × ☐ = _____

4. Use the number line to fill in the blank.

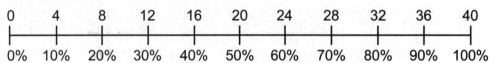

a) 20% of 40 is _____

b) 50% of 40 is _____

c) 85% of 40 is _____

d) 15% of 40 is _____

e) _____% of 40 is 12

f) _____% of 40 is 18

5. A class wrote a science test with 40 possible marks. Help the teacher record the grades as percentages.

a) $\dfrac{32}{40}$ = _____%

b) $\dfrac{38}{40}$ = _____%

c) $\dfrac{14}{40}$ = _____%

d) $\dfrac{20}{40}$ = _____%

e) $\dfrac{22}{40}$ = _____%

Bonus ▶ $\dfrac{21}{40}$ = _____%

6. Use the number line to find 5%, 15%, and 65%.

a)
```
0    50   100  150  200  250  300  350  400  450  500
├────┼────┼────┼────┼────┼────┼────┼────┼────┼────┤
0%  10%  20%  30%  40%  50%  60%  70%  80%  90%  100%
```

5% of 500 is _____   15% of 500 is _____   65% of 500 is _____

b)
```
0    3    6    9    12   15   18   21   24   27   30
├────┼────┼────┼────┼────┼────┼────┼────┼────┼────┤
0%  10%  20%  30%  40%  50%  60%  70%  80%  90%  100%
```

5% of 30 is _____   15% of 30 is _____   65% of 30 is _____

c) You will need to finish the number line yourself.

```
0                                                      60
├────┼────┼────┼────┼────┼────┼────┼────┼────┼────┤
0%  10%  20%  30%  40%  50%  60%  70%  80%  90%  100%
```

5% of 60 is _____   15% of 60 is _____   65% of 60 is _____

7. In Question 6, why should your answers to part c) be double your answers to part b)?

8. At a restaurant, Ted wants to tip the waiter 15%. If his meal cost $30, how much tip should he leave?

9. A bike costs $500. A 5% tax is added. How much is the tax?

Ratios and Proportional Relationships 7-19

RP7-20 More Percentages

35% is short for $\frac{35}{100}$. To find 35% of 27, Marta finds $\frac{35}{100}$ of 27.

Step 1: She multiplies 27 by 35.

```
    2  3
       2  7
  ×    3  5
    1  3  5
    8  1  0
    9  4  5
```

Step 2: She divides the result by 100.

$945 \div 100 = 9.45$

So 35% of 27 is 9.45.

1. Find the percentage using Marta's method.

   a) 25% of 44

   Step 1:

   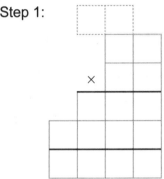

   Step 2: _____ ÷ 100 = _____

   So _____ of _____ is _____.

   b) 18% of 92

   Step 1:

   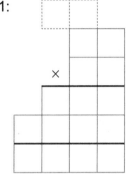

   Step 2: _____ ÷ 100 = _____

   So _____ of _____ is _____.

   c) 18% of 95

   Step 1:

   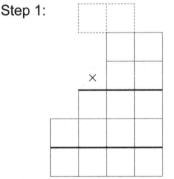

   Step 2: _____ ÷ 100 = _____

   So _____ of _____ is _____.

   d) 26% of 84

   Step 1:

   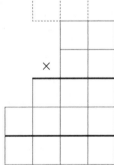

   Step 2: _____ ÷ 100 = _____

   So _____ of _____ is _____.

2. Find the percentage using Marta's method.

   a) 23% of 23   b) 15% of 26   c) 26% of 15   d) 64% of 58

   e) 58% of 64   f) 50% of 81   g) 81% of 50   h) 92% of 11

Amy says 35% is short for 0.35. To find 35% of 27, she multiplies 0.35 × 27.

3. Use Amy's method to find the percentage of the number.

   a) 23% of 47 = 0.23 × 47 = _____

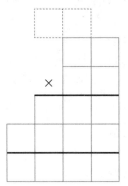

   b) 92% of 49 = 0.92 × 49 = _____

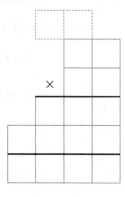

   c) 11% of 70 = _____ = _____

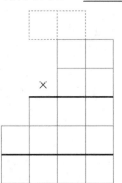

   d) 18% of 30 = _____ = _____

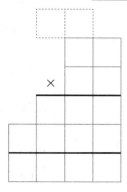

4. a) Find 18% of 23 using two methods:

   i) by writing 18% as a decimal

   ii) by writing 18% as a fraction

   b) In what ways are the methods the same?

5. Calculate 13% of 72 and 72% of 13.

   Compare your answers. What do you notice?

   Why is this the case?

6. a) Calculate 24% of 32.

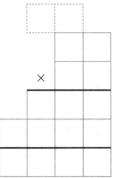

   b) Is your answer more or less than $\frac{1}{4}$ of 32? Why does this make sense?

RP7-21 Mental Math and Percentages

> You can calculate 25% of a number by dividing the number by 4 because $25\% = \dfrac{25}{100} = \dfrac{1}{4}$.
>
> Examples: 25% of 80 is $\dfrac{1}{4}$ of 80 $= 80 \div 4 = 20$.

1. Calculate 25% of the number. Do your rough work in your notebook.

   a) 25% of 60 = _____

   b) 25% of 300 = _____

   c) 25% of 40 = _____

   d) 25% of 30 = _____

   e) 25% of 70 = _____

   f) 25% of 90 = _____

   Bonus ▶ 25% of 1,000,000 = _____

> You can add and subtract percentages the same way you add and subtract fractions.
>
> Example: $\dfrac{10}{100} + \dfrac{5}{100} = \dfrac{15}{100}$ so 10% + 5% = 15%.

2. Add or subtract the percentages.

   a) 20% + 5% = _____

   b) 30% + 20% = _____

   c) 10% + 10% = _____

   d) 20% − 5% = _____

   e) 50% − 20% = _____

   f) 75% − 10% = _____

> To find 5% of a number, first find 10% of the number, then divide by 2.
>
> To find 20% of a number, first find 10% of the number, then multiply by 2.

3. Complete the chart. Start by finding 10% of each number. Make sure your answers agree with your answers to Question 1.

		60	300	40	30	70	90	Bonus ▶ 1,000,000
a)	5%	3			$\dfrac{3}{2} = 1.5$			
b)	10%	6	30		3			
c)	20%	12						
d)	25% = 20% + 5%	15						

4. 10% of a number is 3. What is the number? _____
   Hint: The number is 100% of the number.

5. Mike wants to leave a 15% tip on a meal that cost $40. How much tip should he leave? _____
   Hint: 15% = 10% + 5%

6. Change the fraction to a percentage. Then find the percentage of the stamp collection that comes from other countries.

a) Anne's collection:

USA	Canada	Other
40%	$\dfrac{1}{2}$	$\dfrac{1}{10}$
= 40%	= 50%	= 10%

b) Brian's collection:

USA	England	Other
80%	$\dfrac{1}{10}$	

c) Juan's collection:

USA	Mexico	Other
$\dfrac{1}{2}$	40%	

7. Calculate the percentages mentally, then add them.

a) 20% of 40 is _____ and 80% of 40 is _____, so 20% of 40 + 80% of 40 is _____.

b) 25% of 32 is _____ and 75% of 32 is _____, so 25% of 32 + 75% of 32 is _____.

c) 40% of 300 is _____ and 60% of 300 is _____, so 40% of 300 + 60% of 300 is _____.

d) 30% of 12 is _____ and 70% of 12 is _____, so 30% of 12 + 70% of 12 is _____.

8. Is 100% of each number in Question 7 equal to the number? If not, find your mistake.

9. a) Find 35% of 40 in two ways. Do you get the same answer both ways?

   i) 35% of 40 = 35 × 40 ÷ 100 = _____ ÷ 100 = _____

   ii) 35% of 40 = 25% of 40 + 10% of 40 = _____ + _____ = _____

   b) 35% is less than 50% or $\dfrac{1}{2}$. Is your answer to part a) less than half of 40?

   c) Is 35% closer to 0 or to $\dfrac{1}{2}$? _____

   Was your answer to part a) closer to 0 or to half of 40? _____

   d) Is your answer to part a) reasonable? Explain.

10. Vicky wants to save 25% of her earnings and spend the rest. If she earns $120 a month,

   how much can she spend each month? _____

11. Jim wants to buy a $400 bike. There is a 5% tax.

   a) How much will he pay in taxes? _____

   b) How much will he pay altogether? _____

RP7-22 Word Problems

1. Cathy buys a tennis racket worth $80. The tax is 7%.

   How much is the tax? _____

2. Anwar wants to leave a 15% tip on a meal that cost $24.

   How much tip should he leave? _____

To encourage sales, stores often pay their salespeople **commission**—a percentage of the price of the item that was sold.

3. If a salesperson receives 3% commission, how much would she receive on the sale?

	Item	Price	Commission Amount
a)	CD	$24	*$0.72*
b)	House	$200,000	
c)	Sweater	$60	
d)	Jacket	$300	

4. Subtract the discount to find the sale price.

	Item	Regular Price	Discount (percent)	Discount ($ amount)	Sale Price
a)	Gloves	$36.00	10%	*$3.60*	*$36.00 − $3.60 = $32.40*
b)	Shoes	$49.92	25%		
c)	CD	$14.90	30%		
d)	DVD	$18.50	20%		

5. May's rent will increase by 2% next year. So will her salary.

   a) If her rent is $500 per month this year, how much will her rent increase be in dollars?

   b) How much will her new rent be?

   c) If her salary is $40,000 this year, how much will her salary increase be in dollars?

   d) How much will her new salary be?

6. Don bought cans of juice for 80¢ each. He raises the price by 20%, then sells the cans. How much does he sell each can for?

A car salesperson gets a 30% commission based on the **profit** on the sale.

Example: If a car is bought for $18,000 and sold for $20,000, the commission is …

30% of $2,000 = $600

$20,000 − $18,000

7. Use 30% commission to calculate the amount the car salesperson gets for the sale.

	Car	Buying Price of Car	Selling Price of Car	Profit	Commission Amount
a)	Sedan	$20,000	$24,000	$4,000	$1,200
b)	Compact car	$15,000	$15,600		
c)	SUV	$43,500	$49,900		
d)	Sports car	$185,000	$197,000		
e)	Pick-up truck	$28,000	$33,000		

8. In the 2012 US presidential election, about 58% of American citizens who were old enough to vote actually voted.

a) What percent of American citizens who were old enough to vote didn't vote?

b) If there were 224,000,000 American citizens who were old enough to vote, how many didn't vote?

9. a) A sweater that usually costs $80 is on sale for 25% off. What is the sale price?

b) How would you estimate the price of a $32.99 shirt that is on sale for 25% off? Hint: 32.99 is close to 32, a multiple of 4.

RP7-23 Tape Diagrams, Fractions, and Percentage Problems

1. What percent and what fraction of the whole is each block?

a) [tape diagram of 5 blocks] $\dfrac{1}{5}$ = __20%__   b) [tape diagram of 4 blocks] [one block] = _____

c) [tape diagram of 10 blocks] [one block] = _____

2. What percent of A is each block? What percent of A is B?

a) A: [20% | | | |]

   B: [20% | 20%]

   B is __40__ % of A.

b) A: [tape diagram of 5 blocks]

   B: [tape diagram of 3 blocks]

   B is _____ % of A.

c) A: [tape diagram of 5 blocks]

   B: [tape diagram of 2 blocks]

   B is _____ % of A.

d) A: [tape diagram of 2 blocks]

   B: [one block]

   B is _____ % of A.

Sometimes, B is more than A. Then B is more than 100% of A.

Example: 25% of A

   A: [tape diagram of 4 blocks]

   B: [tape diagram of 5 blocks]

            125% of A

3. What percent of A is B?

a) A: [tape diagram of 4 blocks]

   B: [tape diagram of 6 blocks]

   B is _____ % of A.

b) A: [tape diagram of 2 blocks]

   B: [tape diagram of 3 blocks]

   B is _____ % of A.

c) A: [one block]

   B: [tape diagram of 4 blocks]

   B is _____ % of A.

d) A: [tape diagram of 2 blocks]

   B: [tape diagram of 4 blocks]

   B is _____ % of A.

4. What percent of the total is A?

a) A: ▢▢

    B: ▢▢▢

    A is _____% of the total.

b) A: ▢

    B: ▢▢▢▢▢▢▢▢▢

    A is _____% of the total.

c) A: ▢▢▢

    B: ▢

    A is _____% of the total.

d) A: ▢▢

    B: ▢▢▢▢▢▢

    A is _____% of the total.

Bonus ▶ A: ▢▢▢▢▢▢▢

    B: ▢

    C: ▢▢

    A is _____% of the total.

5. Draw a tape diagram to show the situation.

a) The number of girls is 25% of the total number of children.

   g:

   b:

b) The number of boys is 25% of the number of girls.

   g:

   b:

c) The number of girls is 80% of the number of boys.

   g:

   b:

d) The number of girls is 80% of the total number of children.

   g:

   b:

e) The number of boys is 75% of the total number of children.

   g:

   b:

f) The number of boys is 125% of the number of girls.

   g:

   b:

6. Which parts of Question 5 have the same tape diagram?

   Parts a) and _____, b) and _____, c) and _____.

7. Draw a tape diagram. Then complete the chart.

		Tape Diagram	Girls	Boys	Total
a)	The number of girls is 80% of the number of boys.	g: b:		30	
b)	The number of boys is 80% of the total number of children.	g: b:	20		
c)	The number of boys is 75% of the number of girls.	g: b:			35
d)	The number of boys is 75% of the total number of children.	g: b:	15		
e)	The number of girls is 120% of the number of boys.	g: b:		40	

8. Use a tape diagram to solve the problem.

a) The number of girls in a classroom is 60% of the number of boys. There are 12 girls in the classroom. How many students are in the class altogether?

b) The number of "yes" votes is 80% of the number of "no" votes. There were 45 votes altogether. How many were "yes" votes?

c) The number of fiction books in a library is 150% of the number of non-fiction books. The library has 4,000 books in total. How many fiction books and how many non-fiction books are in the library?

d) Students in a class read a book and watched the movie based on the book. 30% of the students preferred the book and the rest preferred the movie. If 21 people preferred the movie, how many people preferred the book?

Bonus ▶ The number of girls is 40% of the number of boys.

So the number of boys is _____% of the number of girls.

RP7-24 Percent More Than

1. What percent of B is the extra part of A?

a) A: ☐☐☐☐☐☐☐

   B: ☐☐☐☐ extra part of A

   The extra part of A is _____% of B.

b) A: ☐☐☐

   B: ☐☐

   The extra part of A is _____% of B.

c) A: ☐☐☐☐

   B: ☐

   The extra part of A is _____% of B.

d) A: ☐☐☐☐☐

   B: ☐☐

   The extra part of A is _____% of B.

e) A: ☐☐☐☐☐

   B: ☐☐☐☐

   The extra part of A is _____% of B.

f) A: ☐☐☐☐☐☐

   B: ☐☐☐☐☐

   The extra part of A is _____% of B.

g) A: ☐☐☐

   B: ☐

   The extra part of A is _____% of B.

h) A: ☐☐☐☐☐☐☐

   B: ☐☐☐☐☐

   The extra part of A is _____% of B.

2. Draw a tape diagram so that the extra part of A is …

a) 20% of B

   A:

   B:

b) 25% of B

   A:

   B:

c) 60% of B

   A:

   B:

d) 150% of B

   A:

   B:

e) 120% of B

   A:

   B:

Ratios and Proportional Relationships 7-24

"There are 25% more girls than boys in a school" means that the number of "extra" girls is 25% of the number of boys.

Girls: ☐☐☐☐☐

Boys: ☐☐☐☐☐

The number of "extra" girls is the same as 25% of the boys.

3. Fill in the blanks.

a) g: ☐☐☐

   b: ☐☐

The number of extra girls is what percent of the number of boys?

There are _____% more girls than boys.

b) g: ☐☐☐☐

   b: ☐☐☐☐☐

The number of extra boys is what percent of the number of girls?

There are _____% more boys than girls.

c) g: ☐☐☐☐☐☐☐☐

   b: ☐☐☐☐☐

There are _____% more girls than boys.

d) g: ☐☐

   b: ☐☐☐☐☐

There are _____% more _____ than _____.

4. Draw a tape diagram to show the situation.

a) There are 50% more boys than girls.

b) There are 20% more girls than boys.

Bonus ▶ There are 120% more boys than girls.

5. Draw a tape diagram to answer the question.

   a) There are 25% more boys than girls in a class. There are 36 students in the class altogether. How many boys and how many girls are in the class?

   g: | 4 | 4 | 4 | 4 |

   b: | 4 | 4 | 4 | 4 | 4 | } 36 altogether

   _____ boys and _____ girls

   b) There are 50% more boys than girls in a class. There are 18 boys in the class. How many students are in the class altogether?

   g:

   b:

   _____ students altogether

   c) There are 20% more girls than boys in a class. There are 30 girls in the class. How many boys are in the class?

   g:

   b:

   _____ boys

6. There are 25% more girls than boys in the school.

   a) Draw a tape diagram to show the situation.

   b) Use your tape diagram from part a) to complete the chart.

Number of Girls	Number of Boys	Total Number of Students
	360	
360		
		360

148 COPYRIGHT © 2015 JUMP MATH: NOT TO BE COPIED. CC EDITION

Ratios and Proportional Relationships 7-24

RP7-25 Ratios, Fractions, and Percentage Problems

1. Fill in the missing numbers for each classroom.

	Ratio of ...				What Fraction ...	
	girls to students	boys to students	girls to boys	boys to girls	are girls?	are boys?
a)	2 : 5	3 : 5	2 : 3	3 : 2	$\frac{2}{5}$	$\frac{3}{5}$
b)	5 : 7					
c)						$\frac{3}{4}$
d)		31 : 50				
e)				8 : 17		
f)						$\frac{1}{2}$
g)			7 : 11			
h)					$\frac{8}{15}$	
i)				31 : 25		

2. Fill in the missing numbers for each classroom.

	Percent That Are Girls	Percent That Are Boys	Fraction That Are Girls	Fraction That Are Boys	Ratio of Girls to Boys
a)	40%	60%	$\frac{40}{100}$	$\frac{60}{100}$	40 : 60
b)		45%			
c)				$\frac{1}{4}$	
d)					11 : 14
e)			$\frac{1}{2}$		
f)	85%				
g)					21 : 29

3. Show your answer with a tape diagram.

a) $\frac{3}{5}$ of the students are girls.

   The ratio of boys to girls is _____ to _____.

   There are _____% more girls than boys.

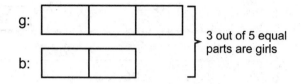

g:

b:

3 out of 5 equal parts are girls

b) $\frac{4}{9}$ of the students are girls.

   The ratio of boys to girls is _____ to _____.

   There are _____% more boys than girls.

c) $\frac{6}{11}$ of the students are boys.

   The ratio of boys to girls is _____ to _____.

   There are _____% more _____

   than _____.

d) $\frac{1}{3}$ of the students are girls.

   The ratio of boys to girls is _____ to _____.

   There are _____% more _____

   than _____.

e) $\frac{7}{12}$ of the students are boys.

   The ratio of boys to girls is _____ to _____.

   There are _____% more _____

   than _____.

f) $\frac{5}{14}$ of the students are boys.

   The ratio of boys to girls is _____ to _____.

   There are _____% more _____

   than _____.

Ratios and Proportional Relationships 7-25

4. Draw a tape diagram, then complete the chart.

		Tape Diagram	Girls	Boys	Total
a)	The number of girls is 80% more than the number of boys.	g: b:		30	
b)	The fraction of students that are girls is $\frac{5}{9}$.	g: b:	20		
c)	The number of boys is 40% of the number of girls.	g: b:			35
d)	The ratio of girls to boys is 5 : 8.	g: b:	15		

5. Show your answer with a tape diagram.

a) There are 20% more boys than girls in a class.

The ratio of boys to girls is _____ to _____.

b) The ratio of girls to boys in a class is 5 : 4. There are _____% more girls than boys.

c) $\frac{3}{5}$ of the students in a class are girls. There are _____% more girls than boys.

6. a) There are 10% more boys than girls in Grade 7. There are 5 more boys than girls. How many boys and how many girls are in Grade 7?

b) The ratio of boys to girls in Grade 7 is 11 : 10. There are 5 more boys than girls. How many boys and how many girls are in Grade 7?

c) Why should your answers to parts a) and b) be the same?

G7-1 Angles

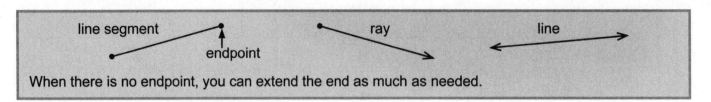

When there is no endpoint, you can extend the end as much as needed.

1. Identify the picture as a line, line segment, or ray.

a)

b)

c)

_____   _____   _____

2. Extend the ends when you can. Circle the points that are on the line, line segment, or ray.

a)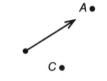

b)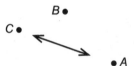

c)

3. Do the lines, rays, or line segments meet? Where possible, extend the ends to check.

a)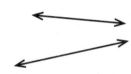

b)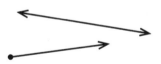

_____   _____

c)

d)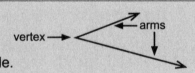

_____   _____

An **angle** is the space between two rays with the same endpoint.
The rays are the arms of the angle, and the endpoint is the **vertex**.

You can extend the arms as much as needed without changing the angle.

4. a) Extend the arms to make them both 2 cm long. Color the space between the arms.

i)   ii)   iii)   iv)

b) Which arms have the most space between them? _____

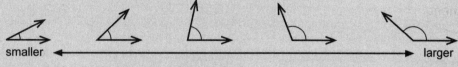

The **size** of an angle is the amount of rotation between the arms.

smaller ←——————————————————————————→ larger

You can measure angles in degrees (°).

5. What is the size of the angle?

a)  $\underline{10°}$

b) 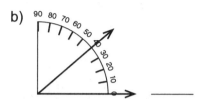   _____

c) 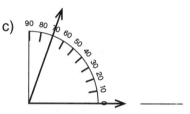   _____

Bonus ▶

d)    _____

e) 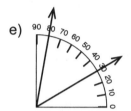   _____

f) 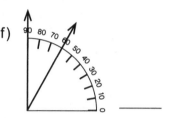   _____

Right angles have square corners and measure 90°.

Acute angles are less than a right angle. They measure between 0° and 90°.

Obtuse angles are greater than a right angle. They measure between 90° and 180°.

6. Identify the angle as acute, obtuse, or right. Hint: Compare the angle to the corner of a sheet of paper.

a)
_____*acute*_____

b)
_____*obtuse*_____

c)
_____

d)
_____

e)
_____

f)
_____

7. Identify the angle measure as an acute angle, a right angle, or an obtuse angle.

a) 35° _____

b) 90° _____

c) 86° _____

d) 100° _____

e) 77° _____

f) 95° _____

G7-2 Measuring and Drawing Angles

To measure an angle, use a **protractor**.

A protractor has 180 subdivisions of 1° around its curved side.
It has two scales, to measure angles starting from either side.

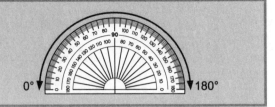

0°   180°

1. Identify the angle as acute or obtuse, then write the measure of the angle.

a)

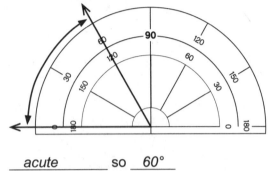

___acute___ so ___60°___

b)

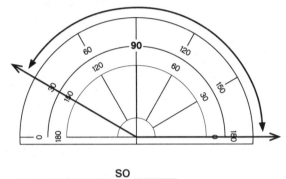

_____ so _____

c)

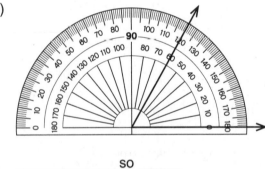

_____ so _____

d)

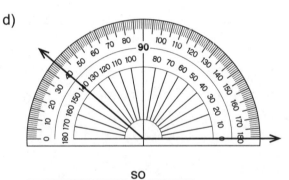

_____ so _____

Each protractor has a **base line** and an **origin**.

To measure an angle, line up the base line with one arm of the angle.
Place the origin of the protractor at the vertex of the angle.

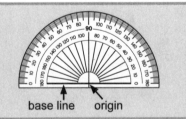

base line   origin

2. a) In which picture is the protractor placed correctly? _____

A.

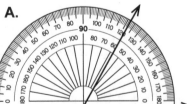

B.

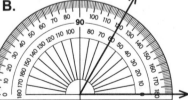

C.

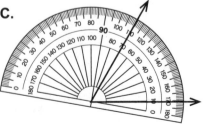

b) What is wrong with the other pictures?

3. Measure the angle using a protractor, and write your answer in the blank. Hint: Use a ruler to extend the arms in parts e) and f).

a)

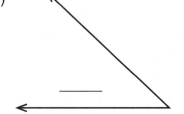

_30°_

b)

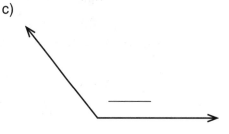

_____

c)

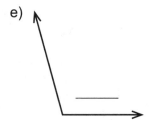

_____

d)

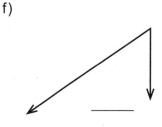

_____

e)

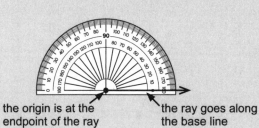

_____

f)

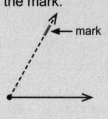

_____

To draw a 60° angle:

Step 1: Draw a ray. Place the protractor as shown.

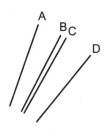

the origin is at the endpoint of the ray

the ray goes along the base line

Step 2: Make a mark at 60°.

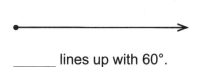

← mark

Step 3: Using a ruler, join the endpoint of the ray to the mark.

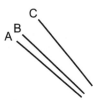

← mark

4. Place the protractor as shown in Step 1. Which mark lines up with the given angle?

a) 60°

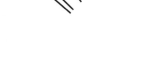

_____ lines up with 60°.

b) 140°

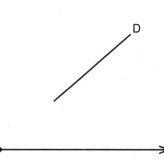

_____ lines up with 140°.

5. Finish drawing the angle.

a) 70°
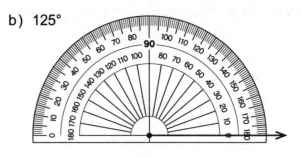

b) 125°

c) 142°
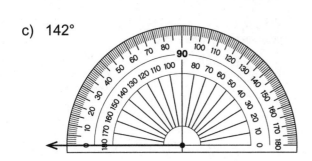

d) 73°
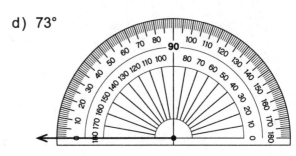

6. Use a protractor to finish drawing the angle.

a) 150°

b) 36°

c) 90°

d) 154°

7. Use a protractor to construct the angle.

a) 35°   b) 80°   c) 70°   d) 125°   e) 32°   f) 167°

G7-3 Constructing Triangles from Angles and Sides

1. a) Are the rays getting closer together, getting farther apart, or neither?

i)

getting closer together

ii)

_____

iii)

_____

iv)

_____

v)

_____

vi)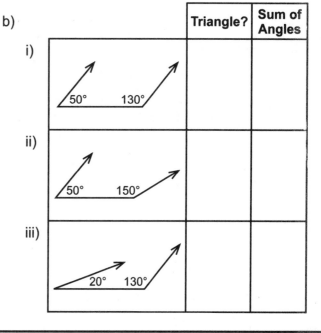

_____

b) Look at the angles in part a) that are not 70°. Write "less than," "greater than," or "equal to."

The rays get closer together when the angle is _____ 110°.

The rays get farther apart when the angle is _____ 110°.

The rays get neither closer nor farther when the angle is _____ 110°.

The rays will meet if extended when the angle is _____ 110°.

2. Decide whether the rays will make a triangle when extended. Then add the angles.

a)

	Triangle?	Sum of Angles
i) 60° 90°		
ii) 120° 60°		
iii) 80° 70°		

b)

	Triangle?	Sum of Angles
i) 50° 130°		
ii) 50° 150°		
iii) 20° 130°		

3. Look at the rays in Question 2. Write "less than," "greater than," or "exactly."

   a) The rays get closer together when the angles add to _____ 180°.

   b) The rays get farther apart when the angles add to _____ 180°.

   c) The rays get neither closer nor farther when the angles add to _____ 180°.

   d) Two angles with a line segment between them make a triangle when the angles

   add to _____ 180°.

> Two shapes are **congruent** if they are **the same size** and **the same shape**. Congruent shapes can have different colors and patterns, and can face different directions.

4. Are the two shapes congruent?

   a) _____   b) _____   c) _____   d) _____

5. Are the two shapes congruent? Explain how you know.

   a)

   _____ , because _____.

   b)

   _____ , because _____.

6. On grid paper, show how many different (non-congruent) shapes you can make by adding one square to the original figure.

   a)   b)   c)   d)

> When two shapes are congruent, you can fit one shape exactly on top of the other with no spaces.

7. Trace Triangle B and cut it out. Is it congruent to Triangle A?

8. Draw a triangle that satisfies the conditions, and cut it out. Compare your triangle with a partner's triangle and decide whether they are congruent.

   a) two angles are 50° and the side between them has length 4 cm

   b) a 30° angle, a 60° angle, and the side between them is 2 inches long

G7-4 Drawing Triangles on Grid Paper

1. Draw the triangle on the 1 cm grid.

   a) two sides of length 4 cm and
      the angle between them is 90°

   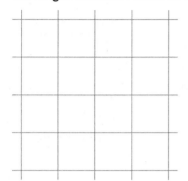

   b) two sides of length 3 cm and 4 cm
      and the angle between them is 90°

   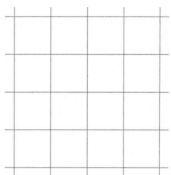

2. a) Use the grid to draw an angle that is half the size of a 90° angle. Start at the dot.

   i)
   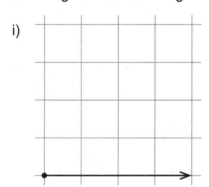

   ii)
   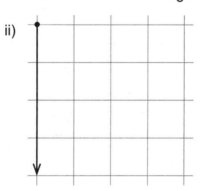

   iii)
   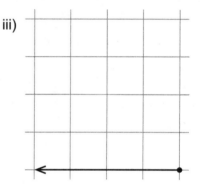

   b) Explain why the angles you drew should be 45°. _____

   _____

   c) Check with a protractor that the angles you drew are each 45°.

3. a) Draw a triangle with two 45° angles and the side between them as shown.

   i)
   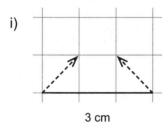
   3 cm

   ii)
   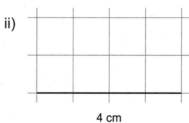
   4 cm

   b) Measure the third angle in the triangles you drew.

   i) _____   ii) _____

When two angles in a triangle are 45°, the third angle is always 90°.

4. a) Match the triangle with the description.

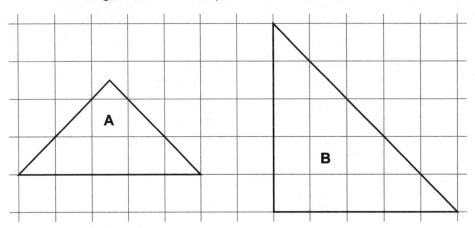

     i)   The 90° angle is between two 5 cm sides. _____

     ii)   The 90° angle is opposite the 5 cm side. _____

   b) Are Triangles A and B congruent? _____

5. Draw a triangle with two 45° angles and a 6 cm side, and with ...

     a) the 90° angle opposite the 6 cm side.   **b)** the 90° angle between the two 6 cm sides.

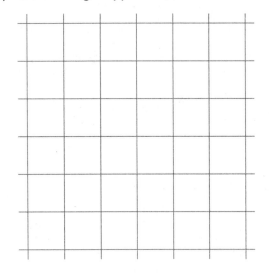 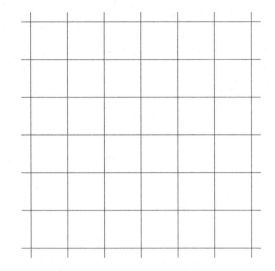

6. On 1 cm grid paper, draw two non-congruent triangles that have:

    • a 90° angle,

    • two 45° angles, and

    • a side of length 7 cm.

G7-5 Constructing Triangles from Three Sides or Three Angles

1. Trace Triangle B onto a piece of paper and cut it out. Is it congruent to Triangle A?
   Write "yes" or "no."

a)
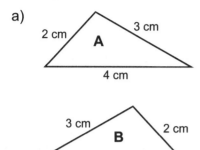

b)
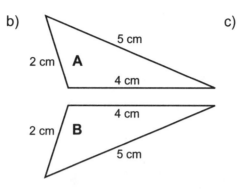

c)
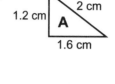

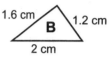

_____   _____   _____

Two triangles are congruent if they have the same three side lengths, in any order. But not any three side lengths can make a triangle.

Example: The side lengths 1 cm, 2 cm, and 4 cm do not make a triangle:

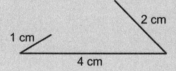   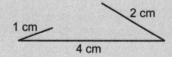   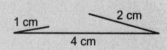

The two shorter sides are too far from each other to make a triangle.

2. Complete the table.

	Triangle	Sum of Two Shortest Sides	Longest Side
a)	4 ft / 5 ft / 6 ft		
b)	5 ft / 11 ft / 15 ft		
c)	1 mi / 4 mi / 4 mi		

	Triangle	Sum of Two Shortest Sides	Longest Side
d)	3 ft / 4 ft / 5 ft		
e)	4 m / 4 m / 7 m		
f)	8 m / 7 m / 2 m		

Three side lengths will make a triangle when the shortest two lengths add to more than the longest.

3. Complete the table.

Three Side Lengths (cm)	2, 3, 5	2, 2, 4	3, 5, 7	2, 5, 6	3, 4, 4	4, 4, 9	Bonus ▶ $\frac{1}{3}$, $\frac{5}{8}$, 1
Sum of Shortest Two Sides (cm)	5						
Longest Side (cm)	5						
Triangle?	no						

4. Abdul says that the lengths 2 cm, 7 cm, and 4 cm make a triangle because 2 + 7 is more than 4. Explain his mistake.

5. a) Finish drawing the triangle. Use a ruler.

   i)

   2 cm

   ii)

   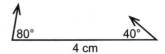
   3 cm

   iii)

   80°   40°
   4 cm

   b) Measure the third angle. What do you notice? _____

   c) Are the three triangles from part a) congruent? _____

6. a) Add the angles in the triangle.

   i)

   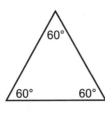

   __180°__

   ii)

   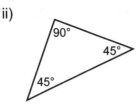

   _____

   iii)

   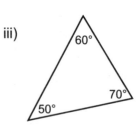

   _____

   b) The angles in a triangle always add to _____.

7. Draw two non-congruent triangles with angles 30°, 70°, and 80°.

Bonus ▶ Can a triangle have side lengths 11 inches, 14 inches, and 2 feet? Explain how you know.

G7-6 Constructing Triangles from Three Measures

1. a) In a triangle, two angles are 30° and 60°. What is the third angle? _____

   b) Finish drawing the three triangles. Each triangle will have:

   • a 30° angle,

   • a 60° angle,

   • a 90° angle, and

   • a 3 cm side.

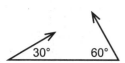 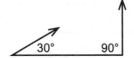 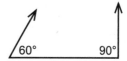

   c) Are the three triangles from part b) congruent? _____

2. Draw three non-congruent triangles with a 40° angle, a 50° angle, and a side of length 6 cm.

3. Can you make a triangle with ...

   a) two right angles? _____   b) two obtuse angles? _____

   c) at least two acute angles? _____   d) exactly two acute angles? _____

   e) a right angle and an acute angle? _____

   f) a right angle and an obtuse angle? _____

   g) an obtuse angle and an acute angle? _____

4. a) Draw a triangle with a 3 cm side, a 4 cm side, and a 90° angle between them.

   b) Draw a triangle with a 3 cm side, a 4 cm side, and a 90° angle not between them.

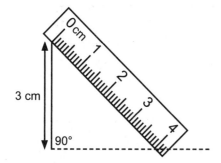

   c) Are your triangles from parts a) and b) congruent?

   d) Draw two non-congruent triangles with a 2 cm side, a 5 cm side, and a 60° angle.

   e) Draw two non-congruent triangles with angles 20°, 70°, and 90°.

5. Do the conditions make a unique triangle, more than one triangle, or no triangle?
Do your rough work in your notebook. Record your results in the table.

		A Unique Triangle	More Than One Triangle	No Triangle
a)	The angles are 50°, 50°, and 50°.			✓
b)	The angles are 75°, 75°, and 30°.			
c)	Two angles are 80° and the side between them is 5 cm.			
d)	Two angles are 80° and one side is 6 cm.			
e)	The sides are 2 in, 3 in, and 4 in.			
f)	The sides are 2 in, 3 in, and 5 in.			
g)	Two sides are 3 cm long and the angle between them is 45°.			
h)	Two sides are 3 cm and 4 cm, and one angle is 90°.			
i)	Two angles are 45° and 90°, and the side between them is 4 cm.			
j)	Two angles are 45° and 90°, and one side is 4 cm long.			

Bonus ▶

k)	Two angles are 90° and the side between them is 5 cm.			
l)	Two angles are 60° and one side is 4 cm long.			
m)	The sides are 2 km, 5 km, and 5 mi. Hint: 1 mi is about 1.6 km.			

The **perimeter** of a shape is the distance around a shape. The perimeter of a triangle is the sum of the three side lengths.

6. Is there a triangle with longest side 5 inches and perimeter 9 inches?
Explain how you know.

Geometry 7-6

G7-7 Counterexamples

1. Circle the picture that shows the claim is not true.

   a) All squares are shaded.

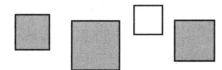

   b) All circles are striped.

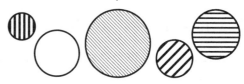

2. Which picture shows the claim is not true?

   a) All triangles are shaded. _____

   b) All triangles have a horizontal side. _____

   c) All triangles have three acute angles. _____

   d) All triangles are labelled with a letter from the word "bead." _____

> An example that shows a claim is not true is called a **counterexample**. To show that a claim is not true, you only need one counterexample.

3. Read from left to right and circle the first counterexample.

   a) All words have a letter "d."

     do   did   kite   rod   rope

   b) All names start with "T."

     Tom   Tara   Sam   Sue   Tony

> Only circles can be counterexamples to this statement: All circles are shaded.

4. Circle all the counterexamples.

   a) All circles are shaded.

   b) All shaded shapes are circles.

   c) All polygons are striped.

   d) All shapes have all sides equal.

   e) All flags have stars.

5. Find a counterexample to the statement using the steps shown.

a) If a word starts with "b," it ends with "t."

Step 1: Circle the words that start with "b."

      boat   bat   bait   rat   rate   bee

Step 2: Find one circled word that does not end with "t." _____

b) If "c" comes right before "e," the "c" sounds like "s."

Step 1: Circle the words where "c" comes right before "e."

      mice   cedar   car   face   soccer   voice

Step 2: Find one circled word where the "c" does not sound like "s." _____

c) If two shapes have the same side lengths, they are congruent.

Step 1: Circle the pairs that have the same side lengths (given in inches).

A. **B.** **C.** **D.**

Step 2: Find one circled pair that is not congruent. _____

d) If a number is a factor of 24, it is also a factor of 8.

Step 1: List all the factors of 24. _____

Step 2: Find one factor in your list that is not a factor of 8. _____

6. Describe a counterexample to the statement.

a) If a shape has four equal sides, it is a square.

    A shape with four equal sides that is not a square.

b) If a number is even, it is a multiple of 4.

    _____

c) If the product of two numbers is a multiple of 9, both numbers are multiples of 3.

    _____

    _____

Bonus ▶ If a shape has a smaller area than another shape, it also has a smaller perimeter.

7. Find a counterexample for each statement from Question 6.

8. a) Sort the shapes by area.

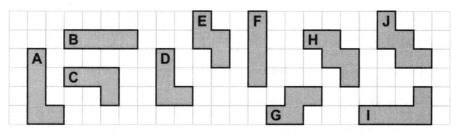

4 squares: ___*B,*_____ 5 squares: _____

b) Sort the shapes into pairs of congruent shapes.

_____ , _____ , _____ , _____ , _____

c) Which statement is true? Find a counterexample for the other statement.

   A. If two shapes have the same area, they are congruent.

   B. If two shapes are congruent, they have the same area.

   Statement _____ is true.

   Statement _____ is false. Here is a counterexample: _____ and _____

9. Which statement is true, A or B? Explain how you know. Find a counterexample for the other statement.

a) **A.** If a triangle has two 45° angles, the other angle is 90°.

   B. If a triangle has a 90° angle, the other two angles are 45°.

   Statement _____ is true because _____

   _____ .

   Statement _____ is false. Here is a counterexample:

b) **A.** If a number is less than 5, it is less than 3.

   B. If a number is less than 3, it is less than 5.

c) **A.** If two triangles have the same three angles, they are congruent.

   B. If two triangles are congruent, they have the same three angles.

d) **A.** If two rectangles are congruent, they have the same perimeter.

   B. If two rectangles have the same perimeter, they are congruent.

G7-8 Scale Drawings and Similar Shapes

1. a) Draw a triangle that has the same shape, but is twice as long and twice as tall.

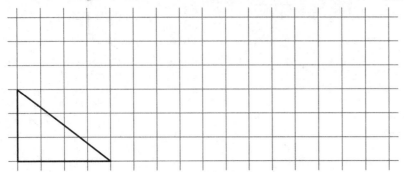

   b) Measure the third side of each triangle. Is the third side twice as long, too? _____

> When you make a new drawing by multiplying every side by the same number, the drawing is called a **scale drawing**.

2. Here are three scale drawings.

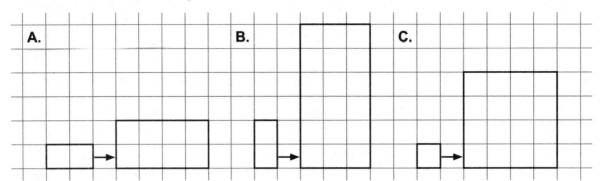

   a) What is the ratio (original length) : (new length)? Hint: The length is the longest side.

   A. _____   B. _____   C. _____

   b) What is the ratio (original width) : (new width)? Hint: The width is the shortest side.

   A. _____   B. _____   C. _____

   c) Are the ratios from part a) and part b) equivalent? If not, find your mistake.

3. Finish the scale drawing.

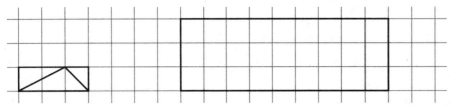

Two shapes are **similar** if they are the same shape, but have different sizes. You can make a similar shape by making a scale drawing.

4. Find the missing side lengths in the similar rectangles. Include the units.

a)

9 mm
5 mm

36 mm

_____

b)

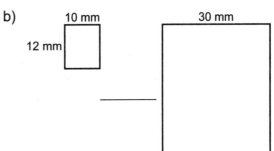

10 mm
12 mm

30 mm

_____

c)

46 mm
5 mm

_____

10 mm

5. The two shapes are similar. Find the missing side lengths. Include the units.

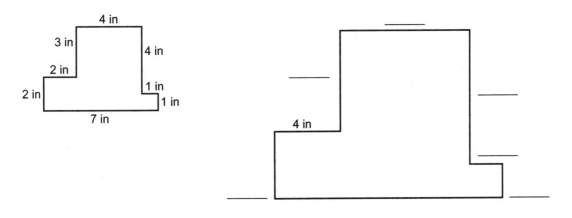

4 in
3 in
4 in
2 in
2 in
1 in
1 in
7 in

4 in

6. Which of these shapes are similar? How do you know?

_____

_____

_____

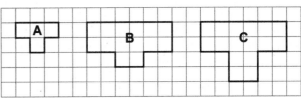

A   B   C

7. On grid paper, draw another rectangle by increasing both the length and the width by 1 unit. Is your drawing a scale drawing of the original shape?

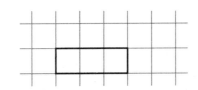

G7-9 Scale Drawings and Ratio Tables

1. Bold the line in the scale drawing that matches the bold line in the original drawing.

   a)

   b)

   c)

2. Jane wants to draw a scale drawing of the shape. Measure the sides of the original shape, then write the lengths of the new lines Jane should draw.

   a) (original length) : (new length) = 1 : 2

	Original Length (mm)	Scale Drawing (mm)
	15	30

   b) (original length) : (new length) = 1 : 3

	Original Length (mm)	Scale Drawing (mm)

   REMINDER: A table is a ratio table if the rows are equivalent ratios.

3. Are the tables in Question 2 ratio tables? How do you know? Hint: What unit ratio is each row equivalent to?

   _____

   _____

   _____

The **length** of a rectangle is the length of its longer side.

The **width** of a rectangle is the length of its shorter side.

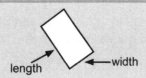

length — — width

4. a) The table shows the measurements of a rectangular field. Complete the ratio table, then draw the field to the scale indicated.

i)

	Actual (m)	Scale Drawing (grid squares)
Scale	15	2
Length	45	6
Width	30	4

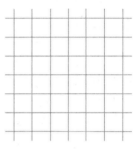

ii)

	Actual (m)	Scale Drawing (grid squares)
Scale	6	1
Length	30	
Width	12	

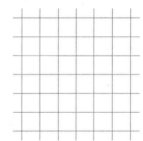

iii)

	Actual (m)	Scale Drawing (grid squares)
Scale	5	2
Length	15	
Width	5	

b) Find the "length : width" ratios from part a).

	i)	ii)	iii)
Length to Width Ratio (actual)	45 : 30		
Length to Width Ratio (scale)	6 : 4		

c) Write the ratios from part b) using the smallest whole numbers you can.

	i)	ii)	iii)
Length to Width Ratio (actual)	3 : 2		
Length to Width Ratio (scale)	3 : 2		

d) Are the length to width ratios equivalent in the actual and scale drawings?

i) _____   ii) _____   iii) _____

The unit ratio (original length) : (new length) = 1 : ? tells you what number to multiply the original length by to get the new length. The unit ratio can be a fraction.

Remember: You can multiply a fraction by a whole number.

$$\frac{3}{4} \times 12 = \frac{3}{4} \text{ of } 12$$
$$= 3 \times \left(\frac{1}{4} \text{ of } 12 \right)$$
$$= 3 \times (12 \div 4)$$
$$= 3 \times 3 = 9$$

5. a) Write the ratio (original length) : (new length) as a unit ratio, then complete the ratio table.

i) $4 : 3 = 1 : $ _____

	Original	Scale
Length (cm)	12	
Width (cm)	8	

ii) $5 : 2 = 1 : $ _____

	Original	Scale
Length (cm)	20	
Width (cm)	15	

b) Are the length to width ratios equivalent in the original and scale drawings?

i)

ii)

_____   _____

When two rectangles are similar, the length : width ratio is the same in both drawings.

6. Find the missing length two ways. Make sure you get the same answer both ways.

Original   Scale

5   4

2 [ ]   →   ? [ ]

a) Make "length : width" ratios the same in both drawings.

Length	Width

b) Make "original : scale" ratios the same for both the length and the width.

Original	Scale

G7-10 Scale Drawings in the Real World

1. On the map, the scale is 1 mm : 50 mi. Use the scale to determine the distances in real life.

Chicago ●

● New York City

Los Angeles ●

● Houston

		Distance on Map (mm)	Distance in Real Life (mi)
a)	From Chicago to Houston		
b)	From Chicago to New York City		
c)	From Chicago to Los Angeles		
d)	From New York City to Houston		
e)	From New York City to Los Angeles		
f)	From Los Angeles to Houston		

2. On the floor plan, the scale is 1 grid square : 20 in. Use the scale to determine the lengths in real life. Include the units in your answers.

		On Floor Plan	In Real Life
a)	How long is the closet?		
b)	How long is the bed?		
c)	What are the dimensions of the washroom?		
d)	How far from the TV is the couch?		
e)	How wide is the table?		

f) The kitchen countertop, which includes the stove, fridge, microwave, and sink along one wall, is shown in gray. If the stove is 30 inches wide, the fridge 28 inches wide, the microwave 24 inches wide, and the sink 32 inches wide, how much countertop space is left?

3. A room is 15 ft wide and 20 ft long. Draw the room to the given scale.

a) 1 grid square : 5 ft

b) 2 grid squares : 5 ft

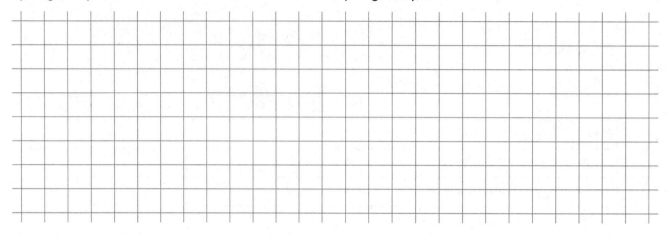

c) 3 grid squares : 5 ft

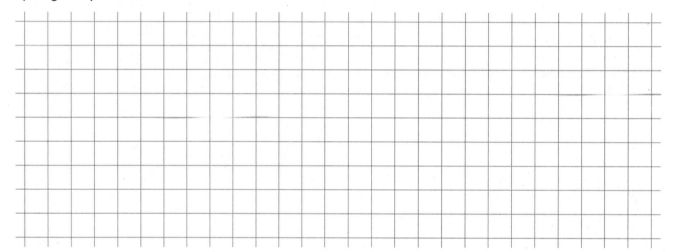

4. A closet is 4 ft wide and 6 ft long. Draw the closet to the given scale.

a) 1 grid square : 2 ft

b) 3 grid squares : 2 ft

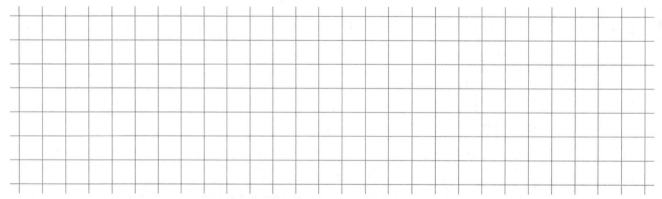

Bonus ▶ A is a scale drawing of B with (original length) : (scaled length) = 1 : 2.

B is a scale drawing of C with (original length) : (scaled length) = 1 : 3.

A is a scale drawing of C with (original length) : (scaled length) = 1 : _____.

5. The scale drawing of a room has the scale 1 grid square : 3 ft.

a) How long is the room? _____

b) How wide is the room? _____

c) Draw the same room to the given scale.

  i) 1 grid square : 6 ft   ii) 1 grid square : 2 ft

  iii) 2 grid squares : 3 ft   **Bonus ▶** 1 grid square : 4 ft

6. The map is drawn using a scale of 3 grid squares to 2 mi.
Draw another map using the scale 1 in to 4 mi.
Hint: Rewrite the scale as _____ in : 1 mi.

7. A window is drawn to the scale
(scale length) : (actual length) = 2 cm : 1 ft.
The drawing is 6 cm high and 10 cm wide.
Draw another picture of the window with scale 1 cm : 2 ft.

Dragon Lair

8. The killer whale is drawn to the scale 1 cm = 6 ft.
How long is the actual whale?

NS7-25 Multiplying Integers (Introduction)

REMINDER: To add integers with the same sign, add their absolute values. The sum has the same
sign as both numbers. Example: $-31 + (-12) = -43$ because $31 + 12 = 43$.

$-31 + (-12)$ can be written as $-31 - 12$.

1. Add the integers.

a) $-3 - 4$

= _____

b) $+17 + 8$

= _____

c) $-5 - 13$

= _____

d) $-200 - 40 - 5$

= _____

e) $-3,000 - 40$

= _____

f) $-1,800 - 7$

= _____

Bonus ▶ $-300,000 - 40,000 - 5,000 - 80 - 7$

= _____

REMINDER: Multiplication is a short form for repeated addition.

Example: $4 \times 5 = 5 + 5 + 5 + 5 = 20$

When you multiply a positive integer and a negative integer, you can use repeated addition.

Example: $4 \times (-5) = (-5) + (-5) + (-5) + (-5) = -20$ or $4 \times (-5) = -5 - 5 - 5 - 5 = -20$

2. Use the number line to add.

a) $3 \times (-2) =$ __−6__

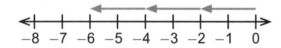

b) $2 \times (-4) =$ _____

c) $4 \times (-3) =$ _____

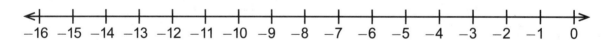

3. Write the product as repeated addition. Then find the answer.

a) $3 \times (-5) = -5 - 5 - 5 = -15$

b) $2 \times (-7) =$

c) $4 \times (-3) =$

d) $4 \times (-2) =$

4. a) Calculate both products using repeated addition.

$3 \times 6 =$

$3 \times (-6) =$

b) What is the same about your answers? _____

What is different about your answers? _____

5. Multiply mentally.

a) $3 \times (-5) =$ _____

b) $4 \times (-2) =$ _____

c) $8 \times (-3) =$ _____

d) $9 \times (-4) =$ _____

e) $5 \times (-8) =$ _____

f) $6 \times (-6) =$ _____

g) $10 \times (-7) =$ _____

h) $3 \times (-7) =$ _____

i) $5 \times (-100) =$ _____

6. Complete the pattern.

a)

3×3	
3×2	
3×1	
3×0	
$3 \times (-1)$	
$3 \times (-2)$	
$3 \times ($ $)$	

b)

2×3	
2×2	
2×1	
2×0	
$2 \times ($ $)$	
$2 \times ($ $)$	
$2 \times ($ $)$	

REMINDER: When you multiply two numbers, the order of the numbers doesn't change the answer.

$$3 \times (-2) = -6, \text{ so } -2 \times 3 = -6$$

This property is called the **commutative property**.

7. Use the commutative property to multiply.

a) $5 \times (-3) =$ _____

so $-3 \times 5 =$ _____

b) $7 \times (-2) =$ _____

so $-2 \times 7 =$ _____

c) $6 \times (-4) =$ _____

so $-4 \times 6 =$ _____

8. Multiply mentally.

a) $-7 \times 3 =$ _____

b) $8 \times (-5) =$ _____

c) $-6 \times 3 =$ _____

d) $2 \times (-5) =$ _____

e) $-5 \times 7 =$ _____

f) $-9 \times 8 =$ _____

g) $-4 \times 5 =$ _____

h) $-6 \times 8 =$ _____

i) $2 \times (-7) =$ _____

9. If $143 \times 26 = 3,718$, what is $143 \times (-26)$? _____

Bonus ▶ Predict how $-143 \times (-26)$ compares to $143 \times (-26)$.

_____

_____

NS7-26 Multiplying Integers

1. Complete the pattern.

a)

−1 × 3	
−1 × 2	
−1 × 1	
−1 × 0	
−1 × (−1)	
−1 × (−2)	
−1 × ( )	
−1 × ( )	
−1 × ( )	

b)

−2 × 3	
−2 × 2	
−2 × 1	
−2 × 0	
−2 × ( )	
−2 × ( )	
−2 × ( )	
−2 × ( )	
−2 × ( )	

2. Use a pattern to show that −5 × (−4) = 20.

When you multiply two negative numbers, the product is positive. Example: −5 × (−2) = 10

3. Multiply mentally.

a) −3 × (−5) = _____

b) −4 × (−9) = _____

c) −8 × (−3) = _____

d) −2 × (−5) = _____

e) −4 × (−8) = _____

f) −7 × (−9) = _____

g) −8 × (−6) = _____

h) −5 × (−11) = _____

i) −9 × (−11) = _____

positive × positive = positive   negative × positive = negative

positive × negative = negative   negative × negative = positive

4. Write whether the product is positive or negative.

a) −5 × 3 _negative_

b) −2 × (−8) _____

c) 8 × (−4) _____

d) 3 × 7 _____

e) −5 × (−7) _____

f) −3 × 4 _____

g) 7 × (−5) _____

h) −4 × (−4) _____

i) −3 × (−4) _____

5. Write "positive" or "negative."

a) Two numbers have the same sign. Their product is _____.

b) Two numbers have different signs. Their product is _____.

6. Write the correct sign ($+$ or $-$).

a) $(+) \times (+) = $ _____

b) $(+) \times (-) = $ _____

c) $(-) \times (+) = $ _____

d) $(-) \times (-) = $ _____

7. Multiply mentally.

a) $2 \times (-3)$

= _____

b) $-5 \times (-6)$

= _____

c) -5×3

= _____

d) 8×4

= _____

e) $-8 \times (-7)$

= _____

f) $6 \times (-6)$

= _____

g) $-7 \times (-7)$

= _____

h) -8×6

= _____

8. Circle the multiplications that have the same answer as $4 \times (-2)$.

-2×4 $\qquad$ -4×2 $\qquad$ -4×-2 $\qquad$ $2 \times (-4)$ $\qquad$ 4×2

> REMINDER: $3 \times \dfrac{4}{5} = \dfrac{12}{5}$ $\longleftarrow$ 3×4

9. Multiply.

a) $2 \times \left(-\dfrac{4}{9}\right)$

= _____

b) $-3 \times \left(-\dfrac{4}{3}\right)$

= _____

c) $-\dfrac{2}{9} \times (-4)$

= _____

d) $\dfrac{3}{7} \times (-2)$

= _____

e) $-3 \times \left(-\dfrac{1}{4}\right)$

= _____

f) $-2 \times \left(-\dfrac{4}{5}\right)$

= _____

g) $-\dfrac{3}{8} \times 3$

= _____

h) $\dfrac{4}{7} \times (-3)$

= _____

10. Write two numbers that multiply to -15. _____ and _____

11. Find as many pairs of integers as you can that multiply to -24.

Bonus ▶ Multiply by keeping track as you go along.

$\square$ $\square$ $\square$ $\square$

$-2 \times 3 \times (-5) \times (-3) \times 2 = \square$

REMINDER: Multiplication distributes over addition and subtraction.

Examples: $6 \times 8 = 6 \times (5 + 3)$ $6 \times 8 = 6 \times (10 - 2)$

$$= \underbrace{30}_{6 \times 5} + \underbrace{18}_{6 \times 3} = \underbrace{48}_{6 \times 8}$$ $$= \underbrace{60}_{6 \times 10} - \underbrace{12}_{6 \times 2} = \underbrace{48}_{6 \times 8}$$

1. Fill in the blanks.

a) $2 \times \underline{\quad 5 \quad} = 2 \times (3 + 2)$

$$= \underbrace{\underline{\;6\;}}_{2 \times 3} + \underbrace{\underline{\;4\;}}_{2 \times 2}$$

$$= \underline{\;10\;}$$

b) $2 \times \underline{\qquad} = 2 \times (3 + 5)$

$$= \underbrace{\underline{\qquad}}_{2 \times 3} + \underbrace{\underline{\qquad}}_{2 \times 5}$$

$$= \underline{\qquad}$$

c) $2 \times \underline{\qquad} = 2 \times (5 - 2)$

$$= \underbrace{\underline{\qquad}}_{2 \times 5} - \underbrace{\underline{\qquad}}_{2 \times 2}$$

$$= \underline{\qquad}$$

d) $2 \times \underline{\qquad} = 2 \times (5 - 1)$

$$= \underbrace{\underline{\qquad}}_{2 \times 5} - \underbrace{\underline{\qquad}}_{2 \times 1}$$

$$= \underline{\qquad}$$

You can write -4 as $0 - 4$. Now you can multiply $2 \times (-4)$ using the distributive property.

$$2 \times (-4) = 2 \times (0 - 4)$$

$$= \underbrace{\;0\;}_{2 \times 0} - \underbrace{\;8\;}_{2 \times 4} = -8 \quad \longleftarrow$$

When you subtract a number from 0, the answer is the opposite of the number.

e) $2 \times \underline{\qquad} = 2 \times (0 - 3)$

$$= \underbrace{\underline{\qquad}}_{2 \times 0} - \underbrace{\underline{\qquad}}_{2 \times 3}$$

$$= \underline{\qquad}$$

f) $2 \times \underline{\qquad} = 2 \times (0 - 5)$

$$= \underbrace{\underline{\qquad}}_{2 \times 0} - \underbrace{\underline{\qquad}}_{2 \times 5}$$

$$= \underline{\qquad}$$

g) $2 \times \underline{\qquad} = 2 \times (0 - 7)$

$$= \underbrace{\underline{\qquad}}_{2 \times 0} - \underbrace{\underline{\qquad}}_{2 \times 7}$$

$$= \underline{\qquad}$$

h) $3 \times \underline{\qquad} = 3 \times (0 - 8)$

$$= \underbrace{\underline{\qquad}}_{3 \times 0} - \underbrace{\underline{\qquad}}_{3 \times 8}$$

$$= \underline{\qquad}$$

To multiply $3 \times (-5)$ or -3×5, you can subtract 3×5 from 0.

So, $3 \times (-5) = -3 \times 5$

$\qquad\qquad = 0 - 15 = -15.$

2. Multiply.

a) $-8 \times 5 = 0 - \underline{\qquad} = \underline{\qquad}$

b) $-3 \times 4 = 0 - \underline{\qquad} = \underline{\qquad}$

c) $-3 \times 6 = 0 - \underline{\qquad} = \underline{\qquad}$

d) $-2 \times 7 = 0 - \underline{\qquad} = \underline{\qquad}$

e) $-4 \times 8 = \underline{\qquad}$ f) $-5 \times 5 = \underline{\qquad}$ g) $-5 \times 6 = \underline{\qquad}$ h) $-7 \times 4 = \underline{\qquad}$

REMINDER: When you take a number away from 0, the answer is the opposite of the number.

Examples: $0 - 8 = -8$ and $0 - (-8) = 8$

3. Use the distributive property to multiply.

a) $-2 \times (-3) = -2 \times (0 - 3)$

$\qquad = \underbrace{\quad 0 \quad}_{-2 \times 0} - \underbrace{\quad (-6) \quad}_{-2 \times 3}$

$\qquad = \underline{\ +6\ }$

b) $-3 \times (-5) = -3 \times (0 - 5)$

$\qquad = \underbrace{\qquad}_{-3 \times 0} - \underbrace{\qquad}_{-3 \times 5}$

$\qquad = \underline{\qquad}$

c) $-2 \times (-9) = -2 \times (0 - 9)$

$\qquad = \underbrace{\qquad}_{-2 \times 0} - \underbrace{\qquad}_{-2 \times 9}$

$\qquad = \underline{\qquad}$

d) $-3 \times (-3) = -3 \times (0 - 3)$

$\qquad = \underbrace{\qquad}_{-3 \times 0} - \underbrace{\qquad}_{-3 \times 3}$

$\qquad = \underline{\qquad}$

e) $-6 \times (-5) = -6 \times (0 - 5)$

$\qquad = \underbrace{\qquad}_{-6 \times 0} - \underbrace{\qquad}_{-6 \times 5}$

$\qquad = \underline{\qquad}$

f) $-3 \times (-9) = -3 \times (0 - 9)$

$\qquad = \underbrace{\qquad}_{-3 \times 0} - \underbrace{\qquad}_{-3 \times 9}$

$\qquad = \underline{\qquad}$

4. Use the distributive property to multiply.

a) $-3 \times 4 = (0 - 3) \times 4$

$\qquad = 0 \times 4 - 3 \times 4$

$\qquad = \underline{\qquad} - \underline{\qquad}$

$\qquad = \underline{\qquad}$

b) $(-2) \times (-3) = (0 - 2) \times (-3)$

$\qquad = (\underline{\quad} \times \underline{\quad}) - (\underline{\quad} \times \underline{\quad})$

$\qquad = \underline{\qquad} - \underline{\qquad}$

$\qquad = \underline{\qquad}$

NS7-28 Multiplying Integers in the Real World

> You can think of an increase as a positive change and a decrease as a negative change.
>
> Example: An increase of $3 is a change of $+3$ dollars. A decrease of $3 is a change of -3 dollars.

1. Describe the change as an integer.

   a) Ben lost $5. __−5__

   b) Ben gained $8. _____

   c) The temperature increased 17°F. _____

   d) The temperature dropped 6°F. _____

   e) Sara's football team gained 20 yards. _____

   f) Sara's football team lost 8 yards. _____

2. Write an integer multiplication equation to show the amount of change.

   a) Jon gained $3 each day for 5 days. __$5 \times (+3) = +15$__

   b) Jon lost $4 each day for 7 days. _____

   c) Jon lost $5 each day for 6 days. _____

   d) The temperature increased by 3°F each hour for 6 hours. _____

   e) The temperature on Mercury dropped 30°C each Earth day for 7 days. _____

   f) Liz's football team lost 5 yards each down for 4 downs. _____

   g) Liz's football team gained 8 yards each down for 4 downs. _____

> You can think of future time as + and past time as −.

3. Describe the time as an integer.

   a) 3 years from now _____

   b) 5 years ago _____

   c) 17 weeks ago _____

   d) 8 days from now _____

4. The temperature is currently 0°F. The temperature increases 2°F each hour. Write an integer equation that shows what the temperature will be or was.

   a) 3 hours from now __$(+3) \times (+2) = (+6)$__

   b) 3 hours ago __$() \times (+2) = ()$__

   c) 5 hours ago _____

   d) 5 hours from now _____

5. The temperature is currently 0°F. The temperature decreases 2°F each hour. Write an integer equation that shows what the temperature will be or was.

   a) 3 hours from now __$(+3) \times (-2) = (-6)$__

   b) 3 hours ago __$() \times (-2) = ()$__

   c) 5 hours ago _____

   d) 5 hours from now _____

6. The temperature is currently 0°F. Write an integer equation to show your answer.

a) The temperature decreases an average of 7°F every hour. What will the

temperature be in 6 hours? _____

b) The temperature increases an average of 5°F every day. What will the

temperature be in 8 days? _____

c) The temperature decreases 4°F every minute. What was the temperature

5 minutes ago? _____

d) The temperature increases 3°F every week. What was the temperature

6 weeks ago? _____

REMINDER: To add two numbers with the same sign, add their absolute values. The sum has the
same sign as both numbers.

To add two numbers with opposite signs, subtract their absolute values. The difference
has the same sign as the number with the greater absolute value.

Examples: $-30 + 25 = -5$ and $-30 - 25 = -55$

7. Add.

a) $-7 + 12 =$ _____

b) $-5 - 8 =$ _____

c) $-5 + 7 =$ _____

d) $12 - 15 =$ _____

e) $-4 + 3 =$ _____

f) $4 + 3 =$ _____

g) $8 - 3 =$ _____

h) $3 - 8 =$ _____

i) $-8 - 3 =$ _____

j) $-5 + 4 =$ _____

k) $-5 - 4 =$ _____

l) $5 + 4 =$ _____

REMINDER: You can subtract a number by adding the opposite number.

$$- (+) = - \qquad - (-) = +$$

Examples: $3 - (+4) = 3 - 4$ and $3 - (-4) = 3 + 4$

$$= -1 \qquad\qquad = 7$$

8. Subtract.

a) $-7 - (-12) =$ _____

b) $-5 - (+8) =$ _____

c) $-5 - (-7) =$ _____

d) $12 - (-5) =$ _____

e) $-8 - (+3) =$ _____

f) $7 - (-8) =$ _____

g) $9 - (+6) =$ _____

h) $13 - (+5) =$ _____

i) $-8 - (-6) =$ _____

j) $8 - (-3) =$ _____

k) $-2 - (-4) =$ _____

l) $-3 - (+6) =$ _____

> REMINDER: Multiplication and division are done before addition and subtraction, unless brackets tell
> you otherwise.
>
> Example: $5 - 2 \times 3 = 5 - 6 = -1$, but $(5 - 2) \times 3 = 3 \times 3 = 9$

9. Evaluate.

a) $10 - 7 \times 3$

= _____

= _____

b) $(10 - 7) \times 3$

= _____

= _____

c) $-5 + 2 \times 3$

= _____

= _____

d) $(-5 + 2) \times 3$

= _____

= _____

e) $-6 - 3 \times 8$

= _____

= _____

f) $(-6 - 3) \times 8$

= _____

= _____

> When you owe money, you can say that you have negative money. This is called a **debt**.
>
> Example: Jay owed \$5, but then gained \$7. After paying his debt, Jay now has \$2 because $-5 + 7 = 2$.

10. Write and evaluate an expression to show the amount that Jen ends up with.

		Expression	Evaluate the Expression	Amount
a)	Jen started with \$5. She gained \$3 each day for 7 days.	$5 + 7 \times 3$	$5 + 21 = 26$	\$26
b)	Jen started with \$8. She lost \$7 each day for 9 days.	$8 - 9 \times 7$	$8 - 63 = -55$	-\$55
c)	Jen started with \$7. She gained \$2 each day for 5 days.			
d)	Jen started with \$6. She lost \$5 each day for 3 days.			
e)	Jen started with a debt of \$3. She gained \$5 each day for 4 days.	$-3 + 4 \times 5$		
f)	Jen started with a debt of \$3. She lost \$5 each day for 4 days.			

11. Glen owes his sister \$100. He earned \$8 per hour for 20 hours of work. After he pays his sister back, will he have enough left over to buy an \$80 sweater?

12. Karen started with a debt of \$100. She earned \$11 per hour for 15 hours of work. Then she bought 12 items that cost \$5 each. Is she still in debt?

The Number System 7-28

NS7-29 Dividing Integers

1. Write the missing sign ($+$ or $-$) in the multiplication equation.

    a) $+2 \times \boxed{} 3 = -6$ b) $-2 \times \boxed{} 3 = +6$ c) $\boxed{} 2 \times -3 = -6$

    d) $-3 \times \boxed{} 5 = 15$ e) $-3 \times \boxed{} 5 = -15$ f) $3 \times \boxed{} 5 = -15$

2. Find the missing number in the product.

    a) _____ $\times 3 = -21$ b) _____ $\times (-2) = -14$ c) $8 \times$ _____ $= -24$

    d) $9 \times$ _____ $= -36$ e) $-7 \times$ _____ $= 35$ f) _____ $\times -2 = -24$

> If you know how to multiply integers, then you can divide integers, too!
>
> Since $4 \times (-3) = -12$, then $-12 \div 4 = -3$ and $-12 \div (-3) = 4$
>
> This is just like whole numbers: since $4 \times 3 = 12$, then $12 \div 4 = 3$ and $12 \div 3 = 4$.

3. Divide by finding the missing number in the product.

    a) $-6 \div (-3)$ b) $12 \div (-2)$ c) $-15 \div 5$

       $-3 \times$ _____ $= -6$ $-2 \times$ _____ $= 12$ $5 \times$ _____ $= -15$

       so $-6 \div (-3) =$ _____   so $12 \div (-2) =$ _____   so $-15 \div 5 =$ _____

> You can use division of positive numbers to divide positive and negative numbers.
>
> $(+) \div (+) = (+)$ $(+) \div (-) = (-)$ $(-) \div (+) = (-)$ $(-) \div (-) = (+)$

4. Use your answer to the first division to do the other three divisions.

    a) $35 \div 5 = \underline{\quad 7 \quad}$ b) $6 \div 2 =$ _____   c) $36 \div 6 =$ _____

       $35 \div (-5) =$ _____ $6 \div (-2) =$ _____ $36 \div (-6) =$ _____

       $-35 \div 5 =$ _____ $-6 \div 2 =$ _____ $-36 \div 6 =$ _____

       $-35 \div (-5) =$ _____ $-6 \div (-2) =$ _____ $-36 \div (-6) =$ _____

5. Divide mentally.

    a) $42 \div (-6) =$ _____   b) $-64 \div 8 =$ _____   c) $32 \div 4 =$ _____

    d) $-28 \div (-7) =$ _____   e) $54 \div (-9) =$ _____   f) $-48 \div (-6) =$ _____

    Bonus ▶ $-3{,}500{,}000{,}000 \div 700{,}000 =$ _____

REMINDER: You can write the answer to a division question as a fraction or decimal.

Examples: $8 \div 5 = \dfrac{8}{5} = \dfrac{16}{10} = 1.6$ $137 \div 50 = \dfrac{137}{50} = \dfrac{274}{100} = 2.74$

6. Use your answer to the first division to do the other three divisions. Write your answer as a decimal.

a) $7 \div 5 = \underline{\dfrac{7}{5} = \dfrac{14}{10} = 1.4}$ b) $5 \div 2 = \underline{\hspace{3cm}}$ c) $11 \div 20 = \underline{\hspace{3cm}}$

$7 \div (-5) = \underline{\hspace{1.5cm}}$ $5 \div (-2) = \underline{\hspace{1.5cm}}$ $11 \div (-20) = \underline{\hspace{1.5cm}}$

$-7 \div 5 = \underline{\hspace{1.5cm}}$ $-5 \div 2 = \underline{\hspace{1.5cm}}$ $-11 \div 20 = \underline{\hspace{1.5cm}}$

$-7 \div (-5) = \underline{\hspace{1.5cm}}$ $-5 \div (-2) = \underline{\hspace{1.5cm}}$ $-11 \div (-20) = \underline{\hspace{1.5cm}}$

7. Divide. Write your answer as a decimal. Do your rough work in your notebook.

a) $12 \div (-5) = \underline{\hspace{1.5cm}}$ b) $-3 \div (-2) = \underline{\hspace{1.5cm}}$ c) $-9 \div 2 = \underline{\hspace{1.5cm}}$

d) $13 \div (-20) = \underline{\hspace{1.5cm}}$ e) $-4 \div (-25) = \underline{\hspace{1.5cm}}$ f) $-3 \div 4 = \underline{\hspace{1.5cm}}$

You can write the answer to an integer division as a fraction of integers.

Examples: $8 \div 5 = \dfrac{8}{5}$ and $-8 \div 5 = \dfrac{-8}{5}$

8. Write the division answer as a fraction of integers.

a) $-9 \div 4 = \dfrac{-9}{4}$ b) $8 \div (-7) =$ c) $-3 \div (-4) =$

d) $-7 \div (-20) =$ e) $3 \div (-25) =$ f) $-5 \div 4 =$

9. Circle the expressions that have the same value as $-\dfrac{4}{5}$.

$\dfrac{-4}{5}$ $\dfrac{-4}{-5}$ $\dfrac{4}{-5}$ $\dfrac{4}{5}$

10. Write the total change and then the average change as an integer. Include the units.

a) A plane rose from -500 ft to $5,500$ ft in 2 minutes.

The plane rose $5,500 + 500 = 6,000$ ft in 2 minutes.

Its average change in elevation was $+3,000$ ft per minute.

b) A plane descended from $8,000$ ft to -100 ft in 9 minutes.

c) The temperature went from $-18°F$ to $-30°F$ in 4 hours.

NS7-30 Powers

Remember: Multiplication is a short form for repeated addition: $5 \times 3 = \underbrace{3 + 3 + 3 + 3 + 3}$

Add five 3s

A **power** is a short form for repeated multiplication: $3^5 = \underbrace{3 \times 3 \times 3 \times 3 \times 3}$

Multiply five 3s

The **exponent** in a power tells you how many times to write the **base** in the product.

base $\longrightarrow 3^5 \longleftarrow$ exponent

1. Write the exponent and base for the power.

a) 2^3 base: ___2___

   exponent: ___3___

b) 8^2 base: _____

   exponent: _____

c) 9^4 base: _____

   exponent: _____

2. Write the product as a power.

a) $7 \times 7 \times 7 =$

d) $5 \times 5 \times 5 =$

b) $2 \times 2 \times 2 \times 2 =$

e) $0 \times 0 \times 0 \times 0 \times 0 =$

c) $9 \times 9 =$

Bonus ▶ $217 \times 217 \times 217 =$

REMINDER: Multiplication is performed from left to right.

3. Evaluate the power. Keep track of the product as you go along.

a) $3^4 = 3 \times 3 \times 3 \times 3 = \square$

b) $2^7 = 2 \times 2 \times 2 \times 2 \times 2 \times 2 \times 2 = \square$

c) $1^{10} = 1 \times 1 \times 1 \times 1 \times 1 \times 1 \times 1 \times 1 \times 1 \times 1 = \square$

d) $10^6 = 10 \times 10 \times 10 \times 10 \times 10 \times 10 = \square$

e) 4^2 f) 3^4 g) 10^4 h) 10^7 **Bonus ▶** Predict: 1^{500}

3^4 means multiply 4 threes: $3 \times 3 \times 3 \times 3$. 3^1 means multiply 1 three: 3, so $3^1 = 3$.

4. Evaluate.

a) $7^1 =$ _____

b) $18^1 =$ _____

c) $237{,}812^1 =$ _____

REMINDER: $(+) \times (+) = (+)$ $(+) \times (-) = (-)$ $(-) \times (+) = (-)$ $(-) \times (-) = (+)$

5. a) Evaluate each term in the pattern.

$(-1)^1 = \underline{\quad -1 \quad}$

$(-1)^2 = (-1) \times (-1) = \underline{\qquad}$

$(-1)^3 = (-1) \times (-1) \times (-1) = \underline{\qquad}$

$(-1)^4 = (-1) \times (-1) \times (-1) \times (-1) = \underline{\qquad}$

$(-1)^5 = (-1) \times (-1) \times (-1) \times (-1) \times (-1) = \underline{\qquad}$

$(-1)^6 = (-1) \times (-1) \times (-1) \times (-1) \times (-1) \times (-1) = \underline{\qquad}$

b) Predict $(-1)^{973}$. $\underline{\qquad}$ Explain your prediction. $\underline{\hspace{6cm}}$

$\underline{\hspace{11cm}}$

6. a) Evaluate the first five powers of 2 and -2.

$2^1 = \underline{\quad 2 \quad}$ $(-2)^1 = \underline{\quad -2 \quad}$

$2^2 = 2 \times 2 = \underline{\qquad}$ $(-2)^2 = (-2) \times (-2) = \underline{\qquad}$

$2^3 = 2 \times 2 \times 2 = \underline{\qquad}$ $(-2)^3 = (-2) \times (-2) \times (-2) = \underline{\qquad}$

$2^4 = 2 \times 2 \times 2 \times 2 = \underline{\qquad}$ $(-2)^4 = (-2) \times (-2) \times (-2) \times (-2) = \underline{\qquad}$

$2^5 = 2 \times 2 \times 2 \times 2 \times 2 = \underline{\qquad}$ $(-2)^5 = (-2) \times (-2) \times (-2) \times (-2) \times (-2) = \underline{\qquad}$

b) Write "even" or "odd." The powers of 2 and -2 with the same exponent are ...

   i) equal when the exponent is $\underline{\hspace{3cm}}$.

   ii) opposite integers when the exponent is $\underline{\hspace{3cm}}$.

c) If 2^{13} is 8,192, what is $(-2)^{13}$? $\underline{\hspace{3cm}}$

d) If 2^{14} is 16,384, what is $(-2)^{14}$? $\underline{\hspace{3cm}}$

REMINDER: You can compare two negative numbers by comparing their positive opposites first.
The answer is the opposite. Example: $3 < 4$, so $-3 > -4$.

A negative integer is always less than a positive integer. Example: $-3 < +2$

e) Order the powers from least to greatest: $(-2)^1$, $(-2)^2$, $(-2)^3$, $(-2)^4$, $(-2)^5$

   $\underline{\qquad} < \underline{\qquad} < \underline{\qquad} < \underline{\qquad} < \underline{\qquad}$

NS7-31 The Order of Operations with Powers and Negative Numbers

1. Evaluate the power first. Then multiply, divide, add, or subtract.

a) 5×2^2

$= 5 \times \underline{\quad 4 \quad}$

$= \underline{\quad 20 \quad}$

b) 2×4^2

$= 2 \times \underline{\qquad}$

$= \underline{\qquad}$

c) $5^2 + 5$

$= \underline{\qquad} + 5$

$= \underline{\qquad}$

d) $3 + 4^1$

$= 3 + \underline{\qquad}$

$= \underline{\qquad}$

e) 10×3^2

$=$

$=$

f) $10^2 \div 4$

$=$

$=$

g) $7^1 - 9$

$=$

$=$

h) $15 - 2^3$

$=$

$=$

> When an expression involves powers, the correct order of operations is:
> 1. Do operations in brackets.
> 2. Evaluate powers.
> 3. Do multiplication and division, from left to right.
> 4. Do addition and subtraction, from left to right.

2. Which operation is done first? Do it, then rewrite the rest of the expression.

a) $4^2 - 5$

$= \underline{\quad 16 - 5 \quad}$

b) $4^3 \div 2$

$= \underline{\qquad}$

c) $5 \times 4 + 3^2$

$= \underline{\qquad}$

d) $36 \times 2 \div 3^2$

$= \underline{\qquad}$

3. Do the operations one at a time, in the correct order.

a) 2×5^3

b) $(2 \times 5)^3$

c) $2 + 5^3$

d) $(2 + 5)^3$

e) $(27 \div 3)^2$

f) $27 \div 3^2$

g) $(22 - 2)^3$

h) $22 - 2^3$

i) $100 \div 5^2$

j) $20 - 4^2 + 3$

k) $6^2 \div (4 + 5)$

l) $7 \times 2^2 + 5$

4. Evaluate both powers. Circle the larger one.

a) $2^5 =$ _____

   $5^2 =$ _____

b) $2^3 =$ _____

   $3^2 =$ _____

c) $1^4 =$ _____

   $4^1 =$ _____

d) $2^{10} =$ _____

   $10^2 =$ _____

REMINDER: $(+) \times (+) = (+)$ $(+) \times (-) = (-)$ $(-) \times (+) = (-)$ $(-) \times (-) = (+)$

5. Evaluate the expression.

a) $(3 - 5)^2$

b) $3 - 5^2$

c) $3^2 - 5^2$

d) $(3 + (-3))^4$

e) $3^4 + (-3)^4$

f) $(3 \times (-2))^3$

g) $3 \times (-2)^3$

h) $4 \div (-2) \times 3$

i) $4 - (-2) \times 3$

j) $-8 \div 2 - 6$

k) $-8 \div (2 - 6)$

l) $(-3)^2 + 4 \times (-5)$

m) $-(3^2) + 4 \times (-5)$

n) $2^3 \div 4 - 8$

Bonus ▶ $(-2)^{(4 + 2) \div 2}$

6. Add brackets where necessary to make the equation true.

a) $2 - 5 \times 3 + 4 = -5$

b) $2 - 5 \times 3 + 4 = -33$

c) $2 - 5 \times 3 + 4 = -21$

7. Evaluate these expressions that all use three 3s.

a) $3^3 + 3$

b) $(3 + 3) \div 3$

c) 33^3

8. Use three 3s to make …

a) 81

b) 24

c) 18

d) 0

e) 11

f) 27

9. Is the product below positive or negative? How do you know?

$(-3) \times 4 \times (-5) \times (-6) \times 7 \times (-8) \times (-9) \times (-10) \times 11 \times (-12)$

10. Evaluate.

    a) $3x$, $x = -4$ b) $-5x$, $x = -2$ c) $5 - 2x$, $x = -4$ d) $2x - 5$, $x = 1$

REMINDER: $3(x + 2)$ and $3x + 6$ are equivalent expressions because

        $3(x + 2) = x + 2 + x + 2 + x + 2 = 3x + 6$ for all values of x.

---

11. Check that $3(x + 2)$ and $3x + 6$ have the same value for the given value of x.

		$3(x + 2)$	$3x + 6$
a)	$x = 1$		
b)	$x = 0$		
c)	$x = -1$		
d)	$x = \dfrac{2}{3}$		
e)	$x = -\dfrac{2}{3}$		
f)	$x = 0.5$		
g)	$x = -3.2$		

SP7-1 Events and Outcomes

Any time you do something that has different possible results, you are doing an **experiment**.

Example: If Rick rolls a die, there are 6 possible results. He could roll a 1, 2, 3, 4, 5, or 6.

The different results of an experiment are called **outcomes**.

1. What are the possible outcomes when you toss a coin?

   ___heads___, _____

2. What are the possible outcomes when you spin the spinner?

   a) 　　b) 　　c) 　　d)

   ___1, 2, 3, 4___　　_____　　_____　　_____

3. What are the possible outcomes when you throw a paper cup?

   It could land _____, or _____,

   or _____.

An **event** is any set of outcomes. For example, when rolling a die, the event "rolling an even number" consists of the outcomes 2, 4, and 6.

4. Lynn rolls a die. What outcomes make up the event?

   a) Lynn rolls an odd number: _____　　　b) Lynn rolls a multiple of 3: _____

   c) Lynn rolls a multiple of 5: _____　　　d) Lynn rolls a prime number: _____

   e) Lynn rolls a number greater than 4: _____

   f) Lynn rolls a number less than 3: _____

5. Shade the outcomes from spinning the spinner that make up the event.

   a) red (R)　　　b) blue (B)　　　c) 7　　　d) a multiple of 3

6. How many outcomes make up the event of spinning …

   a) the letter N _____   b) the letter W _____

   c) the letter C _____   d) a letter in "NEW YORK" _____

An event is **impossible** if there are no outcomes that produce it.

Example: Rolling a 7 on a regular die is impossible because there is no side with 7 dots.

An event is **certain** if all possible outcomes produce it.

Example: Rolling a number less than 10 on a regular die is certain because all sides are numbered with less than 10 dots.

Any other event is **in between** certain and impossible.

---

7. The spinner can spin red (R) or blue (B). Is the event certain, impossible, or in between?

   a) Spinning red is _____.

   b) Spinning green is _____.

   c) Spinning blue is _____.

   d) Spinning a color used to make purple is _____.

8. Should the spinner land more often on white or gray?

   a)   b)   c)   d)

   _____   _____   _____   _____

An outcome or event is **more likely** than another if it should happen more often.

---

9. Write "more likely than," "as likely as," or "less likely than." Spinning green (G) is …

   a) _____ spinning blue (B).

   b) _____ spinning red (R).

   c) _____ spinning yellow (Y).

   d) _____ spinning orange (O).

   Bonus ▶ Which is more likely: spinning a primary color (R, B, Y) or a secondary color (G, P, O)?

   _____

You can use a **probability line** to show how likely an event is. An event has an **even** chance of happening if it happens half the time.

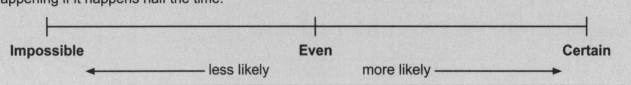

| Impossible | Even | Certain |

←————— less likely   more likely —————→

10. Mark a point on the line to show how likely each event is.

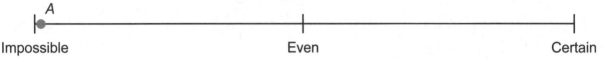

A

Impossible   Even   Certain

A. It will snow in New York City in August.   **B.** You roll a 6 on a regular die.

C. You will see a stranger today.   **D.** You will see a wolf today.

E. You get heads when tossing a coin.   **F.** You roll an 8 on a regular die.

G. The sun will set in the East.   **H.** The sun will set in the West.

When all the outcomes are equally likely, you can compare how likely two events are by counting their outcomes.

Example: On the spinner, spinning red (3 outcomes) is more likely than spinning blue (2 outcomes) because 3 is more than 2.

11. a) List all of the outcomes that are …

   i) even numbers _____

   ii) odd numbers _____

   iii) greater than 5 _____

   iv) a factor of 5 _____

b) Which event is more likely?

   i) an odd number or an even number _____

   ii) a number greater than 5 or a factor of 5 _____

12. Carlos says that spinning red is more likely than spinning blue because two outcomes are red and only one outcome is blue. Is he correct? Explain how you know.

Bonus ▶ Can you create a spinner where spinning a number greater than 3 is less likely than spinning a number greater than 5? Explain.

SP7-2 Probability

The probability of an **impossible event** is **0**. The probability of a **certain event** is **1**. The probability of any event is a number between 0 and 1.

Example: When tossing a coin, getting heads is 1 out of 2 equally likely outcomes. So the probability of getting heads is $\frac{1}{2}$.

1. Fill in the blanks. What is the probability of spinning red?

    a) _____ out of

    _____ outcomes is red.

    The probability of spinning red is _____.

    b) _____ out of

    _____ outcomes is red.

    The probability of spinning red is _____.

    c) _____ out of

    _____ outcomes are red.

    The probability of spinning red is _____.

    d) _____ out of

    _____ outcomes are red.

    The probability of spinning red is _____.

When all outcomes are equally likely, the probability of an event is:

$$\frac{\text{\# of outcomes when the event happens}}{\text{\# of outcomes in total}}$$

2. a) What is the probability of spinning the color?

    i) red _____   ii) blue _____   iii) green _____

    b) Show the probability of each event on the probability line.

    A. Spinning red   **B.** Spinning blue   **C.** Spinning green

    0   A   1

3. Hanna plays on a basketball team. Write each probability as a fraction.

    Impossible   Certain

    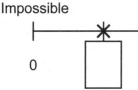   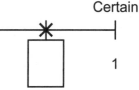

    0   1

    Hanna's team wins   Hanna's team   Hanna scores
    the championship.   wins today.   a basket.

4. The six outcomes from rolling a regular die are: 1, 2, 3, 4, 5, or 6.
Complete the table. Write the probability as a fraction in lowest terms.

	Event	Outcomes When the Event Happens	Probability of Event
a)	Rolling an even number.	2, 4, 6	$\frac{3}{6} = \frac{1}{2}$
b)	Rolling a number greater than 4.		
c)	Rolling an odd number.		
d)	Rolling a prime number.		
e)	Rolling a multiple of 5.		
f)	Rolling a factor of 12.		

5. When Zack spins the spinner, he says the probability of spinning red is $\frac{1}{3}$ because it is 1 out of 3 possible outcomes. Explain his mistake.

6. A class has 12 boys and 13 girls. A student is chosen to make the morning announcements.

a) How many students are in the class? _____

b) What is the probability the student is a girl? _____

c) What percent of the students are girls? _____

d) Are your answers to b) and c) equivalent? _____

REMINDER: You can write a fraction as a decimal or a percentage.

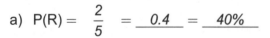

Examples: $\frac{3}{10} = 0.3 = 30\%$ $\frac{4}{5} = \frac{8}{10} = 0.8 = 80\%$ $\frac{3}{4} = \frac{75}{100} = 0.75 = 75\%$

7. Write the probability as a fraction, a decimal, and a percentage.

a) P(R) = $\frac{2}{5}$ = __0.4__ = __40%__   b) P(B) = ____ = _____ = _____

c) P(G) = ____ = _____ = _____

8. Write the letters A, B, and C on the spinner so that the probability of spinning an A is 0.3, a B is 0.5, and a C is 0.2.

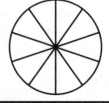

9. The probability of rain is often given as a percentage. Write a fraction for the prediction. Reduce your answer to lowest terms.

   a) 60% chance of rain   b) 35% chance of rain   c) 75% chance of rain

   _____   _____   _____

10. Describe an event that has the given probability of occurring.

   a) 100% _____

   b) 50% _____

   c) 0% _____

> In baseball, a **batting average** is the ratio of the number of hits to the number of times a player has a turn at bat. Batting averages are decimals that can be changed to fractions out of 1,000.
>
> Example: A batting average of .427 ($= \dfrac{427}{1,000}$) means a player had 427 hits in 1,000 times at bat.

11. Find the probability of a hit given a player's batting average. Write your answer as a fraction in lowest terms.

   a) .125   b) .300   c) .475   d) .256   e) .324

12. Which player is most likely to have a hit?

   a) Player A: batting average .425   b) Player A: hits one quarter of pitches

      Player B: hits 4 out of 10 pitches   Player B: batting average .230

      Player C: hits 42% of pitches   Player C: hits 23% of pitches

13. Write numbers on the spinner to match the probability. The probability of spinning …

   a) a 3 is 50%   b) a 2 is $\dfrac{1}{3}$ c) a 3 is 0.4   d) an even number is $\dfrac{5}{6}$

14. Draw lines to cut the spinner into equal parts. Write the probability of the given event.

   a)   b)   c)   d)

   P(B) = _____   P(R) = _____   P(Y) = _____   P(G) = _____

SP7-3 Expectation

Sharon plans to spin the spinner 15 times to see how many times it will land on yellow.

Since $\frac{1}{3}$ of the spinner is yellow, Sharon expects to land on yellow $\frac{1}{3}$ of the time.

Sharon finds $\frac{1}{3}$ of 15 by dividing: $15 \div 3 = 5$.

So she expects the spinner to land on yellow 5 times.

1. If you flip a coin repeatedly, what fraction of the throws would you expect to be heads? _____

2. How many times would you expect to flip heads if you flipped a coin ...

   a) 12 times? _____   b) 40 times? _____   c) 68 times? _____

3. a) Divide.

   i) $96 \div 2 =$ _____   ii) $96 \div 3 =$ _____   iii) $96 \div 4 =$ _____   iv) $96 \div 6 =$ _____

   b) To do the division in part a), did you ...

   A. divide mentally?   **B.** use a calculator?   **C.** use long division?

   i) _____   ii) _____   iii) _____   iv) _____

   c) How many times would you expect the spinner to land on red after 96 spins?

   i)   ii)   iii)   iv)

   _____   _____   _____   _____

4. How many times would you expect to land on yellow if you spin the spinner ...

   a) 18 times? _____
      69 times? _____

   b) 24 times? _____
      92 times? _____

   c) 15 times? _____
      40 times? _____

   d) 8 times? _____
      80 times? _____

   e) 12 times? _____
      30 times? _____

   f) 12 times? _____
      30 times? _____

5. Place the point of your pencil inside a paper clip in the middle of the spinner. Be sure to hold the pencil still so you can spin the paper clip around the pencil.

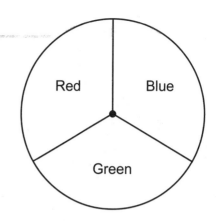

a) If you spin the spinner 30 times, how many times would you predict spinning red?

b) Spin the spinner 30 times. Make a tally of your results. Were your results exactly the same as your expectations? Were they close?

6. If you spin the spinner 18 times …

a) how many of your spins would you expect to be green? _____

b) which of the charts shows a result you would be most likely to get? _____

	A		**B**		**C**
Green	**Red**	**Green**	**Red**	**Green**	**Red**
卌 ‖	卌 卌 丨	卌 卌	卌 ‖‖	卌 卌 卌 ‖	丨

c) which result would surprise you? _____

REMINDER: Since $\frac{1}{3}$ of 15 is 5, we know that $\frac{2}{3}$ of 15 is $2 \times 5 = 10$.

---

7. How many times do you expect each spinner to land on red if you spin each 300 times?

a) _____ and _____

b) _____ and  _____

8. How many times would you expect the spinner to land on red in 300 spins? Explain how you found your answer.

SP7-4 Tree Diagrams

At a sports camp, David can choose from the following activities:

Morning: gymnastics (G) or canoeing (C)

Afternoon: hockey (H), soccer (S), or rugby (R)

David draws a tree diagram so that he can see all of the combinations of options.

Step 1: He writes his two morning options at the ends of two branches.

Step 2: Under each of his morning options, he adds three branches—one for each of his afternoon options.

Step 3: Follow any path along the branches (from the top of the tree to the bottom) to find one of David's options.

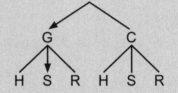

The path highlighted by the arrows shows gymnastics in the morning and soccer in the afternoon.

1. Follow a path from the top of the tree to a box at the bottom, and write the sports named on the path in the box. Continue until you have filled in all the boxes.

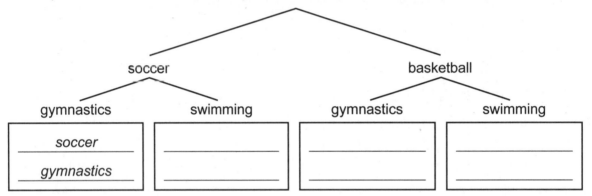

2. Complete the tree diagram to show all of the possible outcomes of flipping a coin twice (H = heads and T = tails).

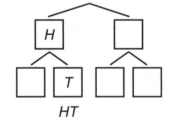

3. Marla's camp offers the following activities:

   Morning: drama (D) or art (A)

   Afternoon: poetry (P) or fiction (F)

   Draw a tree diagram (like the one in Question 1) to show all the combinations of options.

Statistics and Probability 7-4

4. Complete the tree diagram to show all of the possible outcomes of flipping the coin then spinning the spinner.

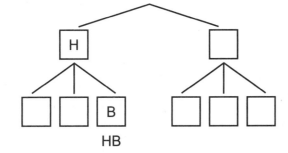

5. a) Complete the tree diagram to show all the outcomes when you toss a coin then roll a die.

b) Complete the tree diagram to show all the outcomes when you roll a die then toss a coin.

6. A restaurant offers the following options for breakfast:

Main Course: eggs (E), muffins (M), or pancakes (P)

Juice: apple (A), tomato (T), orange (O), or grape (G)

Draw a tree diagram to show all the different breakfasts you could order.

7. a) Use the tree diagrams you drew for Questions 4, 5, and 6 to fill in the chart.

Question	Number of Branches at the First Level	Number of Branches at the Second Level	Total Number of Paths
4	2	3	6
5.a)			
5.b)			
6			

b) How can you calculate the total number of paths from the number of branches at each level? Explain.

SP7-5 Charts and Organized Lists

1. Ross flips a coin twice. Shade the given event. Then find the probability.

   a) two heads

    $\dfrac{1}{4}$

   b) two tails

   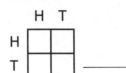 _____

   c) one head and one tail

   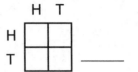 _____

2. Micky rolls two dice. Shade the given event. Write the probability as a fraction in lowest terms.

   a) rolls a sum of 7

   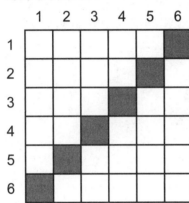 $\dfrac{6}{36} = \dfrac{1}{6}$

   b) rolls a sum of 4

   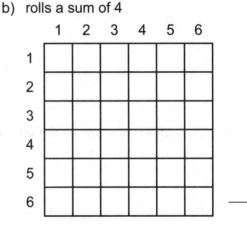 _____

   c) rolls a 3 and a 4

   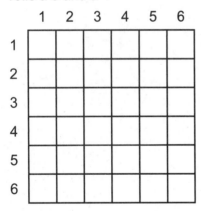 _____

   d) rolls double 6s

   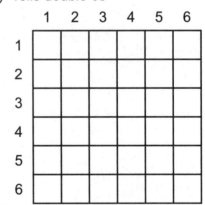 _____

   e) both dice show the same number

   f) rolls at least one 3

   g) rolls an even total

   h) the numbers are 1 apart

3. a) If you roll two dice, how many outcomes are there? _____

   b) If you roll a die twice, how many outcomes are there? _____

   c) Are your answers to parts a) and b) the same? Why does this make sense?

Will wants to make an **organized list** of all the outcomes from spinning Spinner A and then Spinner B.

Step 1: There are **3 outcomes** on Spinner B, so Will lists each outcome on Spinner A **3 times**:

Spinner A   **Spinner B**

1   1   1   2   2   2

Step 2: Beside each outcome from Spinner A, Will writes the 3 outcomes from Spinner B:

1R   1Y   1B   2R   2Y   2B

The list shows there are **6 outcomes** altogether.

4. Blanca tosses a coin then rolls a die. Finish making an organized list to show all the outcomes.

H1   H2   H3   _____   _____   _____   _____   _____   _____   _____   _____   _____

5. Sal tosses a coin then spins the spinner.

a) Make an organized list to show all the outcomes.

i)

H1 H2 T1 T2 _____

ii)

_____

iii)

_____

iv)

_____

b) How many outcomes does each event from part a) have?

i) _____   ii) _____   iii) _____   iv) _____

A game is **fair** if the chance of winning equals the chance of losing.

6. Randi rolls a die then spins the spinner.

a) Make an organized list to show all the possible outcomes.

b) Greg plays a game where he wins and loses as follows:

He wins if he rolls an even number then spins yellow.
He loses if he rolls a multiple of 3 then spins red.

Find the probability of winning and losing. Is the game fair?

7. Anne's camp offers the following activities:

Morning: swimming (S), or tennis (T)

Afternoon: canoeing (C), baseball (B), or hiking (H)

Anne needs to bring her running shoes if she chooses tennis, baseball, or hiking.
She needs to bring a towel if she chooses swimming or canoeing.

Circle the outcomes that show the event.

a) Anne needs her running shoes.

     SC   SB   SH   TC   TB   TH

b) Anne needs a towel.

     SC   SB   SH   TC   TB   TH

c) Anne needs her running shoes
and a towel.

     SC   SB   SH   TC   TB   TH

d) Anne needs her running shoes for
the morning and the afternoon.

     SC   SB   SH   TC   TB   TH

8. If the activities are chosen randomly, find the probability of each event in Question 7.

    a) _____   b) _____   c) _____   d) _____

> A contest between two people is **fair** if they both have the same chance of winning.

9. a) Make an organized list of all the possible outcomes of spinning both spinners.

b) Find the probability that the outcomes from the two spinners ...

    i)   add to 6   ii)   multiply to 6   iii)   add to 4

    _____   _____   _____

c) Ed and Beth play a game in which they each spin one of the spinners. Ed wins
if the results add to 6. Beth wins if the results multiply to 6. Is the game fair?
If not, who has the better chance of winning?

d) Make up a fair game for Ed and Beth to play using the spinners.

10. A tetrahedral die has 4 vertices numbered from 1 to 4. When you roll this die, there is
always a vertex on top. Make a chart to show all the combinations for rolling a pair of
tetrahedral dice.

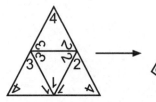 This is a "4" vertex.
There is a 4 hidden
on the back face.

            Statistics and Probability 7-5

SP7-6 More Tree Diagrams, Charts, and Organized Lists

1. Bo plays a game with two spinners. Draw a chart to show all the outcomes. Then fill in the blanks.

   a) Spinner 1 has ___2___ outcomes.

      Spinner 2 has ___3___ outcomes.

        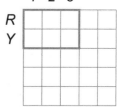

      Spinning both spinners has ___6___ outcomes.

   b) Spinner 1 has _____ outcomes.

      Spinner 2 has _____ outcomes.

      Spinning both spinners has _____ outcomes.

   c) Spinner 1 has _____ outcomes.

      Spinner 2 has _____ outcomes.

       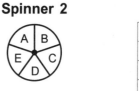 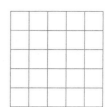

      Spinning both spinners has _____ outcomes.

2. Make an organized list to show that there are 2 groups of 5 outcomes when spinning the two spinners.

3. a) How can you find the number of outcomes for spinning both spinners from the number of outcomes for spinning each spinner?

   _____

   b) If Spinner 1 has 100 outcomes and Spinner 2 has 50 outcomes, how many outcomes would there be for spinning both spinners?

   _____

4. Jenny rolls a die with 20 faces, then a die with 12 faces. How many possible outcomes are there?

5. Make an organized list of all the outcomes.

a)

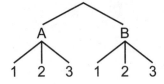

b)

6. In a role-playing game, Jay's character is exploring a tunnel in a cave.

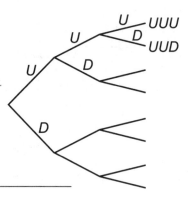

a) Complete the tree diagram that shows all the paths through the cave. (U = up, D = down)

b) How many paths are there through the cave? _____

c) A monster is waiting at the end of one path. Do you think it is likely or unlikely that Jay's character will meet the monster? Explain.

_____

_____

7. Tess has two sets of paints:

Set 1: red, blue, and yellow   **Set 2:** red and blue

She chooses one color from each set at random and mixes them.

a) Make a chart, a tree diagram, and an organized list to show all the possible outcomes.

b) Find the probability that Tess makes ...

   i) green   ii) blue   iii) yellow   iv) purple

c) Did you use the chart, the tree diagram, or the organized list from part a) to do part b)?

8. Find the probability by making a tree diagram or a chart. Explain your choice.

a) Rolling two dice results in at least one 3.

b) Tossing four coins results in at least 3 heads.

9. Cereal boxes come with a picture of either a cat or a dog inside. There are the same number of boxes with each picture. You win a prize if you collect one of each picture.

a) Use a tree diagram to find the probability that you will win a prize if you buy …

   i) 2 boxes   ii) 3 boxes   iii) 4 boxes

b) Does the probability of winning a prize increase with the number of boxes you buy? Did you expect this?

SP7-7 Empirical Probability

> REMINDER: Two quantities are proportional if the T-table comparing their values is a ratio table (i.e., the rows are equivalent ratios).

1. a) Complete the chart.

i)

Spins	Expected Red
30	
60	
150	

ii)

Spins	Expected Red
40	
120	
240	

iii)

Spins	Expected Even Numbers
5	
50	
200	

iv)

Spins	Expected Prime Numbers
10	
40	
65	

b) Are the tables in part a) ratio tables?

i) _____   ii) _____   iii) _____   iv) _____

If you don't know what a spinner looks like, you can use what actually happens to estimate it.

Example: A spinner lands on red 17 times in 20 spins. How many times would you expect it to land on red in 100 spins?

You can use equivalent ratios to find out:

$$\times 5 \left(\begin{array}{c} 17 : 20 \\ ? : 100 \end{array} \right) \times 5$$

You would expect the spinner to land on red 85 times in 100 spins.

---

2. Billy randomly picked 100 of the 800 students at his school and asked them how they get to school. 12 of them said they bike. How many students at his school should he expect to bike to school?

3. A bag contained 10,000 red chips and white chips. Amy reached in and grabbed a chip. She looked at it, then put it back. She did this 40 times and got red 9 times. How many red chips do you estimate are in the bag?

4. A spinner landed on red 12 times in 50 spins. How many times would you expect it to land on red in 1,000 spins?

5. A baseball player had 24 hits in 96 times at bat. How many hits would you expect the player to get in 1,000 times at bat?

The **theoretical probability** is what should happen. The **empirical probability** is what does happen.

$$\text{Empirical probability of A} = \frac{\text{\# of times A happened}}{\text{\# of experiments performed}}$$

When you don't know the theoretical probability, you can estimate it by repeating an experiment many times and using the empirical probability.

6. Do the experiment 25 times. Record your results in the table. Ask three other people for their results. Complete the table. Make sure your "Total" row adds to 100.

a) Toss a coin.

	Heads	Tails
My results		
Partner 1		
Partner 2		
Partner 3		
Total		

b) Toss a paper cup.

	Lands Upright	Lands Upside Down	Lands on Its Side

Use your answers to Question 6 to answer Questions 7, 8, and 9.

7. a) What is the theoretical probability of getting heads? _____

   b) What is your total empirical probability of getting heads? _____

   c) Ethan flipped a coin 5 times and got 4 heads. What is Ethan's empirical probability

   of getting heads? _____

   d) Whose empirical probability is closer to the theoretical probability, yours or Ethan's? Why does that make sense?

   _____

8. Write "as likely as," "more likely than," or "less likely than."

   a) A coin landing on heads appears to be _____ a coin landing on tails.

   b) A paper cup landing upright appears to be _____ a paper cup landing upside down.

9. Estimate the probability that a paper cup will land …

   a) upright _____   b) upside down _____   c) on its side _____

Statistics and Probability 7-7

10. A bottle cap was tossed 1,000 times, with the following results:

Lands Flat Side Down	Lands Flat Side Up	Lands on Its Side
894	65	41

a) What is the empirical probability of the outcome? Write the answer as a fraction and a decimal.

    i) lands flat side down   ii) lands flat side up   iii) lands on its side

_____   _____   _____

b) Place the probabilities approximately on the number line from 0 to 1.

    A. lands flat side up   **B.** lands flat side down   **C.** lands on its side

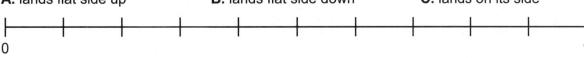

  0   1

c) What is the most likely outcome? _____

d) What is the least likely outcome? _____

e) If you tossed the bottle cap 10,000 times, how many times would you expect it to

land on its side? _____

11. a) How many times would you expect the spinner to land on red if

    you spin it 15 times? _____

b) Kathy spins the spinner 15 times and it lands on red 8 times.
Explain why this doesn't contradict your result from part a).

_____

_____

c) Kathy thinks that if she spins the spinner 1,500 times, it will land on red 800 times.
Explain her mistake.

_____

_____

_____

12. A school goes from Grades 1 to 5 and has 800 students in total. Jack asked the
25 students in a Grade 5 class how they get to school. Ten of them said they bike.

Jack predicted the number of students who bike to school would be $\dfrac{10}{25} \times 800 = \dfrac{2}{5} \times 800 = 320$.

In fact, only 135 students bike to school. What was his mistake? Hint: Are all students
equally likely to bike to school?

SP7-8 Simulating Real World Problems

1. The experiment "Pick a random number from 1 to 5" was repeated 10 times, with the following results:

    1   3   1   2   1   1   5   3   5   5

    a) What is the empirical probability that a random number from 1 to 5 is …

       i) 1   ii) 2   iii) 3   iv) 4   v) 5   vi) even

       _____   _____   _____   _____   _____   _____

    b) What is the theoretical probability that a random number from 1 to 5 is …

       i) 1   ii) 2   iii) 3   iv) 4   v) 5   vi) even

       _____   _____   _____   _____   _____   _____

    c) Is the empirical probability close to the theoretical probability?

       i) _____   ii) _____   iii) _____   iv) _____   v) _____   vi) _____

2. The experiment "Pick a random number from 1 to 5" was repeated 100 times, with the following results:

5	4	5	2	3	5	3	3	2	5
4	4	5	1	2	2	2	3	1	1
2	2	2	1	4	4	3	1	3	5
4	2	3	1	4	3	5	2	5	1
2	5	5	3	3	1	3	5	2	5
5	4	4	5	5	5	5	1	3	5
3	4	5	5	4	1	1	5	3	5
5	3	3	1	2	3	3	5	2	3
4	1	3	3	3	2	3	4	5	5
5	1	2	4	3	1	2	5	3	1

   a) Circle all the even numbers. Check with a partner that you found all the same numbers.

   b) _____ out of 100 experiments resulted in an even number.

   c) What is the empirical probability that a random number from 1 to 5 will be an even

       number? _____

   d) What is the theoretical probability that a random number from 1 to 5 will be an even

       number? _____

   e) Are your answers to c) and d) exactly the same? _____ Are they close? _____

3. A random number generator generated 300 numbers from 1 to 5. 122 of them are even numbers.

a) What is the empirical probability of a number from 1 to 5 being even? _____

b) Use an online random number generator to generate 1,000 numbers from 1 to 5.

c) Copy your list to a file.

Search for 2. How many matches are there? _____

Search for 4. How many matches are there? _____

d) How many even numbers were generated in total? _____

e) Write the empirical probability that a random number from 1 to 5 will be an even number when using ...

i) 10 numbers: $\dfrac{1}{10}$ } from Question 1.a)   ii) 100 numbers: $\dfrac{}{100}$ } from Question 2.b)

iii) 300 numbers: $\dfrac{}{300}$ } from Question 3.a)   iv) 1,000 numbers: $\dfrac{}{1,000}$ } from Question 3.d)

f) What is the theoretical probability that a random number from 1 to 5 will be an even number?

$\dfrac{}{5}$

g) Which empirical probability from e) is closest to the theoretical probability from f)?

You can model spinning a spinner using a random number generator.

The spinner has 4 outcomes, so randomly generate numbers from 1 to 4.

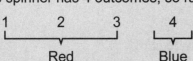

The number generator choosing 1, 2, or 3 has the same probability as the spinner landing on red.
The number generator choosing 4 has the same probability as the spinner landing on blue.

---

4. Circle the numbers that represent landing on red.

a)   1   2

b)   1   2   3

c)   1   2   3   4   5

d)   1   2   3   4
      5   6   7   8

5. Write the numbers you would randomly generate to model the spinner. Then circle the numbers that would represent landing on gray.

a)

b)

c)

d)

> You can model any probability using a random number generator.
>
> Example: There is a 60% chance of an earthquake each year.
>
> **Step 1:** Write the probability as a fraction in lowest terms: $60\% = \dfrac{60}{100} = \dfrac{3}{5}$.
>
> **Step 2:** Randomly generate numbers from 1 to 5 (the denominator of the reduced fraction). Use the numerator to decide which numbers represent which outcome.
>
> $$\underbrace{1 \qquad 2 \qquad 3}_{\text{Earthquake}} \qquad \underbrace{4 \qquad 5}_{\text{No earthquake}}$$
>
> The number generator choosing 1, 2, or 3 has the same probability as an earthquake occurring. The number generator choosing 4 or 5 has the same probability as no earthquake occurring.

6. Write the numbers you would randomly generate. Then write the numbers that would represent each event.

a) A hockey player scores a goal in 50% of the games. ___1, 2___

The player scores: ___1___   The player doesn't score: ___2___

b) A hockey player scores a goal in 75% of the games. _____

The player scores: _____   The player doesn't score: _____

c) 40% of donors have Type O blood. _____

A donor has Type O: _____   The donor doesn't have Type O: _____

7. There is a 25% chance of a flood each year. How would you use a random number generator to represent the probabilities of a flood occurring or of no flood occurring?

8. A student is randomly chosen from a class. How would you use a random number generator to represent choosing a girl if the ratio of girls to boys is …

a) 1 : 2   b) 2 : 3   c) 1 : 4   d) 4 : 3

SP7-9 Simulating Repeated Experiments

Rolling a die is one way to pick a random number from 1 to 6.

Another way is to use a random number generator. You can use a random number generator to simulate rolling two dice by picking 2 numbers from 1 to 6.

Random Numbers	Dice Roll Simulated
1,4	
2,3	
4,1	

1. The experiment "Pick 2 numbers from 1 to 6" was repeated 72 times, with the following results:

4,3	5,3	5,1	1,3	6,6	6,1	1,1	3,4	6,3
3,5	3,6	1,2	1,1	5,6	5,3	5,5	2,5	2,5
4,1	6,6	2,6	4,3	2,1	3,4	1,2	6,2	2,2
5,1	1,4	2,2	1,3	3,6	4,6	2,5	6,4	5,5
2,3	4,6	1,4	6,1	1,3	1,6	3,2	6,6	2,3
4,3	1,4	6,6	4,5	3,1	1,5	6,2	1,1	6,3
6,6	6,5	3,4	2,1	3,6	2,2	5,5	1,4	5,2
6,6	1,5	1,1	1,3	3,4	4,2	4,3	4,1	6,1

a) Find the empirical probability that there is at least one 6.

b) Find the theoretical probability that there is at least one 6. Use a chart, a tree diagram, or an organized list.

c) Is the empirical probability you found in part a) exactly the same as the theoretical probability you found in b)? Is it close?

When the theoretical probability is hard to determine, you can estimate it using the empirical probability.

Example: You can use a random number generator to estimate the probability of various events when rolling three dice by picking 3 numbers from 1 to 6.

2. The experiment "Pick 3 numbers from 1 to 6" was repeated 50 times, with the following results:

1,6,6	2,5,1	6,4,3	6,1,4	1,4,4	5,3,1	1,6,4	1,4,4	1,5,2	4,1,3
1,6,3	4,2,5	2,5,6	5,2,4	6,3,3	6,1,1	1,1,2	3,6,5	6,1,3	2,6,4
6,3,3	6,4,5	3,6,1	6,1,4	2,1,1	6,2,4	3,1,5	4,5,5	3,2,5	4,2,1
3,2,6	6,2,1	3,1,2	3,2,3	4,3,6	6,5,5	4,4,3	6,5,3	5,6,1	2,4,3
1,2,5	3,1,5	1,2,1	6,2,6	4,4,5	6,6,2	1,5,2	6,3,2	2,4,3	2,4,3

a) Circle all the groups that show 3 consecutive numbers. (The numbers don't have to be in order, so you would circle 2,4,3, but not 2,4,5).

b) Underline all the groups that show at least 2 numbers the same.

c) Estimate the probability that, when you roll 3 dice, you will get ...

i) 3 consecutive numbers

ii) at least two numbers the same.

3. A class has 25 students. Each week, one student is chosen randomly to help the teacher. This repeats for 5 weeks. Don wants to find the probability that he will be chosen at least once. He uses a random number generator. There are 25 outcomes, so he randomly picks a number from 1 to 25, and uses 1 to represent himself.

The experiment is repeated 5 times, so Don tells the computer to pick five numbers from 1 to 25, with the following results:

23   5   3   21   21

a) Was Don chosen? _____

b) Was the same student chosen more than once? _____

c) Don repeated the experiment 50 times. Of those 50 experiments, "1" was chosen once in nine experiments, and twice in one experiment. Estimate the probability that Don will be chosen at least once in the 5 weeks. Write your answer as a percentage.

_____

4. a) Use a random number generator to pick 3 numbers from 1 to 30. Are all 3 numbers between 1 and 15? Do this 25 times and record your results in the first row of the table. Ask three other people for their results, then complete the table. Make sure your "Total" row adds to 100.

	Are all three numbers between 1 and 15?	
	How many "yes" answers?	How many "no" answers?
My results		
Partner 1		
Partner 2		
Partner 3		
Total		

b) What is the empirical probability that when you pick 3 numbers from 1 to 30,

all three numbers are between 1 and 15? _____

c) In a class of 30 students, 15 are girls and 15 are boys. A student is randomly chosen each week for 3 weeks. Estimate the probability that, in all 3 weeks, each student chosen is a girl.

_____

d) Justify your estimate from part c). _____

_____

_____

_____

Over many years, a river floods each spring about 30% of the time. You can model this using a random number generator. For each year, pick a number from 1 to 10.

```
1     2     3     4     5     6     7     8     9     10
|-----v-----|     |-----------------v-----------------|
    Flood                        No flood
```

a) How would you model the question?

   i) In the next two years, will at least one year have a flood?

   Pick two numbers from 1 to 10. Is at least one of them a 1, 2, or 3?

   ii) Will the next three years be without a flood?

   _____

b) In the next five years, will there be at least 2 floods?

   _____

c) In the next five years, will there be a flood for at least 3 years in a row?

   _____

6. Use a random number generator to solve the problem.

a) In a class of 30 students, 10 are girls. Each week for three weeks a student is chosen randomly. Estimate the probability that a girl is chosen in at least two weeks.

b) Helen scores a goal in 75% of the games she plays. Estimate the probability that she will ...

   i) score a goal in neither of her next two games

   ii) score a goal in at least four of her next five games

c) If 40% of donors have Type O blood, estimate the probability that it will take at least four donors to find one with Type O blood. Hint: This means none of the first three donors have Type O blood.

7. Which part of Question 6 has the same answer as the problem below? Explain how you know.

   Peter has a 0.400 batting average (he hits 40% of his attempts at bat). What is the probability that it will take him at least four times at bat to get a hit?

8. Which of these problems could you answer using a random number generator? Explain.

   A. What is my chance of getting the correct answer to the next multiple choice question?

   B. What is my chance of getting the correct answer to the next multiple choice question if I guess randomly?

   _____

   _____